Buccaneer

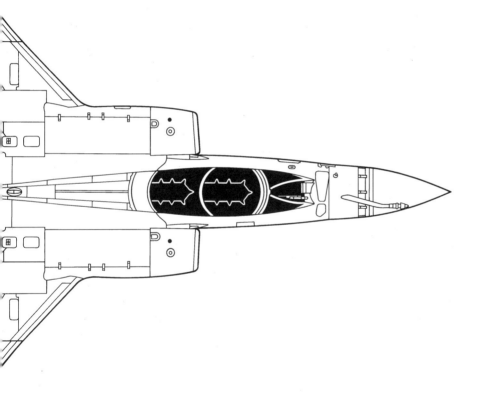

Metres

Scale

Feet

Buccaneer

XK487 and XK489 pictured en route to Farnborough on 4 September 1960. The Buccaneers drew a great deal of attention at the SBAC show, not only from the British public, but from the less-visible 'visitors' from the Soviet Union. The early nose profile of XK487 contrasts with the definitive shape fitted to XK489 although this aircraft also still carries a non-standard instrumentation boom.

Other books by the same author:

The Vulcan Story
RAF Fighter Pilot
Tiger Squadrons
Swing Wings
Fight's On
The Royal Air Force Manual
C-130 Hercules
V-Bombers

Buccaneer

The story of the last all-British strike aircraft

Tim Laming

Patrick Stephens Limited

AN IMPRINT OF HAYNES PUBLISHING

An interesting low-angle view of the first Buccaneer to enter RAF service (XV347), illustrating the sturdy naval undercarriage and distinctly nautical folding wings. The bolt-on refuelling probe became a distinctive sight on virtually all of the UK-based RAF Buccaneers, and glossy camouflage soon gave way to matt colours and toned-down national insignia.

© T. Laming 1998

First published in 1998

British Library Cataloguing-in-Publication Data:
A catalogue record for this book is available from the British Library

ISBN 1 85260 478 6

Library of Congress catalog card No. 98 – 70523

Patrick Stephens Limited is an imprint of
Haynes Publishing, Sparkford, Nr Yeovil, Somerset, BA22 7JJ

Tel. 01963 440635   Fax: 01963 440001
Int. tel: +44 1963 440635   Fax: +44 1963 440001

E-mail: sales@haynes-manuals.co.uk
Web site: http://www.haynes.com

Haynes North America Inc.
861 Lawrence Drive, Newbury Park,
California 91320 USA

Typeset by J. H. Haynes & Co. Ltd.

Printed in Great Britain

Contents

Acknowledgements   6

Introduction   7

Chapter 1   Building a bomber   9

Chapter 2   Airborne   28

Chapter 3   In the Navy   55

Chapter 4   Export success   83

Buccaneer in Colour   97

Chapter 5   The Royal Air Force   107

Chapter 6   From the cockpit   135

Chapter 7   Conclusion   153

Appendices

I   The Buccaneer S.Mk.2 described   162

II   Buccaneer production   179

Index   199

Acknowledgements

The story of the Buccaneer is a long and fascinating one. Researching this project took a long time (much longer than even I had anticipated), and it is hardly surprising therefore, that many individuals and organisations assisted me at some stage. It would be impossible to identify everyone by name, but to all those people who gave so freely of their time, I must extend a very genuine 'thank you'.

However, I must make specific mention of the following individuals who have provided contributions, information, and advice. Stan Field and his colleagues at the Brough Heritage Centre who allowed me to spend so many Thursdays wading through their files. Jack Pearson who provided numerous photographic contributions and fascinating recollections from the Buccaneer's development programme. My thanks also to Roy Boot, for his supply of extensive information, more of which can be found in his own book *From Spitfire to Eurofighter*, published by Airlife. Thanks also to Wing Commander G. R. Pitchfork, whose extensive knowledge of both FAA and RAF Buccaneer operations proved to be invaluable. Also, my thanks to Lt-Col. Dave Knoesen, SAAF, for his long-distance supply of fascinating information and photographs.

Finally, my thanks to the following: Norman Roberson, Terry Wong-Lane, John Hale, Paul Jackson, Phil Claydon, Dave Becker, and Mark Swann (for all the cups of tea consumed during this project!), FAA Museum, 12 Squadron, 15(R) Squadron, 16(R) Squadron, 208(R) Squadron and 216 Squadron.

As is often the case with book projects of this nature, the amount of available information is almost overwhelming, and one of the biggest (and unenviable) tasks associated with the project, is deciding what information (and illustrations) should be included, and which have to be excluded. With an unlimited amount of space, the 'definitive' Buccaneer book might well have been twice the size of this one, but I hope that within the following pages I have provided a detailed and balanced account of the Buccaneer's colourful history, combined with a selection of photographs which are mostly published for the first time, and drawings taken directly from the Buccaneer's technical publications, all of which are published for the first time. I hope that I have also clarified some parts of the Buccaneer's history which have often been wrongly described in the past, although I'm sure that I will have added a few new mistakes all of my own! However, I do hope that this book will serve as a tribute to the many people who designed and built the Buccaneer, and to the many people who crewed the magnificent beasts throughout their service life.

Tim Laming, Sheffield

Introduction

Although a considerable number of land-based aircraft have been modified for naval operations, the reverse situation is comparatively rare. Certainly, many RAF types have later served with the Fleet Air Arm, but how many Fleet Air Arm types have been adopted by the Royal Air Force? As a high-ranking officer once said to a curious journalist; "My dear chap, the Royal Air Force has *never* bought a Fleet Air Arm aircraft". That was indeed the case until Blackburn designed and built their B.103 – the Buccaneer.

Selected from a whole range of competing designs, the B.103 was developed into an excellent low-level maritime strike aircraft with one vital primary task – to destroy the Soviet's capital warships. Good though the first-generation Buccaneer was, it suffered from a lack of power which often made operations from the Navy's carriers very difficult. The answer was the Buccaneer S2, the definitive variant which had more than enough power to give the Buccaneer a range, speed and load-carrying capability which is still unbeatable more than 30 years later.

Although the Royal Navy realised that it had an unbeatable aircraft, the Royal Air Force showed no interest in it. Keen to procure the ill-fated TSR2, the idea of purchasing a naval aircraft was never seriously considered. Even when TSR2 was cancelled, the RAF pinned its hopes on the American F-111. When that too was abandoned by the British government, the RAF was effectively forced to buy the Buccaneer. Of course, the RAF was to be pleasantly surprised, and the aircraft which they reluctantly purchased became one of the best strike aircraft ever to have joined their ranks. When defence expenditure reductions ended the Buccaneer's RAF service, there was no doubt that it could have continued in the maritime strike role for many more years, and still have out-performed any other aircraft.

A classic piece of Yorkshire craftsmanship, Blackburn's Buccaneer could never have been described as graceful, but it flew fast and low, and could carry more weapons over a longer distance than any other aircraft. It was also immensely tough, and even when the RAF's pilots tortured the airframes until they began to fracture, they were fixed, and soon they were back in the air, as powerful and manoeuvrable as they always had been.

This is the story of the Buccaneer – the last of a long line of Fleet Air Arm strike aircraft, and the last in an even longer line of all-British bomber designs. Following in the fine traditions of aircraft such as the Heyford, the Lancaster and the Vulcan, the Buccaneer was the very last British Bomber.

Three Buccaneers from No. 15 Squadron, pictured on a training sortie shortly after the unit reformed at RAF Laarbruch. The bolt-on refuelling probes were not normally carried by RAFG Buccaneers, and like their UK counterparts, the glossy camouflage and full-colour insignia soon gave way to matt colours and toned-down markings. By the 1980s RAF Germany's Buccaneers were housed in individual concrete hardened aircraft shelters.

CHAPTER ONE

Building
a bomber

As the Cold War gradually fades into history, it is sometimes difficult to imagine how Britain, together with her NATO allies, stood poised to wage nuclear war with the Soviet Union for many years. During the 1960s and 1970s the concept of Mutually Assured Destruction – appropriately abbreviated to MAD – seemed to be the only viable means of self defence against the military might of the Soviet armed forces. The threat of a devastating reciprocal nuclear attack was obviously a risky means of defence, but with hindsight it would appear to have been a remarkably successful posture to have assumed. In reality however it was the only posture which NATO – and Britain in particular – could seriously adopt. Matching the massive postwar Soviet military build-up on a tank-for-tank basis was never a practical proposition, but the development of nuclear weapons enabled NATO to provide a relatively inexpensive means of deterring the Soviets from embarking upon any serious expansionist adventures without running a very serious risk of starting a war which neither side could ever hope to win.

It was against this background that the Buccaneer was born. As part of the Soviet's post-war rearmament programme, a significant amount of resources were put into naval power, with new types of destroyers, submarines or cruisers appearing almost on an annual basis throughout the 1960s. The British government was particularly concerned when the Soviets introduced the first in a planned fleet of 24 new 'Sverdlov' class heavy cruisers, armed with twelve 5.9in guns in triple turrets, twelve 3.9in guns in twin turrets and a pair of 21in torpedo launchers, each capable of launching five weapons. Displacing a staggering 17,000 tons when fully laden, these fearsome vessels could achieve a speed of 34 knots and a radius of action of some 5,000 miles. They also carried twin guided missile launchers and no less than 32 anti aircraft guns. Although little more than half of this planned fleet actually entered service, their very existence was enough to convince Britain's naval chiefs that they would pose a very serious threat to merchant shipping, if Britain was ever to fight a war with the Soviet Union.

Providing a means of defence against these new cruisers was by no means easy. Traditionally, the Admiralty would have ordered the production of similarly-equipped warships to counter the threat, but in a climate of postwar cash shortages the prospect of building bigger and more powerful ships to simply match or better the Soviets, was no longer a realistic option. It was Admiral A. S. Bolt of the Naval Staff's Air Warfare Division who suggested that a more cost effective solution would be to develop a strike aircraft which could be launched from the Navy's carriers, to carry nuclear bombs at high speed and ultra-low level, in order to avoid detection by the Soviet's increasingly sophisticated radar systems. Suitably armed with a nuclear store, the new strike aircraft would not have to rely upon pinpoint delivery accuracy, and even one bomb would be more than enough to destroy any one of the Soviet's treasured 'Sverdlov' cruisers.

Consequently, the first draft of Naval Staff Requirement NA.39 was produced in October 1953, outlining the Admiralty's need for a new strike aircraft capable of carrying both nuclear and conventional stores, and with a top speed and range well in excess of that which was already achievable by other aircraft. This was translated into Issue One of Specification M.148T, released on 27 March 1954, which called for a twin-seat and twin-engined strike aircraft able to fly at an altitude of just 200ft, at 550 knots or more, with a radius of action beyond 400 miles (800 miles at altitude). Maximum take off weight would be 40,000lb (but with an overload weight of 45,000lb), with equivalent landing weights of 30,000lb and 35,000lb respectively. Folded dimensions of the aircraft would not exceed a length of 51ft and a width of 20ft. The normal weapons load would be 4,000lb, and the primary weapon for the new aircraft would be Green Cheese, a guided nuclear bomb which was being designed by Fairey for employment against naval targets. The alternative primary armament would be Red Beard, a free fall tactical nuclear bomb which was being developed for the Royal Air Force (to be carried by the ill-fated TSR2). Secondary armament would be 24 air-to-surface (OR.1099) rockets, two 2,000lb bombs or four 1,000lb bombs, a 4 x 30mm Aden cannon

Russia's 'Sverdlov' class cruisers posed a major threat to Britain's merchant shipping and created a need for a high-speed and low-level attack aircraft. In essence, the 'Sverdlov' was the catalyst which led to the development of the Buccaneer.

pack or four Red Angel 'special' bombs. The aircraft would also be required to act as an in-flight refuelling tanker, and would be ready for service introduction by 1960.

The Admiralty requirement was particularly ambitious when one considers that low-level attack was still a relatively new concept. The Royal Air Force had already considered the possibility of developing a low altitude bomber but had subsequently abandoned the idea, and for the time being was confidently relying upon high flying V-Bombers (Valiant, Vulcan and Victor) to fulfil the long range bombing mission. The Admiralty's decision to opt for an ultra-low level strike aircraft was therefore surprisingly far-sighted, even though the practicality of performing the low level mission over the sea was obviously greater than for a similar overland mission. Invitations to tender for the design and production of ten or twenty development aircraft (there was to be no prototype as such) were sent to Armstrong Whitworth, Blackburn,

Fairey, Shorts and Westland, towards the end of March 1954, with submissions being required some six months later. A further eleven companies received copies of the invitation to tender and some three months later Percival requested permission to produce a semi-complete design, bearing in mind the remaining time in which a submission could be prepared. Percival were subsequently given permission to produce a 'ghost' design which would investigate a means of generating and deploying engine compressor gases to aerodynamic advantage, and although this design would be geared towards the Naval requirement, the associated engineering detail would not be required.

During September, the various companies issued their design brochures and models, while a late bid arrived from Hawker. Sydney Camm had originally been reluctant to become involved in what was essentially a bomber project, when Hawker was traditionally a designer of fighter aircraft. However, following a direct approach from the Admiralty, the Hawker design team produced a proposal

Hawker's M.148T submission, the P.1108, bore a remarkable resemblance to the A-4 Skyhawk.

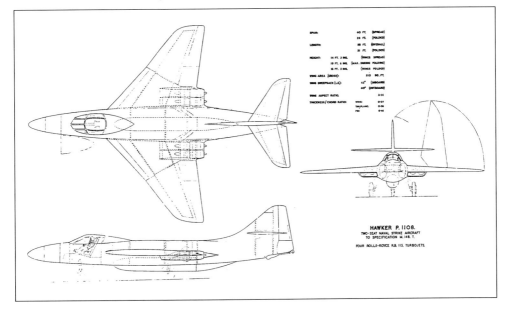

to meet the requirement, even though it was not backed-up by much enthusiasm from the company. Because Hawker traditionally utilised Rolls-Royce engines, a power plant which was still being designed was chosen to power Hawker's M.148T submission (there being no other suitable Rolls-Royce engine at the time). The design featured no less than four RB.115 engines positioned under the inner wing (a preliminary design even featured six engines), and Rolls-Royce's John Fozard had great difficulty convincing Hawker that the additional safety of four engines would be worth the direct trade-off against additional weight and complexity. Looking remarkably similar to an enlarged Douglas A-4 Skyhawk, the Hawker P.1108 was designed to carry the Green Cheese guided bomb in a semi-recessed position under the fuselage, but without complete information on projected construction schedules, the design was placed at a distinct disadvantage when compared with the other submissions, right from the start.

Armstrong Whitworth produced a relatively conventional design to meet the Navy's requirement, built around two de Havilland Gyron Junior engines, housed in nacelles positioned under the inner wing. It would have been possible to house the engines close to the fuselage, producing better drag characteristics, but this would have necessitated a restriction on the size of the internal fuel tanks or the bomb bay, which had to be large enough to carry Green Cheese. Placing the engines in nacelles slung under the wing was a better option, although the need to house the main undercarriage inside the inner wing effectively forces the engines further out on the wing, resulting in a potentially catastrophic single-engine asymmetric performance. Consequently, the undercarriage was repositioned in an unusual arrangement,

outboard of the engines. The restriction on take off weight to 40,000lb was one of the most important points which Armstrong Whitworth had to address. Keeping the wing span as small as possible enabled the design to rely upon just one wing fold joint, resulting in a significant weight saving thanks to the reduction in the number of heavy operating jacks and linkages which would have been required for a double wing fold. The design team also investigated the new concept of bleeding-off engine compressor air to flow over the wing flap upper surfaces, in order to prevent airflow breakaway and thus reduce the required landing speed (or conversely, increase the landing weight). This system was being used on the Supermarine Scimitar and was recognised as being ideal for carrier-borne aircraft. The flap blowing system didn't improve the design's take off performance however, and so Armstrong Whitworth proposed a jet deflection system, with cowls positioned to deflect the engine exhausts downwards through 45 degrees, thus reducing the necessary take off speed. The system was only to be employed during the catapult launch, as once airborne the engines would be required to provide the aircraft with as much forward thrust as possible, in order to achieve a safe speed (necessary in case of engine failure).

The AW.168 was capable of meeting both the range and maximum speed requirements, and the ingenious lift augmentation devices would have also enabled the aircraft to meet the specification's weight restriction. A full-sized wooden mock up of the aircraft was constructed (featuring folding wings and nose section), and Armstrong Whitworth proposed that two aircraft should be built as simple flying 'shells', with no lift devices, fold mechanisms or even bomb bay. These would be used to gather aerodynamic data, after which another aircraft

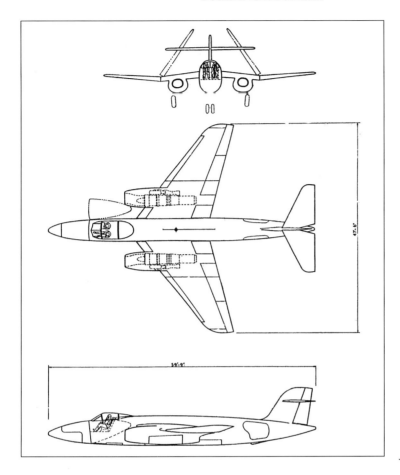

The Armstrong Whitworth M.148T design, the AW.168, was considered very seriously and came a close second to the winning submission from Blackburn.

would be introduced with wing flap blowing and jet lift systems. The subsequent development aircraft would then be fully equipped machines. Although Armstrong Whitworth was already committed to production of the Sea Hawk fighter, the company had sufficient resources to handle another major project, and the design team's capabilities were second to none, having only recently produced the very impressive AW.166 to meet the terms of specification ER.134T (which was only narrowly beaten by the successful Bristol 188). On the other hand, Armstrong Whitworth's production had in recent years been confined to the manufacture of aircraft designed by other companies, chiefly in the shape of the aforementioned Sea Hawk, and also the Meteor night

fighter. Even so, the AW.168 looked like a practical design worthy of serious consideration.

Fairey's submission was to say the least, somewhat unusual in terms of overall appearance, even though the configuration of the airframe was quite conventional. Following experience with the outstanding Fairey Delta 2 supersonic research aircraft, the choice of a delta wing layout enabled the aircraft to achieve a good high speed performance whilst possessing the same structure weight as a conventional swept winged design. The twin Gyron Junior engine installation was positioned inside the fuselage, mounted above the weapons bay resulting in a very deep slab-sided fuselage. The design brochure indicated that

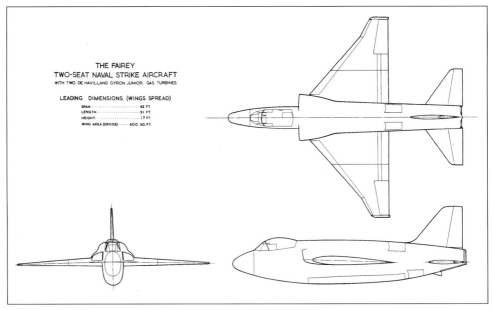

THE FAIREY
TWO-SEAT NAVAL STRIKE AIRCRAFT
WITH TWO DE HAVILLAND GYRON JUNIOR GAS TURBINES

LEADING DIMENSIONS (WINGS SPREAD)
SPAN·· 42 FT
LENGTH······························· 51 FT
HEIGHT······························· 17 FT
WING AREA (GROSS) ······ 500 SQ.FT

Fairey's unusual submission for Specification M.148T.

the bomb bay (which featured inward-retracting doors) would have to incorporate a lowering device or 'push-off' mechanism for the nuclear stores, while the wing's low speed lift devices (comprising supersonic engine compressor air bled over double-slotted flaps) had clearly not been developed sufficiently (the Ministry's assessor described the system as 'half-hearted'). On the credit side, the airframe was designed to be immensely strong, and with both fuselage and wing fuel tanks, range could be extended to 1,660 miles, or 2,130 miles with the addition of overload external tanks. Fairey believed that it would be impossible to meet all the requirements laid out in M.148T, and their design reflected what they considered to be the best compromise between the various specified figures. They outlined a three-year schedule for the production of the first aircraft (which was to be built to the specification standard but without the complete internal systems fit) and a six-year schedule for the completion of the 20th example. Although designed to be

both rugged and easily maintainable, the Fairey submission's conservative performance figures and poorly researched wing devices placed the aircraft at a disadvantage when compared with the other designs submitted.

Perhaps the most imaginative M.148T design was that submitted by Shorts, in the shape of their P.D.13. Some years previously, Shorts had produced a design to meet specification B.35/46 (which produced the Vulcan and Victor). Some properties of swept wing design were already well-established, including trailing edge control surface flutter, which prompted the Chief Designer, David Keith-Lucas, to choose a pivoting wing layout which would require the incorporation of a tail fin and rudder. Swept wings also have a tendency to twist under loads, altering the aerodynamic shape to such an extent that lift properties become seriously affected. In a tight turn, wing-tip lift diminishes, while a greater load is absorbed by the rest of the wing. The resulting aeroelastic effect pulls the tips upwards towards each other. However, by moving the wing structure's torsional box further aft, the wing's torsional and flexural axes coincide, so that when the wing flexes, the twisting moment is eliminated. Conversely, when the wing twists, the wing incidence is not affected. This new design was first described by Professor Geoffrey Hill at Westlands, who dubbed it the 'isoclinic' wing.

Although the Air Ministry opted for the Handley Page and Avro bomber designs in preference to the submission made by Shorts, the company decided to pursue the design and funded their own third-scale flying model of their proposed bomber, designated S.B.1. It was completed early in 1951 and made its first flight from Aldergrove (launched by winch) on 14 July of that year, with Tom Brooke-Smith at the controls. The S.B.1 was a relatively cheap and simple aircraft, manufactured mostly from spruce, featuring a shoulder-mounted wing (with a span of 38 feet) with a leading edge sweep of 42.5 degrees. However, the wing trailing edge began with an inboard sweep of zero degrees, sweeping back to 30 degrees at mid-span, before decreasing to just 18 degrees on the outer section. More than a third of the wing was pivoted, acting as ailerons in opposition, or as elevators in unison. Painted silver with black and yellow bands, the sole S.B.1 was serialed G-14-1, and after two test flights, preparations were made for the first towed flight launches. Fortunately, Shorts already had a company-owned tug aircraft in the shape of Sturgeon TT2 prototype VR363 which had been retained by the company after production of 24 Sturgeons for the Fleet Air Arm. On 20 July the S.B.1 was launched from the Sturgeon's tow cable at 10,000 feet, and performed perfectly. The only problem encountered by Brooke-Smith was the severe turbulence generated by the prop-wash generated by the Sturgeon's 2,080hp Merlin 140

engines, each driving huge six-bladed contra-rotating propellers. Brooke-Smith suggested that the towline be extended to keep the glider well away from the Sturgeon, but on the next flight (on 14 October), the problem was found to be even worse, and Brooke-Smith was forced to cut the glider from the towline at low altitude, causing the glider to hit the runway in a nose-down attitude at more than 80mph. He was injured quite severely, but the S.B.1 escaped relatively unscathed, although Brooke-Smith was less than keen to fly the glider and Sturgeon combination again. Having taken note of their Chief Test Pilot's views, the Shorts team decided to manufacture a redesigned fuselage to which the S.B.1's wing and tail could be fitted. The new design would incorporate a pair of Turbomeca Palas turbojets each developing 353lb static thrust. The new aircraft, designated S.B.4 was slightly longer than the glider and on 4 October 1953 the isoclinic wing took to the air again. Test flying was undertaken from both Aldergrove and Sydenham, and although the decidedly underpowered S.B.4 was limited to a top speed of 250mph and an altitude of 5,000 feet, the aircraft was a very useful research tool, indicating an impressive performance for the full-scale P.D.1 which would have had a wing span of 114 feet and a top speed of around Mach 0.87.

The S.B.4 was named 'Sherpa' before appearing at the 1954 SBAC display, where the little aircraft generated a great deal of interest. However, the Ministry of Supply still saw little point in developing the project any further, not least because a variety of rather less exotic solutions to high-speed flight were being discovered. After Shorts completed their research, the Sherpa was given to the College of Aeronautics at Cranfield where further research was conducted on a fairly low-key basis until 1964 when the Sherpa's engines reached the end of their fatigue life. Having gained so much knowledge of the isoclinic wing, it was no surprise therefore, that it formed the basis for the company's M.148T submission. Their P.D.13 was a tailless design with swept wings, featuring rotating wing controllers at one-third of the span. Two Rolls-Royce RA.19 engines were proposed which would feature a jet deflection facility, giving the aircraft a better low-speed lift, and with a Green Cheese weapon on board, the all-up weight was estimated to be 40,520lb. The first aircraft was to have been ready for flight in some 30 months, with the 20th pre-production machine flying within five years. Although a fairly radical design, the P.D.13 proposal was (unlike the competing submissions) based on data gleaned largely from a practical flight test programme, in the form of the Sherpa.

Westland also submitted a design to meet M.148T, the company being particularly keen to secure a contract for the aircraft which would eventually replace the Wyvern, an earlier Westland design which was approaching the end of a successful career with the Fleet Air Arm. Although fairly unusual for the time, the company's twin-finned proposal was remarkably similar in terms of airframe layout to Chance-Vought's Cutlass, with a short fuselage, a twin boom tail layout and fuselage-buried engines (Gyron Juniors) with a simple tricycle undercarriage, although the aircraft also had the addition of a small tail bumper wheel for projected carrier launches, enabling the aircraft to be raised off its nose gear to achieve a good launch angle of attack. With folding wings, the design's stumpy fuselage and short tail didn't require a folding nose section in order to meet the restrictive dimensions required for carrier handling. Like the Short P.D.13, the Westland design also featured

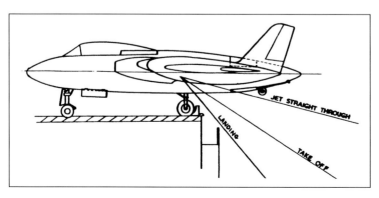

The Westland M.148T design resembled Chance-Vought's Cutlass, but featured a new jet-deflection system.

a jet deflection system (the engine exhausts emerging mid-fuselage, rather than at the tail, as in the Cutlass), with the twin engines being rotated downwards for take-off, and further downwards for approach and landing. The delivery schedule offered a first aircraft in 27 months, with the 20th example within five years.

Blackburn, a company with a long tradition of naval aircraft design, also submitted their proposal as Blackburn's Chief Engineer Roy Boot (often regarded as "Mr Buccaneer") recalls; "Sitting in my corner of the Brough Project Office in 1952, directly after the substantial effort expended on the N114T fighter design which was abandoned, I had attempted to anticipate the need and had drawn up the initial B.103 design. I had also caused a low speed wind tunnel model to be constructed. Of course at this time the modus operandi and its ramifications, weapons and equipment to be carried were a matter of guesswork. It seemed obvious to me that to do a worthwhile job a twin engined aircraft was necessary and of those on which information was available, the 11,000lb thrust Armstrong Siddeley Sapphire AS.Sa.7 engine offered the best characteristics. The problem was, within severe carrier constraints of weight and dimensions, to produce an aircraft with the stipulated radius of action with a high subsonic performance with a strong emphasis on high speed low level characteristics and with a large weapons bay, capable of use at much higher speeds than had previously been practicable."

Blackburn's B.103 was developed around a wing design which was based on the company's experience with the HP.88 (Blackburn designation YB.2), a unique experimental aircraft which was built for Handley Page during the design and development phase of the Victor bomber. The huge bomber's complex wing platform was manufactured to one-third scale, and attached to a Supermarine 510 fuselage resulting in VX330, an unorthodox design by any standards, which first flew on 21 June 1951. The compound sweep wing interested the Brough design team, and the concept was incorporated (in simplified form) into a series of designs for naval fighters which the company were producing at the time. Two angles of wing sweep were adopted, together with a continuous (straight) trailing edge and a thickness-to-chord ratio which decreased from wing root to tip. This layout caused the inner wing to stall first at high speeds, while a slatted

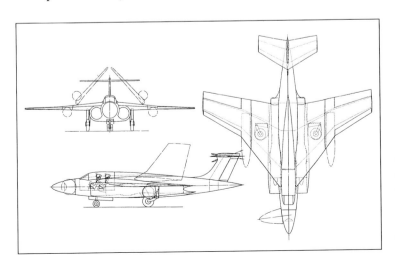

The 1952 Blackburn design study drawing which shows how the basic layout of the NA.39, particularly the wing plan form, was already established.

outer wing eliminated the risk of a low speed stall, thus avoiding any pitch-up problems throughout the flight envelope. The tailplane was positioned on top of the B.103's fin, even though Gloster were experiencing design problems with their Javelin fighter's high-set tailplane at the time, leading to much debate at Brough.

In order to avoid a heavy and complicated double wing fold, the B.103's wing span was restricted to 45 feet, with a total wing area of 650 sq ft. However, in order to do this, the wing's low speed lift had to be enhanced and jet lift trials, which were being conducted on a Meteor, seemed to offer a solution to the problem. Blackburn calculated that a 60-degree deflection of the Sapphire's engine thrust would reduce the approach speed by 25 knots. On the other hand, the system couldn't be easily adapted to catapult take-offs, and there was always the question of how the system could safely operate in the event of an asymmetric landing approach caused by a single engine failure. Consequently, the B.103 design was carefully drawn-up to allow for the incorporation of the jet deflection principle even though Blackburn remained ambivalent towards its usefulness. The deflected thrust line had to be close to the aircraft's centre of gravity, therefore the engines had to be positioned well forward relative to the wing. This arrangement enhanced the structural strength of the design by allowing wing spar rings to encompass the jet pipes, rather than having to run the spar loads across the engines. Likewise, the load bearing structure was bent over the weapons bay, resulting in a very robust construction, ideal for low level operations.

Even with the addition of jet lift, the B.103's all-up weight was projected to be some 42,000lb, which was still fairly high for carrier operations. However, early in 1954 a great deal of official interest was being directed towards a new lightweight engine which promised a thrust of 7,500lb. This appeared to be more suitable for Blackburn, who concluded that, at least in theory, a saving of up to 5,500lb in weight might be achieved with this engine. Consequently, design work was based on this power plant, resulting in a lighter aircraft with a span of 42 feet. However, additional wing lift was still a priority, and it was the United States which eventually caught Blackburn's attention. John Attinello (working for the US Navy and the NACA) had produced some valuable data on the possibilities of bleeding high pressure air from an aircraft's engines, over the upper surface of wing flaps, so as to prevent airflow separation over these surfaces at low speeds, thus creating extra lift. Dr John Williams at the National Physical Laboratory and Lewis Boddington at the Ministry of Supply investigated the concept and recommended that Blackburn should develop the idea still further. Some flight testing on a modified Grumman Panther had already been done, and the principle was being incorporated into Supermarine's Scimitar. The Blackburn design team established that air could be bled from the B.103's engines at a sufficiently high pressure to 'choke' the outlet slits and thus create an even air distribution across the wing flaps. They calculated that approach and launch speeds could be reduced by up to 15 knots.

Roy Boot recalls that, "Purely instinctively, I had a horror of terminating blowing at the outboard end of the flap and so I proposed to avoid this by extending the blow over the whole of the wing span, in the hope that we could eventually droop the ailerons to effectively obtain a full span flap. One day our Technical Director (N. E. Rowe) looked over my shoulder and asked what lift coefficient I thought we might get if the ailerons were drooped. I took a deep breath and looked

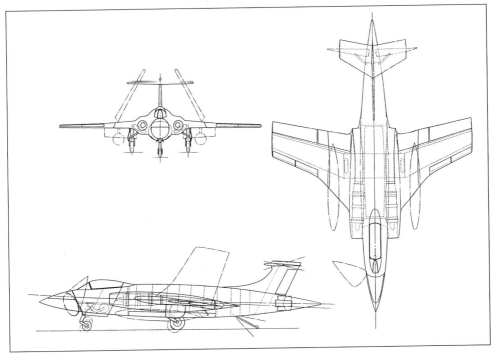

The 1954 drawing of the B.103, prior to the introduction of area ruling, which developed the design into the definitive shape of the first NA.39.

into my proverbial crystal ball and said 'about two'. There and then the decision was made to go for it, right from square one." Normal flaps would occupy roughly 65 per cent of the wing span. The wing fold break was to be at 45 per cent of the span, and this meant that the flaps would have to be made in two sections. Now that the team had decided to droop the ailerons this seemed like a wasteful arrangement, so the ailerons were extended inboard to the wing fold position. The Naval Staff had insisted that the new strike aircraft should have full anti-icing protection and this requirement was influential in the eventual design of the aircraft's wing blowing system. Blackburn's designers initially looked at electrical anti-icing, but the relatively crude systems possible at the time would have required a considerable amount of power. Consequently, engine bleed air seemed like a more prac-

tical idea, although the design's wing leading edge slat would prevent anti-icing ducting being fitted in that area. Therefore, it was decided that the wing leading edge should be fixed, incorporating a slit along the upper surface through which high pressure air would re-energise the local airflow in much the same way as a slat would, but at the same time provide hot air for anti-icing protection.

Not surprisingly, this seemingly simple concept had some complications, not least the need to shut-off the blowing system on the wing trailing edge, when only anti-icing was required. Likewise, for conditions outside of the launch and landing configuration, when the system pressure would be higher, a regulation system would be needed to avoid damaging the pressurised ducts. To add to the complications, the air bleed system was then extended to the tailplane. Wing blowing over the flaps combined with drooped ailerons would effectively triple the aircraft's pitching moment when compared with a more traditional unblown part-span flap configuration. This required the tailplane to provide much more lift in order to counter the pitching moment and the large trim changes associated with flap selection. Fitting a trailing edge flap to the tailplane (geared directly to flap and aileron droop selection) would partially solve the problem, but the combination of decreasing speed and increasing load would create the risk of a leading edge stall on the tailplane. Thus, the anti-icing duct along the tailplane was similarly modified to provide high pressure blowing, this time across the under surface.

With much of the design now fixed on paper, Blackburn produced a one-fifth scale representation of a half wing, in order to gain some practical experience with the wing blowing system, before submitting the final design tender. A Palouste engine was already on site at Brough, and this was used to produce high pressure air across both trailing and leading edge slits, giving the design team some valuable data, which confirmed that the system would work. There was some doubt as to how accurate the data was, bearing in mind the possible scale effect of the wing model, but further analysis by experts at RAE Farnborough suggested that the figures were right and that wing blowing would provide a significant amount of lift, albeit at the expense of engine thrust. At this stage in the design's development, a final choice of power plant for the aircraft had yet to be made; the Sapphire seemed to be the best choice, scaled down from 11,000lb thrust (which would have made the aircraft too heavy to meet the Naval requirement) to around 7,000lb. This lower thrust would meet the strict requirement specifications, but it was already acknowledged

that an 11,000lb thrust engine would have been ideal, if the aircraft's all-up weight could have been allowed to increase accordingly. On 4 December 1953, Rolls-Royce outlined plans for a new light-weight engine which was expected to deliver up to 7,500lb thrust, and as described previously, Blackburn quickly tailored the B.103 design around this engine. Just a few weeks later however, Rolls-Royce decided not to proceed with the programme, leaving Blackburn to look elsewhere for a suitable power plant. By this stage, Armstrong Siddeley were now able to offer a new design in the shape of the P151 which offered good thrust and weight characteristics, but also delivered variable thrust in relation to forward speed, something which quickly prompted Blackburn to look more seriously at de Havilland's scaled-down version of their Gyron engine.

Estimated at 8,000lb thrust, the Gyron Junior seemed ideal for the B.103, and it appeared prudent to de-rate the thrust to 7,000lb in order to run the engine at a lower temperature to provide better fuel consumption and fatigue life. Unfortunately, the boundary layer wing blowing system was expected to require some twelve per cent of the engine's mass flow, which would reduce maximum thrust to just 6,000lb – too little to meet the necessary performance figures. Consequently, the original higher temperature design was restored and after some re-working of the control system, the Gyron Junior could provide 6,500lb thrust with full wing blowing in operation, and the development of turbine blade cooling later enabled the full 7,000lb thrust to be achieved. Bristol also proposed a new engine design, their BE33, promising to provide a very respectable 11,400lb of thrust. Larger and somewhat heavier than the Gyron Junior, the BE33 did however possess a good fuel consumption figure, and was clearly much more adaptable for future developments, and was ideal for supplying boundary layer control air. On the down side, the BE33 development programme was likely to be fairly long, and maybe a year longer than the Gyron Junior's (the latter being a smaller version of an existing power plant). Blackburn attempted to design the B.103 around both engines, but in view of the BE33's delay and the production of the Gyron Junior already underway, the design team opted to build the B.103 airframe around only the Gyron Junior, and as part of the weight saving process, the wing spar rings (through which the engines would be slotted) were made only wide enough to accommodate the Gyron Junior, the BE33 being three inches wider in diameter. The BE33 programme was eventually abandoned, and with the benefit of hindsight, Blackburn had made the right decision to opt for the Gyron Junior, a less-than perfect powerplant for the B.103, but by far the best power plant available at the time.

While Blackburn continued working on the B.103 design, the Ministry of Supply carefully gathered information on the capabilities of each company which submitted a design to meet M.148T, having wisely concluded that the chosen design would not only have to be the best available, but would also have to be manufactured by a company with the expertise and resources necessary for such an advanced project. Armstrong Whitworth were identified as being one of the companies less suited to the task. For some years they had concentrated on the production of aircraft which had been designed by other companies, most notably the Meteor night fighters and their recent work was largely devoted to development and manufacture of Sea Hawks. Conversely, they had a good design staff which had produced unusual aircraft such as the experimental tailless

AW.52, and their AW.166 (submitted to meet specification ER.134T) was regarded as a very close second choice to the Bristol 188 (which was selected for that particular requirement). Their submission for M.148T was technically sound and very detailed, but their current status conspired against them.

Fairey was a relatively small company, and their workload was already very high. Apart from continuing development of their hugely successful Gannet, they were also devoting a great effort towards helicopters in the shape of their Ultra-Light and the huge Rotodyne. They also had the unique Fairey Delta 2 programme to handle, and the Design Conference felt that it would be unwise to over-stretch the company still further, despite Fairey's acknowledged background in naval aircraft design and high speed flight research. It was agreed that the Gannet programme was likely to suffer if Fairey's resources were required for the M.148T and so the company's submission was placed at a disadvantage. Shorts, on the other hand, had relatively little work to handle. They were busy producing the Seamew and the revolutionary S.C.1 vertical take-off experimental aircraft, and they had considerable experience in the production of naval aircraft design. They also had the S.B.5 and Sherpa programme to offer as concrete proof of their capabilities and their design staff was regarded as being second to none. To be judged against this were the technical aspects of their P.D.13 design, especially the development of a jet deflection system and their unique wing design. Despite this, the Shorts submission was certainly a firm favourite.

Hawker were heavily committed to development of the Hunter and although the company had a long history of quality design and production, they had traditionally concentrated on single seat fighter designs, whereas M.148T was a much larger and more ambitious project. More importantly, the proposed RB.115 engines required for their submission were unlikely to be available within the necessary timescale. Likewise, Westland also looked unlikely to be capable of producing a suitable aircraft, as they even admitted in their submission brochure. To successfully develop their design, they would require at least another 100 staff or alternatively, would have to sub-contract more than half of the programme to another company. They had produced the unique jet deflection Meteor and they also had direct experience with their Wyvern, the aircraft which M.148T would effectively replace, but without sufficient staff, their projected development and flight schedule was deemed to be overly optimistic, possibly by more than nine months.

The Blackburn submission appeared to be more practical, in that the company was approaching the end of their Beverley freighter production programme, and they had a strong and experienced design staff. The company also had a very long tradition of naval aircraft design (their factory was sited next to the Humber estuary to facilitate flight testing of seaplanes) and some experience of high speed design, having produced the HP.88 for Handley Page. Although their B.103 design was fairly straightforward, it did include the potentially problematical boundary layer control system, and the proposed machined skin and huge centre section forgings appeared to be quite ambitious. However, the latter features were also recognised as being the basis of a very sound design proposal, and on balance, the Blackburn submission looked very favourable. Assessment of the companies was completed on 18 November 1954 and the Tender Design Conference took place at the Ministry of Supply on 3 December of the same year.

At the conference, both the Hawker and Westland designs were immediately excluded from further consideration. Hawker hadn't submitted a formal tender in any case, and the Westland design didn't offer more than modest performance, even if the company's production capabilities could be expanded. Consequently, the choice laid between the designs submitted by Armstrong Whitworth, Blackburn, Fairey and Shorts. Bearing in mind the production assessments which had already been made, the conference also looked at projected performance figures, handling qualities, weapons carriage and structure, as part of their detailed deliberations. Fairey was eventually dropped from further consideration, chiefly because the company lacked sufficient design capacity but also because their proposed aircraft wouldn't meet the necessary high altitude cruise limits laid down by M.148T and was inferior to the other designs in terms of overall predicted performance. Shorts was the next casualty, largely because their design was very advanced, and featured many revolutionary aspects of design which had yet to be explored in detail. The unusual isoclinic wing certainly raised a few proverbial eyebrows, and the very fact that no tailless design had yet proved to be an operational success, suggested that the idea of producing such a revolutionary aircraft for deck operations was at best a risky proposition. The team of Royal Aircraft Establishment experts preferred the Armstrong Whitworth proposal, despite some doubts as to the company's weight estimates for the aircraft. Their design reputation and the promise of service deliveries in 1960 put them ahead of Blackburn's submission, which was likely to be completed a year later, largely because of their requirement for new machine tools which would have to be procured or manufactured. However, the

Naval Staff believed that it although the Armstrong Whitworth design was good, it would be worth waiting another year for the Blackburn aircraft, which promised to be superior, with better performance, ease of maintenance and good development potential.

The design conference failed to reach a definitive conclusion, as it was eventually agreed that the ambitious nature of the project should be reflected in the selection of two designs, which after a period of further wind tunnel and design work, could be narrowed-down to just one aircraft for full production. However, Blackburn were unofficially informed that they were now almost certain to be selected, and were already on a 'short list' with just one other company. During February 1955 they were given the go-ahead to proceed with the initial design process and to begin work on preliminary production tasks. At the next conference meeting the whole matter was reappraised and the decision was made to adopt just one design right from the start. Much to the surprise of the various competing companies, the Blackburn submission was accepted as being the best all-round proposal, with the right combination of advanced design balanced with sound technical knowledge, which convinced the Naval Staff that they wouldn't necessarily get the most technically advanced aircraft, but they would at least be certain of getting an aircraft into service at the earliest opportunity which would be able to perform all of the necessary tasks allocated to it, while still being adaptable to further development at a later stage. Letters of rejection were sent to the remaining companies and during July 1955 an order was placed with Blackburn for a batch of 20 development aircraft, now referred to by the company as the NA.39, reflecting the original Naval Requirement designation. This order was something of a departure from the normal practise of building just one or two prototypes of any new combat aircraft. Experience with aircraft such as the Hunter and Swift had illustrated how advanced aircraft design necessitated a very long and thorough development programme which couldn't be effectively handled by just a couple of aircraft. Consequently, the first three NA.39s would be conventional prototype 'flying shells', the first nine machines being assigned to development flying, with a further five for clearance trials at Boscombe Down. The remaining six would be allocated to service trials with the Royal Navy. As Roy Boot explains, "Within batches of three in sequence of build there was sufficient slack to make up for the loss of one of these aircraft, but the loss of two within the same batch would have had serious consequences. The one exception to this was the second aircraft which contained elaborate special instrumentation for flight flutter and strength testing. Fortunately no such misfortune befell us but with the inevitable mishaps, the flexibility built into the original programme was fully utilised before we finished and in fact it was just adequate."

The production of an initial developmental fleet is now common practice within the aerospace industry. Likewise, the concept of the Weapons System was first applied during the production of the NA.39, and unlike every previous production contract, Blackburn were responsible for a much greater part of the complete product, involving extensive liaison with equipment suppliers. The use of both analogue and digital computers was also introduced during the programme, and the dramatic growth in electronics and avionics development led to a technical staff expansion of more than three times the company's size prior to the NA.39 contract. In many ways, the new naval aircraft also ushered-in the basis of the modern defence aerospace industry. The

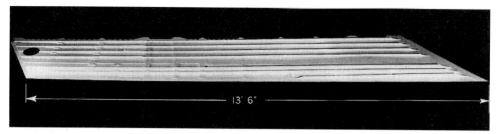

13' 6"

Blackburn adopted radical new manufacturing techniques for their NA.39. In order to make the strike aircraft's wing as strong as possible whilst still remaining relatively light, many panels were milled from solid blocks of metal, the stringers being created as an integral part of the structure.

manufacturing process was also equally ambitious, and the aircraft's projected operating environment required the design to be immensely strong and capable of withstanding severe buffeting and load reversals during almost every flight. Extensive use was to be made of integrally-machined spars, ribs and skin panels, effectively cutting the required components out of solid blocks. The US Air Force had already commissioned a programme to enable machine tool manufacturers to produce skin mills and stretch presses, having studied the advantages of such processes since 1948. However in the UK there was nothing of a comparable nature, and Blackburn had to go directly to the USA to find a suitable skin mill. Unfortunately it quickly became clear that it would take between two and three years for a suitable machine to be delivered to the UK, by which time the first NA.39 would have to be ready to fly. Consequently, and probably with more than a little Yorkshire determination, Blackburn simply decided to manufacture their own skin mill, and less than a year later it was fully operational, and three more machines were subsequently built. Blackburn also made plans to build a stretch press, but thankfully the Ministry of Supply managed to locate and import a suitable machine directly from the USA. Even with the huge machines in place, production of huge components from solid billets was by no means easy, and

Blackburn devoted a great deal of effort towards the production process. Their efforts were rewarded, as the completed aircraft was stronger and more rugged than anything which had hitherto been produced.

The design process went ahead smoothly, despite a great deal of early uncertainty surrounding various aspects of the overall weapons system. The radar, for example, was initially expected to be a twin installation to locate distinctive 'sore thumb' targets at long range, and also provide ranging information for the final attack run. It wasn't until some way into the programme that the Ferranti Blue Parrot radar was selected to fulfil both roles and it was fortunate that the system could be incorporated into the aircraft without any significant redesign being necessary. The projected weapons fit was a rather more certain aspect of the programme however, and from the outset it was clear that the Green Cheese and Red Beard bomb (the latter referred to rather euphemistically as a TMB – Target Marker Bomb) would be better housed inside an internal weapons bay, rather than on an external weapons pylon. The bomb bay would require a central store station for both types of atomic weapon, and two more positioned side-by-side for medium-sized conventional stores, and two smaller pairs of stations for 1,000lb bombs. The size of the weapons bay was thus established, based on the specified

The main load bearing structure of the NA.39, shortly after completion at Brough. The main spars are bolted to the rings through which the Gyron Junior engines would later be positioned. Not surprisingly, the structure made the aircraft immensely strong, and able to withstand a full operational life at low level.

dimensions of Green Cheese and Red Beard. However, the Green Cheese bomb had to acquire its target before release, and would therefore have to be presented externally. Other conventional stores couldn't be suspended from a bomb bay roof as was traditional in bomber design, simply because the high speed aerodynamics of the new aircraft wouldn't allow for the use of conventional two-piece bomb bay doors and in any case, this system wouldn't have allowed Green Cheese to be lowered before launch. Some thought was given to inward-tracking

The primary armament of the NA.39 was the Red Beard free-fall atomic bomb, euphemistically referred to as a 'Target Marker Bomb' or 'TMB'. This photograph, taken on 22 April 1959, illustrates a wooden mock-up of the bomb used for engineering work at Brough during development of the aircraft's bomb bay.

doors (and a lowering roof) but the best option was to attach stores to a one-piece door which would rotate though 180 degrees, as used on both the Voodoo and Martin B-57. In order to present the homing bomb, the door's rotation gearing was connected to a rack and pinion arrangement which lowered the door as it rotated. However, as the NA.39 programme progressed, the naval staff abandoned the complicated Green Cheese bomb in favour of the free fall Red Beard store, and Blackburn redesigned the bomb door with a simple hinge fit. There were still some reservations as to how the door might affect aircraft handling during rotation, even though wind tunnel tests confirmed that when fully open or closed, the door was satisfactory. The Blackburn design team's solution was to rotate the door at high speed, so that any noticeable effects simply wouldn't have time to develop.

Shortly before the final B.103 design was submitted, some preliminary information on Area Rule became available from studies conducted in the USA. It had been discovered that aerodynamic drag over the airframe of a high performance aircraft could be reduced if the aircraft's fuselage was suitably shaped to cause the airflow to smoothly and gradually expand as it moved from nose to tail. Although the precise nature of the phenomenon was still not known, the basic knowledge obtained suggested that by redesigning the NA.39's fuselage to produce a 'Coke bottle' effect, the distribution of airflow across the whole aircraft would be more even. To some extent the NA.39's contours couldn't be altered too drastically, especially around the weapons bay which had to be the shape and size already determined. However, the sides of the forward fuselage could be pulled in to compensate for the drag of the canopy area. The wing's trailing edge sweep was increased from 10 to 20 degrees and the

area behind the wing was enlarged to produce the NA.39's characteristic 'waisted' appearance. With hindsight it is debatable whether the very basic application of Area Rule contributed significantly to the type's performance, but the resulting enlargement to the rear fuselage did at least produce a very useful equipment stowage area at no aerodynamic cost.

Another striking feature of the NA.39's design was the dive brake installation. The naval requirement laid down a very stringent dive performance which called for a drag increase much larger than anything previously achieved. The use of conventional fuselage-mounted doors wouldn't be sufficiently effective, nor would spoiler-type devices attached to the wings. Instead it was proposed to split the extreme rear fuselage into two petals, sliding along a crosshead with drag links. This was certainly capable of producing a huge amount of drag, even if it was still somewhat short of the Admiralty's ideal, but it was hoped that the installation would provide very effective brakes without creating large trim changes when the petals were opened. In fact, the brakes later proved to be particularly troublesome in terms of trim problems, which were only solved after a lengthy flight development programme. More significantly, the air brakes greatly improved the aircraft's carrier approach handling qualities. Although aerodynamic (profile) drag increases with speed, another form of drag which is lift-dependant, actually increases as airspeed decreases. Consequently, at minimum drag speed the two drag components are equal, but below that speed the total drag increases and begins to affect the aircraft's handling qualities. The NA.39's huge airbrakes significantly reduced the minimum drag speed to such an extent that it was well below the type's approach speed. The brakes also increased overall drag however, but this was easily compensated for by increasing engine thrust, which in turn improved engine mass flow and pressure supplied to the boundary layer control system. Yet another benefit was the reduction in the fuselage length when the brakes were opened, enabling the aircraft to easily meet the Admiralty's stowed length specification.

As production of the NA.39 got under-way, it quickly became clear that the task of machining skin panels and structural members from solid billets would be far from easy. Although the process was fairly simple in theory, the Blackburn design staff were particularly concerned with the long-term strength of the airframe which was to be operated in the harshest conditions imaginable, at ultra low level and at high speed with a sizable weapons load.

Clearly, a tough aircraft could be manufactured, but if the aircraft was to survive ten or maybe 15 years of severe buffeting and load reversals, great attention would have to be paid to possible sources of stress failures. Consequently, every effort was made to avoid small radii and sharp changes of section, where stress would otherwise be concentrated. Of course, the Blackburn staff's far-sighted approach was invaluable in later years, when their creation continued to remain in service far beyond its originally anticipated withdrawal date. Once the production process was properly established however, the construction of the first aircraft (XK486) proceeded fairly smoothly, the huge fuselage centre section emerging from its jig in just three months.

The Blackburn B.103 nearing completion in the Brough factory. Like most prototypes, the airframe's clean lines have yet to be broken by a series of 'bolt-on' attachments developed during the aircraft's operational life. Note also the contours of the nose section which have yet to be revised to house the Blue Parrot radar.

CHAPTER TWO

Airborne

As the prospect of a first flight drew closer, attention turned to the choice of test airfield for the aircraft's flight development programme. Although the Brough factory was adjacent to Blackburn's private airfield, the short concrete runway was woefully inadequate for a jet-powered strike aircraft. The NA.39 would probably have got safely airborne within the space available but a much longer runway would be needed for regular test flying, and the nearest to Brough was a disused former RAF base at Holme-on-Spalding Moor, some ten miles away (18 miles by road). There the main runway was 6,000 feet long and was resurfaced, together with a connecting taxy track and there were a small number of offices and laboratory buildings. One J-type hangar was refurbished, two

Aerial view of Holme-on-Spalding Moor, the operations centre for the Buccaneer programme. The three hangars used by Blackburn are clearly visible, together with a pair of NA.39s to the rear of the control tower. A former World War Two bomber airfield, Holme-on-Spalding Moor was reactivated for Buccaneer operations and remained active into the 1980s until both the Buccaneer and Phantom (another aircraft for which Brough was responsible) were phased-out of RAF service. The airfield has now reverted to agricultural use.

The route from Brough to the RAE airfield at Bedford had to be examined very carefully prior to the delivery (by road) of the first NA.39. The ingenious and simple calibration device used by Blackburn was a truck-mounted wooden frame, matching the dimensions of the aircraft. The vehicle was used to trace the route which would be taken from Brough to Bedford, and from Brough to Holme-on-Spalding Moor.

T-type hangars being brought back into use some time later, one to house test aircraft and the other for support equipment.

Even though Holme-on-Spalding Moor was ideal for test flying, the Air Ministry was still uneasy at the prospect of a valuable prototype making its first flight there, and it was agreed that a runway in excess of 9,000 feet would be preferable. This effectively left Blackburn with the choice of either the RAE airfield at Thurleigh (Bedford) or the A&AEE's airfield at Boscombe Down. Not surprisingly, the former was chosen simply because it was much closer to Brough and preparations were made to transfer the completed aircraft by road, ready for a first flight during April 1958. After completing resonance tests and engine runs at Brough, XK486 was painstakingly dismantled again and loaded onto a trailer truck, ready for the

long journey by road, under huge shrouds to hide its identity. In 1958 an almost obsessive concern for security meant that as much of the NA.39's programme as possible was kept secret. Early publicity photographs of the aircraft were carefully positioned so that surrounding buildings would not give any clue to the aircraft's size. Likewise, plan views of the aircraft's wings were not released, and the paint scheme applied to the early test aircraft varied slightly on each airframe (particularly the size of national insignia), in order to 'confuse the enemy'. Even so, one leading journal was able to produce a three-view drawing of the aircraft which was accurate to within a few inches.

Following reassembly at Bedford, the aircraft began making high speed taxy runs on the airfield. In order to reach the end of the huge runway, XK486 had to be taxied for more than two miles along a

Hidden under protective wraps, the first NA.39 heads for Bedford on top of an articulated truck. For security reasons, the aircraft remained shrouded throughout the journey, and in order to avoid arousing too much attention, the truck retained its civilian haulage titles and travelled without a conspicuous security escort. Who could have imagined that the truck was carrying a nuclear bomber?

(downhill) perimeter track. Because of some early problems with the two engines when set at idle rpm, thrust was set slightly higher than would have otherwise been necessary and in order to keep the aircraft within safe taxy speed limits, frequent brake application was required. Test pilot Derek Whitehead eventually lined-up XK486 on the runway and opened up the throttles to full power, quickly accelerating to 100 knots at which stage he cut power and applied full brake pressure. As the aircraft began to slow the brakes

NA.39 XK486 out in the open air in January 1958 after being painted prior to its first flight. Early engine trials were carried out on the airfield at Brough, after which the aircraft was partially dismantled to be transported to Bedford, Brough's runway being far too short and unsuitable for any significant extension.

April 30, 1958 and XK486 roars into the air for the first time, from Thurleigh's 10,000-foot runway. The first flight was completely successful and presented few surprises for test pilot Derek Whitehead.

overheated dramatically and a spectacular fire ensued while Whitehead steered the aircraft off the runway onto the grass. When the aircraft came to a standstill the starboard main tyre burst, fusible plugs (which melt as the tyre overheats) not having been installed at this stage. The resulting explosive force was unfortunately directed upwards, causing severe damage to the inner wing, requiring repairs which were anticipated to require possibly three months of work. Thanks to the efforts of the repair team however, the aircraft was back on the airfield on 29 April, to recommence taxy trials. The following day, Derek Whitehead (with Bernard Watson as observer) taxied XK486 back onto the runway and executed a perfect take-off with a Meteor acting as chase plane. A trouble free flight ensued lasting for 39 minutes during which Whitehead took the aircraft to 17,000 feet. The landing was achieved with the use of the aircraft's huge airbrakes, much to the surprise of the Meteor chase pilot who immediately overshot his target once the brakes were deployed. Everyone was delighted with the aircraft's performance and Blackburn were particularly proud that the first flight had been achieved just 33 months after the production contract was placed

with them. Having met all of their target dates for the programme, they were more than keen to begin flight testing.

The second flight didn't go quite to plan however. As XK486 approached Bedford the undercarriage was lowered, only to find that the nosewheel remained locked up. Despite emergency selections and fairly severe manoeuvring designed to shake the wheel loose, it refused to budge and it was decided that the aircraft would be landed with the main wheels down, allowing the aircraft to settle onto its nose as the landing speed decreased. As the aircraft was turned on to finals the airbrakes were deployed and, much to everyone's astonishment and delight, the nosewheel suddenly popped down, enabling Whitehead to make another perfect landing. Subsequent investigation revealed that part of the nosewheel steering mechanism had been incorrectly installed, allowing the nosewheel to move as the rudder pedals were operated in flight. Eventually this jammed the wheel against the bay sill. However, when the air brakes were opened, so much hydraulic power was required that there was a momentary drop in hydraulic power to the rest of the airframe, and this had allowed the nosewheel to centre itself and thus extend. Needless to say, modifications to the system were quickly made. Subsequent tests flying at Bedford concentrated on the aircraft's wing blowing system, and despite the complex nature of the system, the test flying proceeded remarkably well. Some excessive yaw and noticeable buffeting was encountered with the ailerons drooped to 30 degrees, but a reduction of five degrees produced much more satisfactory handling without any loss of lift. The only major problem Blackburn had, was trying to obtain approval to transfer test flying to Holme-on-Spalding Moor, and XK486 remained at Bedford for some three months.

During July 1958, test flying began at Holme-on-Spalding Moor, when XK486 arrived from Bedford. The aircraft was more than capable of safe operation on the 6,000-ft runway, but as a precautionary measure, arrester gear (initially nylon pack type but later replaced by a more modern hydraulic type) was installed. The system was used occasionally, and on one memorable test 'flight' the system was inadvertently brought into operation during a take off run, when the aircraft's tail hook was accidentally dropped, causing the pilot some concern when he quickly came to a standstill, despite having had both engines at full throttle. One of the first tasks to be undertaken at the airfield was a canopy jettison test under a full flight load. The Bedford trials had all been placed under a 350 knots speed restriction until this test was completed, so once the aircraft was back in Yorkshire, the aircraft was rigged for the test. A representative metal canopy was fitted, and rigged to a jack system inside the newly-refurbished hangar. Catch nets were installed and the canopy jettison gun seats were linked to a string which was fed out from the aircraft to a safe position from where the test could be

initiated. The design team were concerned that the valuable aircraft might be damaged and great tension surrounded the test. There was too much tension all round in fact, as the string broke. Fortunately, the test was re-rigged and proved to be successful, enabling test flying at more representative speeds to begin.

The NA.39's flight envelope was quickly extended to 450 knots, much of the flying being performed at low level over East Yorkshire, there being few airspace restrictions in the area. The only major airspace user was RAF Leconfield where Hunters and Javelins occasionally competed for ATC routings. Many of these flights were accompanied by a Meteor or Hunter chase aircraft, Blackburn having adopted what was an American practice. Indeed, a considerable amount of the NA.39's test programme owed much to American expertise as the aircraft was supported by the US Mutual Weapons Development Programme, designed to provide funds for armament projects being pursued by friendly nations. Some $13 million was allocated to flight test instrumentation for the NA.39 in the form of trace recorders for data, magnetic tape for flutter testing and film for weapon release, such equipment being readily available in the USA. The flutter tests were conducted on aeroelastic models in a 'blow down' wind tunnel at Langley in Virginia. This specialised wind tunnel enabled the test team to induce flutter up to the point of destruction, at which stage the model's broken parts would pass harmlessly away. Blackburn studied the tunnel and its operating systems very carefully and built a British equivalent at Brough during 1956, the tunnel still being in use to this day. During September 1958 XK486 was flown to Boscombe Down, from where it was to perform daily demonstration flights at the SBAC show.

Pictured over the huge Royal Aircraft Establishment airfield at Bedford, XK486 sweeps majestically past the cameraman, accompanied by Meteor WS667, the chase plane assigned to the first flight trials. Although the NA.39 handled fairly predictably, the aircraft's sizeable air brake produced a phenomenal deceleration which, on the first flight, took the Meteor pilot by surprise, the chase plane quickly overtaking the NA.39 as soon as XK486's brake petals opened.

For security reasons the aircraft wouldn't land at Farnborough, and a few weeks after the show, XK486 returned to Boscombe Down to enable naval test pilots to have a first preview of the aircraft. For much of the time while the aircraft was with the A&AEE, the prevailing weather conditions were fairly turbulent, as the aircraft had yet to be fitted with an autostabiliser system, the test pilots found that the aircraft was quite a handful during landing approaches. As most of the pilots were used to flying Sea Vixens and Scimitars, they felt that the NA.39 was somewhat under-powered, but in other respects they were quite impressed with the aircraft.

Early in September, the second NA.39 (XK487) had been completed at Brough, and it was towed on its landing gear to Holme-on-Spalding Moor, from where it first flew on 12 September. It was a slightly more robust aircraft than XK486, fitted with strain gauges and flutter exciters, known as 'bonkers' which were basically small explosive cartridges fitted into the aircraft's wing tips. Flutter was found to be a minor problem, the only major modification found necessary

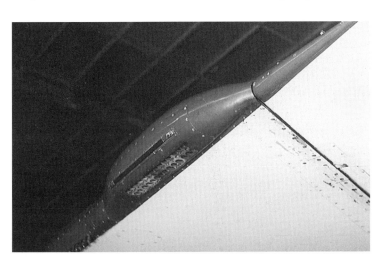

Various aircraft in the NA.39 test fleet were fitted with 'bonkers', the explosive charges fitted to the aircraft's wing tips. Contained inside a fairing, these small charges were detonated to artificially induce wing flutter for various airframe and weapons trials flights.

being balance weights for the tip of each tailplane. The tailplane jack strain gauge was also used when the aircraft began flight testing at transonic speeds. Because the aircraft's airspeed and Mach No. instruments were somewhat inaccurate, a technique was evolved which required the aircraft to enter a dive at high altitude, pulling out when a specific strain gauge reading was achieved. Combined with other readings and sonic booms heard over the airfield, the team quickly built up the transonic calibrations. Much of the flutter testing was performed at low level and calm air conditions were required in order to obtain accurate data. The calmest air was found shortly after sunrise or just before sunset and so the bulk of this test flying (done during the early summer of 1959) was done around 9pm, some two or three hours after other test work had been completed. The intervening idle period

was normally spent in the nearby Red Lion pub, where Blackburn's staff became regular and valued patrons.

A few months previously, the test fleet increased still further when XK488 made its first flight on 13 November 1958, followed by XK489 on 28 January the following year. The latter aircraft was assigned to performance and handling trials and also flew a number of canopy-off test flights, as well as exploring the aircraft's bomb door operation. XK488 was put through a flight clearance programme before being dispatched to de Havilland at Hatfield, to undertake engine trials work. The winter months drastically reduced the amount of test flying possible, and improvements to the temporarily grounded airframes were made in less than ideal conditions, as the flight test hangar was unheated. One early task was to revise the shape of the airbrake petals, as the initial shape

Buccaneer manufacturing sequence table.

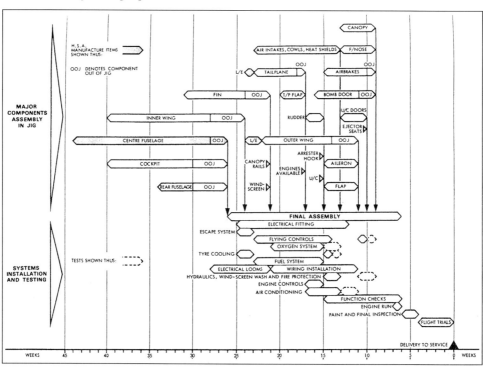

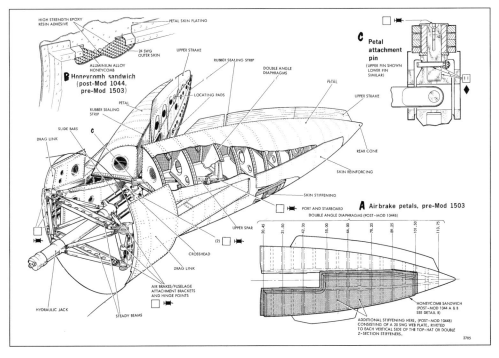

Buccaneer S1/S2 airbrake construction drawing.

(recommended by the RAE and tested in the Brough wind tunnel) proved to be unsatisfactory in certain conditions. Transient airflow conditions and the influence of the engine efflux made wind tunnel tests pointless, the only effective approach being to fly various test shapes attached to the brake petals. The test programme wasn't as straightforward as expected, and trim changes through the brake's operating cycle became an annoying problem, especially when complete trim reversals could occur under some conditions. After a great deal of trial and error, vertical strakes of differing areas were fitted to the top and bottom of the brake petals. Further modifications to the basic airframe included the addition of vortex generators along the upper wing leading edges. Development of the aircraft's flying controls continued too, and after a great deal of work the final standard was recognised as being impressive.

McDonnell's Dwight Bennett, responsible for installing an experimental fly-by-wire control system in the Phantom, asked Blackburn's Roy Boot how they had managed to develop such responsive and harmonised controls. Roy Boot replied, "the hard way".

The first major incident in the development programme occurred while XK489 was on final approach to RAE Bedford. Test pilot G. R. I. (Sailor) Parker reported a severe tailplane control restriction which forced him to struggle with the controls until he made a safe landing at Thurleigh. Investigation revealed that potting around a coiled restrictor had collapsed, causing a differential lock to engage, after which the movement of the control column simply stretched the input cables rather than effecting any movement. Modifications were made but Sailor Parker was soon to encounter another problem, this time on XK486. He

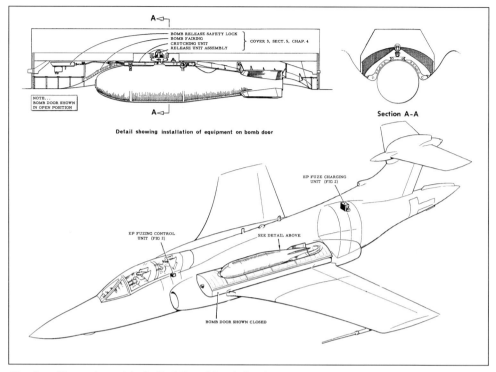

Carriage illustration, with the Red Beard bomb fitted.

encountered similar aileron restrictions and made a diverted landing at Elvington. Investigations didn't reveal a definite cause, but Blackburn's Roy Boot believed that a hydraulic leak caused the aileron's differential lock to behave abnormally. Parker later remarked that even though in principle a tailplane failure would be much harder to handle than an aileron failure, the reverse was actually the case. He also added that after having nursed the aircraft back on two occasions, he would bale out if there was a third incident. Some time later, he did.

XK490 joined the test fleet after flying for the first time on 23 March 1959. Primarily assigned to armament carriage and release trials, it was ready for use some time before the equipment it was intended to carry, and so it was reassigned to handling and cooling system trials which required a deployment to Malta, where it was soon

established that the cooling system needed a significant amount of reworking. As a direct result of the Malta detachment an improved cold air unit and control system was eventually developed, and cooling air directed into the radio bay was re-routed to individual items rather than simply being distributed over the whole area. After returning to the UK, XK490 was still unable to resume armament trials and so it was assigned to general handling investigations. As part of this programme the aircraft was sent to Boscombe Down, where an American NACA pilot, W. H. (Bill) Alford, was tasked with an assessment of the aircraft, as part of the agreement through which the US financed part of the aircraft's development. The aircraft was due to be deployed on board HMS *Victorious* for the NA.39's initial deck trials programme and the stay at Boscombe Down was to be a work-up period for the aircraft and crews. On 12 October, Alford was airborne in XK490 when the aircraft crashed in the New Forest, killing both him and his observer John Joyce. Investigation of the accident relied on wreckage examination and eyewitness accounts. Locals who had seen the crash revealed that the aircraft had dived into the ground at an angle of approximately 60 degrees, in an inverted position. The centre fuselage had exploded upon impact but the rear fuselage and air brakes had remained intact and had buried themselves along with the instrumentation recorders inside them. Eventually, they were recovered from a 35-ft deep pit. Combined with the eyewitness accounts, the instrumentation confirmed that Alford had flown the aircraft in a low speed configuration with wing blowing in operation, but with a simulated single engine failure. This was a condition which hadn't yet been explored by the company test pilots and Alford had stalled the aircraft at approximately 10,000 feet, from where he had insufficient height to recover. Although both crew ejected, the inverted dive was beyond the safe limits of their ejection seats. Having established the cause of the accident, a great deal of exploration was devoted to establishing why the aircraft had stalled. It was eventually concluded that a non-return valve may have failed, leading to a major engine malfunction at a very critical moment.

Like any naval aircraft, the Buccaneer had to be capable of withstanding deck launches and landings. Catapult launch and arrester gear trials were conducted at RAE Bedford, where a test rig and representative 'carrier deck' was available for test flying. The aircraft (XK489) was launched at various speeds and angles of incidence, in order to establish the minimum speed at which the aircraft could be safely launched and flown clear. Some of these catapult launches (an acceleration of just 0.5 knots per second was attempted) were pretty exciting, and occasionally the aircraft would refuse to get airborne and settle back onto the runway ahead of the catapult. The pilot was then left with the unenviable choice between attempting to climb away at a perilously low speed, or flying into the crash barrier positioned ahead of the launch area. On every occasion the aircraft was flown clear, although on one test the aircraft settled heavily onto the runway after launch, bounced over the crash barrier and finally struggled into the air.

January 19, 1960, XK523 sweeps majestically over the deck of HMS Victorious *for the first time, during the NA.39's initial deck trials. With the tail hook still retracted, this first pass was a 'bolter' to give test pilot Derek Whitehead an opportunity to make a 'dry run' prior to making the first 'trap'.*

Following delays caused by the tragic loss of XK490, the first deck launch trials took place in January 1960 with XK489 on board HMS *Victorious*, operating in the English Channel in company with the seventh NA.39, XK523 which first flew on 29 July the previous year. The latter aircraft was the first to reach *Victorious*, flying directly from Holme-on-Spalding Moor, while XK489 was snowbound at Boscombe Down. A total of 31 launches were made over a three-day period, mostly in poor weather conditions but despite some attention-grabbing moments when the aircraft occasionally sank below the level of the flight deck after launch, the trials progressed smoothly. The NA.39 was the biggest and heaviest aircraft to land on *Victorious* and its arrival was just as impressive for the crews below deck (who certainly felt and heard the landing) as well as those watching the spectacle above. It was probably at this stage that the trials team recalled an early Admiralty specification

that the NA.39 should have hand holds fitted to the wing tips, so that the deck crew could run out and bring the aircraft to a halt, should it appear to be in danger of rolling overboard after landing. Needless to say, some Admiralty chiefs had failed to appreciate what a mighty beast the new strike aircraft would be. In terms of size, it was barely capable of fitting into the carrier's deck lift, and even with nose, tail and wings folded, it had a clearance of just two inches. One important development which did emerge as a result of the deck trials was the NA.39's 'hands-off' launch technique which required the pilot to preset the tailplane position prior to launch and then allow the aircraft to get into the air before taking a firm grip of the control column. This avoided the risk of excessive back pressure on the control stick which would easily cause the aircraft to pitch up into a stall. The trials aircraft were also fitted with incidence indicators which included audio

XK530 just about to get airborne from RAE Bedford's steam catapult, during trials on 3 August 1961. Although the catapult trials were successful, some of the launches at Bedford were fairly exciting, especially those made at the lower end of the aircraft's launching speed, when the NA.39 barely lumbered into the air. In one instance the aircraft crashed back onto the runway, bounced over the crash barrier ahead of the catapult, and then lifted into the air.

Despite miserable weather, XK523 arrived on board Victorious *without any problems, to begin the first series of deck launches and landings. With just one deck handler visible in the photograph, one is reminded of the Naval Staff's early insistence that the aircraft should be fitted with hand holds for the deck crews, so that they could grab the aircraft and bring it to a halt. Not a good idea for an aircraft of this size and weight!*

Tail hook down, landing gear extended, XK523 in the hands of test pilot Derek Whitehead, about to touch down on HMS Victorious. *As can be seen by the turbulent wake being left by the carrier,* Victorious *was steaming into wind in order to give Whitehead a few extra knots of wind for his first approaches.*

The Buccaneer's size was dictated by the size and weight of the 'TMB' weapons which was to be her primary armament. However, the aircraft's dimensions were constrained by the size of the Navy's carrier deck lifts. After some careful design work which enabled the nose radome to hinge, the Buccaneer cleared the deck lift limits 'comfortably' by a few inches.

warnings when the aircraft reached a critical value, and after the trials it was decided to incorporate a warning system into production aircraft.

The deck trials were a great success, although there were some moments for concern. The flights were made at relatively light weights with partial fuel loads, as the Blackburn design team weren't able to guarantee the accuracy of the aircraft's fuel system at that stage. As a precaution, a flow meter had been shipped aboard *Victorious* so that the precise amount of fuel being loaded into the aircraft could be measured. Additionally, the aircraft's tanks were chain-dipped before and after each flight, the results of which caused some concern. The recorded data suggested that as well as putting fuel into the aircraft, the refuellers were actually taking it out at times. The cause was eventually traced to the actions of the Blackburn ground crew, who were accustomed to operating a typical fuel bowser, and often left the fuel hose attached to the aircraft after refuelling, until such a time that the fuel truck or

aircraft were to be moved. They had done this on board *Victorious*, unaware of the way in which the carrier's internal fuel system differed, by sucking standing fuel from the lines back into the main tanks after refuelling was complete. Luckily, the fuel hose hadn't been left connected for too long at any one time, otherwise a very serious accident might have occurred. Following completion of the first deck trails, some modifications to the aircraft were made, including the arrester hook design, the rebound ratio of the main undercarriage (the aircraft tending to bounce over the arrester wires), the design of the tailskid damper (which occasionally struck the catapult shuttle during launch) as well as the autostability gearings. These problems were relatively simple to fix and were proved on later deck trials although they collectively contributed to delays, and considerable frustration for the design staff.

The Blackburn test fleet continued to grow, with XK491 having flown for the first time on 29 May 1959, followed by XK523, and then XK524 on 4 April 1960. All of the aircraft handled well although

Holme-on-Spalding Moor, 7 August 1960 with six NA.39 development aircraft on display for Blackburn's cameraman. By this stage, XK486 had received a large area of white paint on her rear fuselage, as part of the ongoing trials programme.

XK489 and XK490 began to develop minor directional 'snaking' problems above 520 knots. This situation didn't cause concern until XK491 began to demonstrate a fairly severe tailplane shake at similar speeds. Investigations quickly followed using cine cameras and wind tunnel tests, and the cause was found to be a shock-induced airflow separation at the fin and tailplane junction. The partial solution was a 'waisted' bullet fairing although the modification was only just agreed in time to modify the aircraft for its final pre-CA release trials, and for the first aircraft due for delivery to the Royal Navy. A complete 'fix' was eventually found by stiffening linkages in the rudder input circuit, but Navy chiefs rejected the modification on cost grounds. By 1960, the Blackburn designers had incorporated a number of changes to the aircraft's final configuration, based on the views of test pilots and a considerable amount of trials data. The eighth aircraft (XK524) was the first to incorporate much of these modifications which included structural weight-saving, cockpit controls and instrument

NA.39 XK524 getting smartly airborne in front of the main test hangar at Holme-on-Spalding Moor. Complete with photographic calibration markings on the nose and tail, the aircraft also carries underwing tanks and is fitted with wingtip 'bonkers'. The aircraft crashed at Holme-on Spalding Moor during a test flight on 13 May 1965.

alterations. In essence, this aircraft was the first production standard aircraft and having been partially redesigned, it was subjected to repeat performances of many of the handling trials which had first been made with the earlier aircraft. During August 1960 the results of Blackburn's search for a suitable name for the aircraft emerged. Many suggestions had been made, some more serious than others, including the term 'ARNA' defined as 'Another Royal Navy Aeroplane'. It's amusement value only became clear when attached to the prefix 'Blackburn' and the 'Banana' nickname (also partially inspired by the aircraft's unusual bulged fuselage) stuck with the aircraft throughout its career. Of course, the final choice of name had a much more apposite definition, described as 'Pirate, or unscrupulous adventurer'. Thus, from mid-1960 the NA.39 became the Buccaneer.

The flight trials programme progressed well, although XK524 was responsible for some considerable delays. In order to bring the aircraft up to production standard, an additional eight months were required which correspondingly delayed the following aircraft. When the aircraft was cleared to fly, after just a few test sorties a hydraulic pump failed causing contamination of the aircraft's entire hydraulic system which had to be completely stripped and cleaned, creating another three-month delay in the programme. XK525 joined the trials after first flying on 15 July 1960, and was the first aircraft to be equipped with a complete weapons system 'package'. XK526, XK527 and XK528 spent periods at both Holme-on-Spalding Moor and Boscombe Down, on handling and performance trials as well as radio and navigation assessments. XK529 and XK530 were earmarked for weapons system development but in order to speed-up preparations for the aircraft's CA Release, they were assigned to more general performance trials. XK529, as the 13th NA.39, caused numerous headaches for the servicing teams and spent a considerable amount of time in the Holme-on-Spalding Moor hangar

A rare photograph of XK528 during weapons trials on 2 November 1965. A dummy WE177 nuclear bomb has just been released from the port attachment point in the aircraft's bomb bay. Unlike the earlier Red Beard 'TMB', the WE177 was the first 'lay down' nuclear bomb available to the Fleet Air Arm, two of which could be carried in the Buccaneer's bomb bay. In practice, the weapon was expected to be released in a toss manoeuvre. This aircraft broke up during another weapons test flight on 30 June 1966.

The Blackburn NA.39 trials fleet on 7 August 1960. In order to 'confuse the enemy' Blackburn adopted a practice of varying the size of national insignia and serial presentation on each development aircraft, so that any aspiring analyst would be unable to make an accurate estimation of the aircraft's proportions. Despite this, one leading aviation magazine produced a near-perfect drawing of the aircraft, the dimensions of which were based on the size of the aircraft's ejection seats.

until it was eventually pronounced fit to fly, redesignated as aircraft number 12A. Sadly, even this deference to superstition didn't save the aircraft from destruction, just a few months later.

Although the initial armament and weapons carriage trials proceeded without any serious problems, the delayed start, problems encountered during the trials and various changes of requirements on the part of the Navy, meant that the programme extended almost two years beyond its projected completion date. Most important to the programme was the Red Beard atomic weapon, officially referred to as the Target Marker Bomb (TMB). By this stage the Green Cheese guided weapon

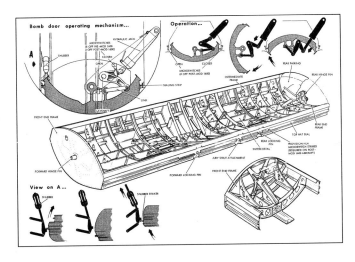

Buccaneer S1/S2 bomb door construction drawing.

had been abandoned because of its complexity and cost, and the TMB was to be the Buccaneer's primary weapon. Blackburn received their first TMB during December 1960, one such example being stored in Holme-on-Spalding Moor's former parachute shed, under armed guard. Carriage and temperature trials on XK523 with the instrumented TMB shell began in January 1961, and it came as little surprise to the design team that the huge 2,000lb finned bomb produced very severe buffeting. This had been anticipated and a special fairing had been designed to fit into the bomb bay, fitting snugly around the bomb and smoothing the airflow. This arrangement proved entirely satisfactory, and level separation trials were conducted on XK523 from West Freugh during February, at 250, 400, 500 and 580 knots. During May and June 1961, further tests were made, releasing TMB's at 350, 450 knots in level flight, and 540 knots for a 30-degree 'long toss' and 105-degree 'over-the-shoulder' delivery. All of the flights were satisfactory, and during April 1962 XK530 was detached to RAE Bedford to fly a series of deck-proofing flights with the TMB, making catapult launches and arrested landings at up to 5g, with an instrumented TMB carcass in the bomb bay. Further trials took place with XK530 and XK536 on board HMS *Hermes* in May 1962, followed by vibration and temperature tests in July and August 1965, with Buccaneers XN974 and XN976 deployed to NAS Pensacola, the instrumented TMB being transported across the Atlantic in a Vulcan. The 25-kiloton Red Beard bomb was very much a 'first generation' atomic weapon, and had to be treated with particular care, as the bomb could explode with a force of up to one kiloton as a result of a 'direct impact or graze'. Emergency clearance (the Cold War was

at its most dangerous stage) was given in 1963 to carry the TMB under Navy Scimitars, although the extremely small clearance between the bomb and the carrier's flight deck meant that Scimitars were not authorised to land on carriers with the weapon (most flights inevitably terminated at Yeovilton) and this less than ideal situation emphasises how urgent the Buccaneer's TMB carriage capability was to the Royal Navy.

Carriage of conventional stores also presented few problems. The first trials revealed that bombs tended to pitch and jostle after release from the four stations, which resulted in a rather inconsistent strike pattern. A simple 'fix' consisted of angled carriers and revised release intervals. Underwing stores were tested without any difficulty, although a great deal of effort was devoted to one particular item, namely the Buccaneer's distinctive external fuel tanks. In order to provide a minimum amount of drag and thus extend the aircraft's range, the tanks were semi-conformal, in much the same style as the Victor's 'slipper' tanks. Although the design was successful, a great deal of time was spent on establishing a safe jettison system, based on an elaborate scissors and hook mechanism which was necessary to eject the tank away from the aircraft at a safe angle. The resulting tank was certainly well engineered but correspondingly expensive, as Roy Boot recalls, "It led to a conversation between myself and Sir Sydney Camm, the Design Director of Hawker Siddeley Aviation. In his typical manner he set about me in no small way concerning this expensive rubbish compared with the simple welded drop tank used on the Hunter, and had I never heard of value engineering, etcetera. The relative cost factor was about seven to one so at first Sir Sydney did have a point. I pointed out to him that due to the relative drag of the two tanks, range with our

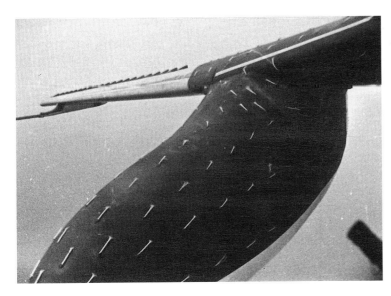

Unusual still frame from a test film taken on 23 May 1967 during trials with the Buccaneer's 'slipper' fuel tanks. Painted matt black, XK526 has a number of wool tufts stuck to the fuel tank in order to illustrate the air flow over the tank surfaces. At Mach 0.7 and 5,000 feet, the tufts demonstrate the unusual up-flow around the wing intersection.

slipper tanks retained under the aircraft was at least as great as with Hunter-type tanks dropped when empty. I added that greater range still could be achieved if the slipper tanks were also dropped when empty. It wouldn't take many sorties for the slipper tank to break even on cost and to me this seemed like value engineering. Gentleman that he was, Sir Sydney graciously conceded."

A rare picture of a Buccaneer S1 releasing an underwing 'slipper' tank during jettison trials. The tank was designed to fall away nose-first, in order to separate cleanly from the aircraft. The tank was only intended to be released in an emergency or during a wartime operational mission, as in practice, the tanks were far too expensive to 'dump' during peacetime.

As mentioned previously, after almost losing XK489 and XK486, Sailor Parker had commented that if he found himself in another equally dangerous situation, he would abandon the aircraft. His prediction came true on 5 October 1960 while flying the first NA.39 prototype, XK486, on an autopilot test. Flying manually in cloud at 16,000 feet near Market Weighton, not far from the Brough factory, Parker felt the aircraft begin to roll, and despite his attempts to level the aircraft, the aircraft failed to respond. True to his word, Parker closed the throttles and ordered his observer Dave Nightingale to eject, after which Parker quickly pulled his own seat firing handle. Nightingale was unable to reach his firing handles because of the 300-knot airflow but after flying a further six minutes, the aircraft had slowed sufficiently for Nightingale to effect his escape, after which the aircraft stalled and descended in a gentle spiral, impacting at a shallow angle and spreading debris (including the tailplane and one wing) over a half-mile area. It then catapulted across a small valley and came to rest in open countryside. The cause of the accident was the aircraft's

The 8th NA.39, XK524, in 'A' Shed at Brough shortly before completion on 24 March 1960. Factory workers are busily attending to the aircraft's starboard main landing gear, while other work progresses in the cockpit. Members of the design staff are examining the interior of the radar bay.

artificial horizon which had failed while the aircraft was in cloud. Slowly spinning spontaneously, Sailor instinctively countered the instrument reading. Believing that he was maintaining level flight, he then perceived a roll which he couldn't control. Without a standby Artificial Horizon Indicator to confirm that he was being fooled by a faulty AHI, he naturally abandoned an aircraft which was perfectly serviceable in all other respects. To add to the confusion still further, Sailor's radio call to say that he was abandoning the aircraft coincided with a call from Holme-on-Spalding Moor to him, effectively blocking out the message. It was only when another air traffic controller telephoned Holme-on-Spalding Moor that the Blackburn team knew what had happened. Luckily for the development programme, much of the tasks assigned to XK486 had already been completed by this stage, and its loss was of little significance.

A more tragic incident was the loss of 'unlucky' aircraft No. 13, XK529. Having been assigned to 'C' Squadron at Boscombe Down (the Royal Naval Test

Unit), the aircraft was detached to HMS *Hermes* for a further series of deck trials, which included development of the 'hands-off' launching technique. On 31 August 1961, Lt-Cdr 'Ossie' Brown together with his observer, Trevor Dunn, were catapulted from the carrier whilst sailing in Lyme Bay, Dorset. Literally no more than a second after launch, the aircraft pitched up violently and immediately stalled, crashing into the sea just one mile ahead of the ship, killing both crew. The cause of the accident was never conclusively established, but it was believed to have been a failure of the BLC system, or a pilot-induced over rotation on take-off (the aircraft was found to be over-trimmed by two degrees).

On a more positive note, much of the work necessary to prepare the aircraft for its first CA Release was complete by March 1961 with XK530 still pushing the type's envelope clearance to the highest speed possible whilst enabling the support team to gain more experience and confidence with the latest (Phase 3) engines made available by de Havilland.

A frustrating amount of time was spent in fitting the new engines, and more time was spent on a troublesome microswitch which indicated to the pilot that turbine blade cooling was in operation (a new feature in the Phase 3 engines). The switch was positioned so that the engine had to be removed in order to reach it and it was only after the switch was repositioned (at the suggestion of Blackburn's Roy Boot, rather than de Havilland) that many months of time-wasting adjustments were saved. The Ministry of Supply were still unconvinced that the Gyron Junior engines were sufficiently reliable to permit a CA Release, and it was only through further progress meetings that Blackburn were able to convince the authorities to forge ahead. In their favour, Blackburn were able to report that the design's weight growth was well within the estimates made for the aircraft. At the same time however, the project's Experimental Manager reported that XK531 and XK532 would be delivered to the Navy with the aforementioned tailplane bullet fairings fitted. The Project Director (who was chairing the meeting) had already ruled that clearance trials for this fit wouldn't be practicable within the available timescale, and so Roy Boot and his colleague, John Stamper, were forced to fake coughing fits in order to comfortably drown out this statement, and move the project forward. This they did quite successfully, and the CA Release was finally given, enabling Buccaneers to be delivered to the Royal Navy's Intensive Flying Trials Unit (IFTU), No.700Z Flight, formed at RNAS Lossiemouth during March 1961. Initially equipped with XK531 and XK532, they were joined by XK533, XK534 and XK535 by the end of the year and, as the unit's name implies, they were assigned to intensive flight trials, operating both by day and night, to

establish the aircraft's performance in terms of range (from sea level to 40,000 feet), speed, engine performance, handling, weapons system and servicing techniques. By the end of the first year, XK531 and XK532 had logged some 340 flying hours which was almost as much as achieved by all of the development Buccaneers flying from Holme-on-Spalding Moor during the same period.

While the Navy began to operate the Buccaneer at Lossiemouth, Blackburn's development programme continued apace. One important part of the programme was the aircraft's in-flight refuelling capability, which would give the aircraft, at least in theory, almost unlimited range with tanker support. In order to minimise airframe drag at every opportunity, Blackburn had designed a fully retractable refuelling probe for the Buccaneer, which rotated through 90 degrees and emerged in the eleven o'clock position ahead of the pilot. Although the system wouldn't be vital for Naval operations (the aircraft had a very respectable range without refuelling), it was believed that a refuelling probe might be valuable in emergency situations, for example when an aircraft was unable to safely land on a carrier in poor weather, etc. The first refuelling trials were conducted with XK491, making 'dry prods' from a Valiant tanker provided by the RAF. At this stage in the Buccaneer's development (October 1959) the aircraft's flying controls were still being refined, and precise longitudinal control wasn't easy to obtain. Worse still, the refuelling probe's extended position was fairly close to the Buccaneer's nose section, and this created a bow wave effect which pushed the Valiant's refuelling basket away from the probe, just before contact. As if this problem wasn't enough, the probe and drogue induced an airflow disturbance which caused the engine compressor to stall.

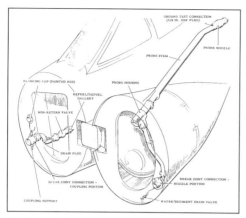

Bolt-on refuelling probe internal layout drawing.

The problems culminated in the arrival of XK491 at Elvington on 29 October, with the tanker's refuelling basket still attached to the Buccaneer's extended probe. Trials continued for some considerable time, but eventually the whole probe system had to be redesigned and re-engineered to enable the probe to extend further from the nose section in a more upright position, and such was the extent of the modification that it wasn't incorporated into early production machines. Much to the horror of the design team, flight trials demonstrated that the modified system was little better than the original fit, as although the bow wave effect was reduced, the engine compressor stall was still evident. The Blackburn designers were forced to abandon the concept, and eventually opted to use a simple bolt-on probe.

An even more important part of the design process which occupied part of the trials programme for a long time, was the aircrew escape system. Because the Buccaneer was designed for low level and high speed operations, there would clearly be very little time for the aircrew to escape in the event of an emergency. The other major consideration was the close proximity of the observer to the pilot, which effectively meant that a single-piece canopy would have to be fitted, covering both crew positions. As the Buccaneer was being developed, Blackburn noted a number of recent incidents during which various aircraft had inadvertantly jettisoned canopies through various malfunctions. Blackburn produced a design which made this impossible, by making the canopy slide along guide rails before being freed. The size and weight (200lb) of the canopy meant that gas pressure was required to unlock the guide rails and push the canopy away from the aircraft by means of vertical rams. The disadvantage of this system was that a time delay had to be built into the jettison sequence to ensure that the canopy had cleared the cockpit area before the ejection seats were fired. Naturally, the designers felt that this was a less than ideal situation for an operating environment where a second could mean the difference between life and death. Trials at Boscombe Down had demonstrated that at speeds above 250 knots, conditions in the rear cockpit became very unpleasant with the canopy removed and a simple plate screen behind the pilot didn't solve the problem. The loss of XK486 in 1960 showed that at high speed it was impossible to escape from the rear cockpit once the canopy was removed and this encouraged the designers to adopt a system which enabled the crew to eject directly through the canopy, with manual canopy jettison provided as a back-up.

Martin Baker made alterations to the Buccaneer's ejection seat, attaching canopy breakers to the top and sides of the assembly to clear a path through the perspex for the seat occupant. Meanwhile, the designers at Brough revised the canopy thickness from half an inch to 5/16 inch to ensure that it broke properly. The new system was tested at Brough and on a rocket-powered sledge at China Lake in California. Initially the

Following some detailed examination of aircrew escape procedures, it was established that the Buccaneer observer's position required a substantial windscreen, in order to clear the airflow from the forward cockpit when the canopy was removed. Blackburn test flew a series of shapes (as illustrated on XK489) before adopting the definitive windscreen used by the Buccaneer fleet.

seats required a forward speed of 60 knots to ensure successful operation, but the later addition of rocket packs allowed the seat to be operated in any speed or altitude combination. Further research suggested that the seat canopy breaker might not create a sufficiently large hole for all circumstances, as the sledge tests had all been done, by necessity, in a level plane. Investigations suggested that in some ejections, particularly if the aircraft was in a spin, a larger hole would be required to ensure a smooth escape. Consequently, Blackburn returned to the Buccaneer's canopy-off conditions, and tried to find a way to improve the turbulent conditions for the observer. Joe Boulger had encountered a similar problem whilst working on the design of the Gnat with Folland. Like the Buccaneer, the Gnat's canopy formed a pressure depression in the front cockpit so that turbulent airflow came not only over the top of the windscreen, but over the sides of the rear cockpit, and then into the front cockpit to form an updraught over the pilot. Boulger suggested that a windscreen be fitted behind the pilot, effectively sealing the space between him and the observer. A variety of shapes were tested by Blackburns and eventually a definitive windscreen was devised and fitted as standard for all Buccaneers, although ejection through the canopy always remained as the primary means of escape.

As a purely naval aircraft, it was very likely that a number of Buccaneers would have to ditch, and designers at Brough were particularly concerned that a Buccaneer without its canopy would quickly find its cockpit filling with water, causing the nose to sink rapidly and drowning the occupants, as had happened in the case of XK529 after launching from HMS *Hermes*. The only practical solution appeared to be to make an ejection through the canopy and

Brough's 'B' Shed on 16 November 1962, with Buccaneer S1s near completion. The aircraft are painted in the Royal Navy's early Buccaneer colour scheme comprising all-white anti-radiation paint, signifying the Buccaneer's nuclear role.

dummy tests were conducted in a huge water tank at HMS *Vernon* and at Glen Fruin. The main concern was that the seat's canopy breaker would punch what was initially a small hole which would allow water to rush into the cockpit at high pressure, possibly breaking the seat occupant's neck, and so an alternative means of breaking the canopy was required. Eventually, the concept of using plastic explosive in thin strips was discussed and it was agreed that this would provide a means to instantly fragment the whole canopy and allow the crew to make a safe escape even when underwater. Of course, the system would also enable the canopy to be cleared much more quickly during an airborne ejection, making through-the-canopy ejections much safer. Designers at Brough studied various canopy break-up patterns, beginning with a strip which surrounded the whole canopy, although this produced large fragments which were almost as dangerous as the whole canopy. Ultimately a wavy pattern across the top

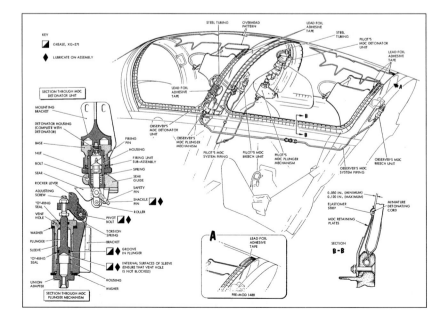

Miniature detonating cord system.

Resplendent in an anti-flash white paint scheme, the 10th development aircraft (XK526) is pictured low over some East Yorkshire moorland, during a test flight on 27 May 1962. The dark shade of the radome indicates that the unit was unpainted, and retains its natural fibreglass colour.

of the canopy was chosen and adopted for the Buccaneer fleet. Such was the effectiveness of this system that the miniature detonating cord (MDC) has now become a standard fit for many combat aircraft including the Hawk, Harrier and Tornado.

The Buccaneer's entry into Fleet Air Arm service was relatively uneventful, and early experience with the aircraft was almost entirely positive. Pilots converting to the type from Scimitars and Sea

Vixens were surprised at the Buccaneer's sluggish take-off performance, especially when compared with other Naval types. This was caused partly by the Buccaneer S1's Gyron Junior engines which were certainly less powerful than the Navy (and Blackburn) might have liked, but the new pilots also often failed to appreciate what a large and heavy aircraft the Buccaneer was. As the unit commander, Lt-Cdr E. R. Anson, commented, "take-offs were adequately exciting, and events

The 13th development aircraft (XK529) thundering by at low level for Blackburn's cameraman on 10 May 1961. The aircraft's upper surfaces have been painted dark sea grey, in anticipation of what was to become the Buccaneer S1's standard Fleet Air Arm colour scheme for many years. Note that this aircraft has yet to receive the fin/tailplane aerodynamic 'bullet' modification.

were frequent enough to avoid a feeling of boredom". They were much more surprised however, to find that the Buccaneer was a magnificent aircraft once settled into the low altitude and high speed regime for which it had been designed. Operating from Lossiemouth, 700Z Flight had immediate access to the open sea, and miles of sparsely populated countryside where the Buccaneers could be flown without restriction. The ride at low level was astonishingly smooth (often referred to as "like riding on rails") and the view from the cockpit was superb, even for the observer who was afforded some forward view by his raised position, and the staggered positioning of the crew seats either side of the fuselage centreline. Manoeuvring was easily accomplished, and any over-exuberance on the part of the pilot would produce a gentle buffet which prompted the pilot to unload the amount of 'g' being applied. Landing performance was good, and the huge airbrakes seemingly brought the aircraft to a standstill when applied. On final approach, the airstream direction detector (ADD) gave the pilot an audible and visual cue to ensure that the aircraft maintained the correct angle of attack at all times and the touchdown was usually fairly firm, with little or no 'flare' being applied. The only potential problem was the loss of the boundary layer control system, although the 700Z Flight pilots commented that this simply required a higher approach speed or a longer take-off run. In truth the loss of the BLC system was rather more serious than that, but certainly not catastrophic provided that the pilot recognised the problem and took appropriate action.

The Buccaneer's first major military exercise (codenamed 'Shopwindow') took place in September 1961 and XK534 (from 700Z Flight) was demonstrated at the Farnborough SBAC show in the same month. A year later, four aircraft from the unit (XK531, XK532, XK533 and XK534) flew formation aerobatics at Farnborough. Display flying did cause the unit (and Blackburn) some problems however. One particular air display routine included an eight-point hesitation roll, and it was proposed to interrupt the roll at the inverted stage, to fly a full 360-degree roll, before resuming the eight-point hesitation roll. The manoeuvre sounded fine in theory, but after the first attempt the aircraft returned to Lossiemouth's flight line with the wing flaps broken from their jacks, and the fin noticeably bent, so much so that the attachment bolts couldn't be withdrawn from the fuselage connection. Indeed, it was a miracle that the pilot brought the aircraft safely back onto the runway. The cause was identified as roll inertia coupling, a potentially dangerous situation in which a simple rolling manoeuvre couples with the aircraft's inclination to the line of flight, resulting in loss of control. The Buccaneer's handling trials had explored this phenomenon and the test programme had included a number of flights during which the test pilots had flown the aircraft in a series of predetermined flight conditions while a stepped input of a given magnitude was fed into the ailerons. This was achieved by attaching a dog chain to the control column, the other end fixed to the cockpit wall. Altering the number of chain links established the amount of control input being applied. Unfortunately, although the tests had been exhaustive, nobody had ever thought about starting a roll in the inverted position.

700Z Flight was quickly absorbed into No. 801 Naval Air Squadron, which formed at Lossiemouth on 17 July 1962. Their first aircraft was XN925, which was quickly followed by new deliveries from Brough. These included XN967 which deserves special mention in view of the astonishing series of multiple failures which the aircraft suffered during a flight on 27 November 1965. Ironically, its pilot was Lt Bill Rice who was making what would have probably been his last Buccaneer flight, having trained students on the Buccaneer simulator at Lossiemouth. If his students had tried to repay him for all the hours of stress he had given them, they couldn't have done a better job than XN967 did. Taking off with a full internal fuel load and underwing fuel tanks, the aircraft climbed away safely from Lossiemouth's runway, the landing gear retracting as expected, with the cockpit indicator lights going out as normal. A moment later the air turbine alternator failed, but a standby inverter in the aircraft didn't take over as designed. Consequently, Rice abandoned the mission and began making his attempt to return to Lossiemouth, selecting undercarriage down again. Instead of a normal extension sequence there was a loud bang followed by a rumbling noise which persisted for a few seconds. The undercarriage lights didn't appear, and so Rice selected an emergency extension. This didn't work either, and after trying a normal sequence selection again his efforts were rewarded with an 'Emergency' caption. The next step was to jettison fuel, and this procedure went as planned. Selecting flaps down and airbrake out was less successful, but Rice did manage to obtain drooped ailerons and wing blowing. The canopy was then jettisoned and Rice carefully brought the aircraft back on to finals for a smooth landing, much to his (and his observer's) relief. Alas, their troubles weren't over, as the port undercarriage leg failed during the landing run, causing the aircraft to veer off the runway and on to the grass. Finally, the aircraft slewed to a halt and a short but memorable flight was over.

After recovering the aircraft from the airfield, a detailed examination was conducted on the airframe at Lossiemouth. The nosewheel had slewed before retracting and had jammed against the fuselage underside. The port main undercarriage had suffered a failure of the leg shortening mechanism, and at the

XK491, the 6th NA.39 on the flight line at Holme-on-Spalding Moor, 24 May 1960. With the nose hinged open, the aircraft reveals an empty radome. Note the air starter unit attached to the port engine and the small counter balances fitted to the tailplane leading edges.

point where the retraction jack is attached to the airframe. The 'undercarriage locked' microswitch had been damaged and undercarriage hydraulic circuits had been severed. One of the port flying control system hydraulic pipes had been severed and both of the general services hydraulic systems had drained dry. Likewise, the port flying control system was approaching the same state. The fuel jettison system had worked, but had failed after just one minute, and other systems were damaged as a result of the various failures. Not surprisingly, the Brough design team were called to investigate, and Roy Boot with undercarriage expert Stan Field duly arrived at Lossiemouth. After listening to air traffic control tapes and interviewing the crew, a detailed account of the flight was assembled. The Buccaneer's air turbine alternator had failed on previous occasions in different aircraft, but a vent plug had worked loose in this instance, and this had fallen into the control box, causing a short circuit, preventing the 107 invertor from taking-over. Completely independent of this failure was the nosewheel's misalignment during retraction, which had gone unnoticed by the pilot because of the undercarriage

warning light's circuit being damaged in the port main wheel bay. With normal and emergency hydraulic pipes severed, the port undercarriage leg was snatched by the surrounding airflow and forced downwards, breaking its retraction jack and damaging the port system flying control pipe. Air loading then centred the undercarriage leg, allowing the spring-loaded downlock to engage. Damage to the gear leg, including scour marks, suggested that a foreign object had become lodged between the leg and the undercarriage bay during retraction, and this would have led to the ensuing failures. The marks on the leg were consistent with an open groundlock falling from the ledge of the gear bay, but as the gear retraction had taken place over the sea, no trace of any groundlock could be found, and station records couldn't account for any missing item. Despite this, the investigators concluded that this was the cause of the main failures, which, by adhering to the principles of Murphy's Law, simply managed to take place at the same time as others occurred elsewhere on the airframe. Despite this monumentally unlucky flight, XN967 went on to enjoy a successful service life, ending her days in the Helston Aero Park in Cornwall.

Interesting forward view of XK527, illustrating the small frontal area of the Gyron Junior's air intakes. This aircraft was later converted to S2 standard. This view also illustrates the bulged canopy shape, and the small air intakes on the inner wing leading edges, which were peculiar to the S1 variant.

CHAPTER THREE

In the Navy

As development and flight trials of the Buccaneer S1 continued through 1959, both Blackburn and the Navy were anticipating further development of the Gyron Junior engine, to provide the aircraft with greater thrust. Although the S1 was undoubtedly going to be a success, the Gyron Junior engines were always regarded as being an 'interim' solution to the aircraft's power plant requirements, until something more suitable came along. Until that time arrived, the Buccaneer S1 would at least provide the Navy with an 'almost-perfect' aircraft in a fairly short timescale. On 12 January 1960 a meeting took place at Brough between Blackburn staff and representatives of both the Ministry of Aviation and Royal Navy. By this stage they had all agreed that the Buccaneer certainly needed to be re-engined at the earliest opportunity, and three options were available. First, de Havilland was (as expected) offering a development of the Gyron Junior engine, with an aft fan which enabled the engine to deliver a thrust of 10,700lb, albeit with a weight penalty of 1,800lb. The engine was expected to be available quite swiftly, but its larger proportions would require fairly extensive modifications to the Buccaneer's airframe structure, for an increase in range of around 25 per cent.

Bristol Siddeley had produced a front fan development of their Orpheus engine, the BS55, which would produce 9,000lb thrust and offer a 30 per cent increase in range. On the down side, the thrust would reduce to 8,340lb when boundary layer blowing was selected, and the delivery timescale was uncertain. Consequently, it looked like a fairly unattractive proposition. The best option however, was that being offered by Rolls-Royce, who had been developing an engine for de Havilland's new airliner, destined for service with British European Airways. A world financial recession caused largely by the Korean War was slowly deepening, and this prompted BEA to change their requirements, resulting in a need for a smaller aircraft and a correspondingly smaller engine with which to power it. The result was the de Havilland Trident, and the engine was the RB163 Spey. Thrust was expected to be 11,380lb which, if fitted in the Buccaneer, would reduce to 9,600lb with BLC selected, and with a weight penalty of 1,100lb. As if these figures weren't exciting enough, the engine would also fit relatively easily into the existing Buccaneer airframe's spar rings, despite an increased mass flow requirement of around 80 per cent. With the aircraft's maximum range also estimated to improve by as much as 80 per cent, there was no doubt that the Spey was the ideal power plant for the second generation Buccaneer, the S.Mk.2.

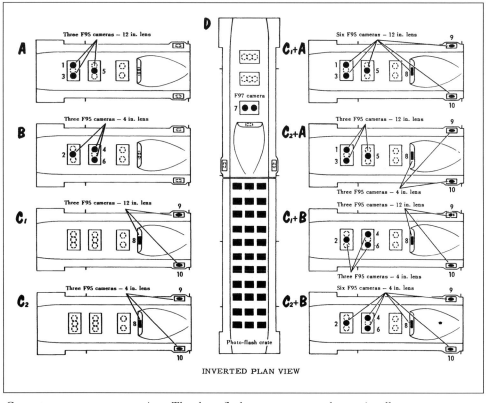

Camera crate arrangement options. The photo-flash crate was not used operationally.

Conversion of an S1 airframe was planned to commence in March 1961, followed by a first flight in December, and the first delivery in October 1963. However, because of the intensive flight trials being conducted for the Buccaneer S1, no suitable airframe was available for conversion. XK526 was selected for conversion, but after having completed tropical trials in August 1961, it was effectively stranded at Singapore until it could be shipped back to the UK and it wasn't until January of the following year that the aircraft was back at Brough, ready for work to commence. A variety of improvements were proposed for the S2 in addition to the new engines. A Honeywell inertial navigation platform with Doppler mixing was proposed (license built by English Electric), together with sideways-looking radar. It

was agreed that the latter system could be installed, but there didn't appear to be sufficient room for installation of the associated cockpit displays which were then available. A ground position marker provided by radar information could be superimposed on the rolling map display, and the Blue Parrot radar could also be operated in a terrain avoidance mode if required. Electrically-signalled flight controls were also considered, as were various electronic warfare fits and a reconnaissance system. Even more ambitious was a fighter development, possibly using a reheated version of the Spey engine. The Navy however, was interested primarily in the possibility of re-engining the aircraft with Speys, and with commendable good sense, decided to opt for an aircraft which could be produced easily, although work already

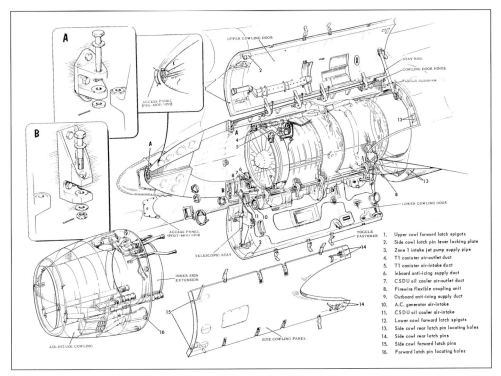

1. Upper cowl forward latch spigots
2. Side cowl latch pin lever locking plate
3. Zone 1 intake jet pump supply pipe
4. T1 canister air-outlet duct
5. T1 canister air-intake duct
6. Inboard anti-icing supply duct
7. CSDU oil cooler air-outlet duct
8. Firewire flexible coupling unit
9. Outboard anti-icing supply duct
10. A.C. generator air-intake
11. CSDU oil cooler air-intake
12. Lower cowl forward latch spigots
13. Side cowl rear latch pin locating holes
14. Side cowl rear latch pins
15. Side cowl forward latch pins
16. Forward latch pin locating holes

Spey engine installation.

done by English Electric on constant speed drives and alternators led to a degree of support for the introduction of a new electrical system for the S2, if nothing else.

Following the January 1960 meeting, the Blackburn designers began to establish the structural changes which would be necessary to accommodate the new engine. The increased mass flow would certainly require a much larger air intake and these were combined with new canted jet pipes which were also directed outwards. It also quickly became clear that the engine installation wouldn't be quite such a simple modification as originally believed, but despite this, the development of the new airframe proceeded swiftly and relatively smoothly. The only major problem encountered was one concerning the engine itself. The Spey's 12-stage compressor produced a much higher

pressure and temperature than the Gyron Junior, and Blackburn realised that the S1's ducting and associated systems for the air bleed wouldn't be able to cope. Consequently, it was agreed that air would be bled from the seventh stage of the compressor, with further air being taken from the 12th stage, and this led to failures of some engines as they were tested on completion at Derby. The compressor blade's torsional frequency was affected by the air being bled, and this occasionally led to blade fractures and failures. Thankfully, Rolls-Royce quickly identified the problem and rectified it. As mentioned, the Buccaneer S1's electrical system was recognised as being less than ideal, and so the S2 included two constant speed drives and 30 KVA alternators. Combined with the new engine gearbox, the revised electrical system would require extensive development and testing, and the delay in

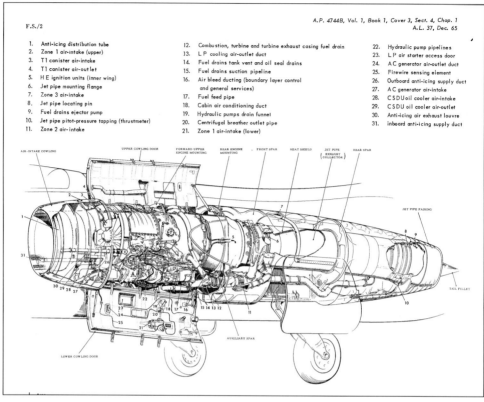

A.P. 4744B, Vol. 1, Book 1, Cover 3, Sect. 4, Chap. 1
A.L. 37, Dec. 65

F.S./2

1. Anti-icing distribution tube
2. Zone 1 air-intake (upper)
3. T1 canister air-intake
4. T1 canister air-outlet
5. H E ignition units (inner wing)
6. Jet pipe mounting flange
7. Zone 3 air-intake
8. Jet pipe locating pin
9. Fuel drains ejector pump
10. Jet pipe pitot-pressure tapping (thrustmeter)
11. Zone 2 air-intake

12. Combustion, turbine and turbine exhaust casing fuel drain
13. L P cooling air-outlet duct
14. Fuel drains tank vent and oil seal drains
15. Fuel drains suction pipeline
16. Air bleed ducting (boundary layer control and general services)
17. Fuel feed pipe
18. Cabin air conditioning duct
19. Hydraulic pumps drain funnel
20. Centrifugal breather outlet pipe
21. Zone 1 air-intake (lower)

22. Hydraulic pump pipelines
23. L P air starter access door
24. A C generator air-outlet duct
25. Firewire sensing element
26. Outboard anti-icing supply duct
27. A C generator air-intake
28. C S D U oil cooler air-intake
29. C S D U oil cooler air-outlet
30. Anti-icing air exhaust louvre
31. inboard anti-icing supply duct

Spey engine installation.

XK526's arrival at Brough was, in this respect, something of a blessing in disguise as it gave Blackburn some valuable time to work on the electrical system prior to installation.

Delays were encountered however, despite Blackburn's attempts to actively avoid them. Remembering problems with the S1's microswitches and relays which had often become unserviceable, equivalent items from civil aircraft development were substituted, these being much more reliable and readily available. Unfortunately these items required suitable clearance forms, and obtaining appropriate documentation from the suppliers created another obstacle for Blackburn to overcome. Another clearance delay was caused because the Buccaneer S2's engine bay was expected to reach a temperature of up to 400 degrees Celsius, twice that which was stipulated by the appropriate guidance rules. Rolls-Royce had carefully researched the matter and had established that the higher figure was perfectly acceptable, but the 'official' Ministry rules had been broken, and eventually Blackburn were instructed to build a fire tunnel in which the engine installation could be demonstrated as being able to run safely at 400 degrees without any risk. The annoying delays and expense did at least provide Brough with a new test facility which became useful on many other projects in later years. With the conversion complete, XK526 was towed to Holme-on-Spalding Moor, from where it made its first flight in S2 form on 17 May 1963. Turning to port immediately after take-off in typically flamboyant fashion, test

XK531 was one of the first NA.39s to be delivered to the Fleet Air Arm, joining 700Z Flight at RNAS Lossiemouth. Pictured on Lossie's flight line on 22 August 1961, the aircraft carried pale blue codes on her nose, and the 'LM' station letters on her tail. A portable air starter unit is in position below the port engine. This unit could be carried under the Buccaneer's wing when necessary.

pilot Derek Whitehead (with Jack Pearson as observer) brought the aircraft back over the airfield for a low-level and high-speed pass in front of the test programme hangars. The S2 programme was truly underway and the definitive Buccaneer – the 'real' Buccaneer – was airborne.

The Royal Navy placed a contract for the Buccaneer S2 on 8 January 1962, they being sufficiently confident in the new variant to place the order before the S1 had even entered service. Having accepted that the S2 was going to be greatly superior to the S1 in almost every respect, the production of Buccaneer S1s

August 21, 1961, and XK531 sweeps low and slow past Lossiemouth's harbour. The Buccaneer was to remain a familiar sight over Lossiemouth for 30 years. Note that the inboard flaps are extended although the ailerons are not drooped. The air brakes are partially open.

was immediately terminated, and S1 airframes which were only partly constructed on the production line at Brough were then completed as S2s. The second S2 prototype (XK527) joined the development programme in September 1963, followed by XN974, XN975 and XN976 in June, July and August of the following year, and all were assigned to an intensive flight trails programme, repeating much of the handling, flutter and general performance testing which had been undertaken by the S1. Apart from the very obvious leap in performance demonstrated by the S2, the flight testing also revealed some minor, but less-desirable changes, including an excessive amount of airflow noise whilst operating at high speeds. Investigation revealed that the source of the noise was disturbed airflow around the area where the huge engine intake met with the fuselage side. In order to rectify what was an annoyance rather than a major deficiency, a variety of differently shaped fairings were attached

to the fuselage, and then test flown. The most suitable fairing didn't please Rolls-Royce however, who believed that it might reduce the engine's fatigue life. Consequently a compromise shape was chosen, which was combined with cockpit sound insulation to produce conditions which were certainly acceptable, and this was adopted for the entire Buccaneer S2 fleet. Even so, the aircraft still remained notoriously noisy at high speed.

More seriously, an excessive amount of drag was produced whilst operating at cruising speed. Blackburn's Roy Boot addressed the problem in a very straightforward manner by simply examining the aircraft in the hangar at Holme-on-Spalding Moor: "I stood near the rear of XK527, looking forward over the nacelles. With the downwards and outwards deflection of the jet pipe, one could see the rapid expansion between rear nacelle and fuselage, and also a large base area from which the jet pipe cooling air emerged. Some swift redesign action

HMS Eagle entering Valletta's historic harbour on 25 August 1965. Four Buccaneer S1s are visible on the forward flight deck, with Sea Vixen fighters to the rear. No. 800 Naval Air Squadron's Buccaneers wore a fairly unusual colour scheme, with the traditional grey upper surfaces and white undersides extending onto the radome which was usually unpainted. The unit's Buccaneers are also carrying refuelling probes - another relatively rare sight on Buccaneer S1s. (Photo via G. Pitchfork)

Pictured at Holme-on-Spalding Moor on 21 August 1961, just two days after making her first flight, XK531 wears the anti-flash white colour scheme as applied to some early Buccaneer S1s and NA.39s. The national insignia are pale blue and pink, the serials and codes being applied in pale blue. The radome is unpainted, and the 'Royal Navy' titles are black, as are the engine intakes. Note also the white 'creep' marks on the nosewheel tyre.

reduced the base area and introduced new rear nacelle lines, the latter not being achieved without a major problem of getting an acceptable shape without causing the jet pipes to become left or right-handed. The minimum degree of downward deflection was defined by the position of the open airbrakes." After making his changes, Roy was christened 'Mr Nacelles' by the Brough drawing room staff. Even with the airframe revisions, the cruise performance at high altitude was still not as good as had been hoped for, as Roy explains, "Of course we blamed the engine, but unlike the situation with the Mark One, there was now an altitude test facility at Derby. When we had some results, a meeting took place at Brough, chaired for the Ministry by Laurie Sterne. The Rolls-Royce representative resisted any suggestions for changes to the engine, and Laurie commented that, 'you remind me of Oscar Wilde when some changes to his play were suggested and he humbly denied being an adequate person to alter a masterpiece'. In the end some improvements to the engine and the engine control system were agreed, and they had some limited success. To further

improve the high altitude cruising performance, the square cut wing tips were replaced with triangular ones which increased span without encroaching on wing folding clearance limits. This did give a worthwhile improvement and checks made at the time on the possible effect on overall strength of the wing showed it to be negligible. Many years later, following a catastrophic failure of the main front spar, a critical local stress which had not previously been detected was found, and the decision taken to remove these extended tips and to revert to the original square cut ones."

The Buccaneer S2's flight testing programme proceeded even more smoothly than the S1's, and on 9 April 1965, 700B Flight formed at Lossiemouth as the Buccaneer S2 Intensive Flying Trials Unit. With a complement of eight aircraft, the unit completed its assigned tasks by the end of September, at which stage it disbanded to be replaced by No. 801 Naval Air Squadron, which formed on 14 October. Just four days later, the unit's commanding officer, Lt-Cdr J. de Winton flew XN980 over Nelson's Column at 1,000 feet, in recognition of

A 1963-vintage illustration of 809 Naval Air Squadron's XK533 and XN950. Both aircraft eventually suffered catastrophic ends to their careers; XK533 crashed into the Moray Firth just short of Lossiemouth's runway whilst making a single-engine approach on 21 October 1963, and XN950 also crashed near Lossiemouth after suffering engine failure on an overshoot, on 28 March 1966.

the 160th anniversary of the Battle of Trafalgar. More units quickly followed, with 809 NAS forming on 27 January 1966, and after a working-up period, the unit was deployed under the command of Lt-Cdr L. Middleton for a stay at Farnborough, from where the unit made a series of formation flypasts for the 1966 SBAC show. The following year, 809 NAS was embarked on HMS *Hermes*, the carrier quickly being assigned to Gibraltar, after Spain had placed airspace restrictions on the area. No. 800 NAS was recommissioned during June 1966, embarking on HMS *Eagle* shortly afterwards, and finally No. 803 NAS was commissioned on 3 July 1967, before embarking on HMS *Victorious*. The carrier conducted a work-up cruise in the Irish Sea before departing for the Far East, where the it took part in a joint exercise with the USS *Enterprise*. US Navy crews refuelled Buccaneers from their Skywarrior tankers during the

700B Flight's XN965 pictured releasing a free-fall 1,000lb HE bomb. Rocket pods are attached to the underwing pylons, while a further two bombs are visible still hung in the bomb bay. As illustrated, toss bombing was a widely-used means of weapon delivery both for conventional and nuclear stores.

exercise. Meanwhile, on 26 March 1965 No. 736 NAS was formed as the Buccaneer land-based training unit, initially equipped with S1s but supplemented by S2s as they became available. Prior to the first operational carrier deployments, the Buccaneer S2 had already gained its 'sea legs' however, as XN974 had undertaken preliminary trials on HMS *Eagle* during September 1964, followed by main trials on HMS *Ark Royal* in March 1965, when 100 catapult launches were completed within a two-week period.

Hot weather trials were conducted with XK527, XN974 and XN976 at NAS Pensacola in October 1965 with two of the aircraft completing a total of 100 launches from the wooden-decked USS *Lexington*. XK527 had already earned a degree of notoriety after having nearly been destroyed during earlier flight testing. As part of a roll inertial coupling investigation, test pilot Paul Millet commenced a test at high altitude, and quickly found the aircraft entering a spin. Many thousands of feet lower, he managed to regain control even though both engines were on the point of flaming-out. It was the only recorded incident of a Buccaneer being successfully recovered from a spin. Returning from the hot weather trials, XN974 then earned itself the distinction of being the first Fleet Air Arm aircraft to fly unrefuelled across the Atlantic, Cdr G. Higgs and Lt-Cdr A. Taylor bringing the aircraft some 1,950 miles from Goose Bay to Lossiemouth in 4 hours 16 minutes. Further proof of the Buccaneer S2's long range performance was provided by Lt K. B. Cross and Lt-Cdr G. Oxley during 803 Naval Air Squadron's work-up on HMS *Victorious*. Launching from the carrier in the Irish Sea, they flew a 2,300-mile non-stop mission to simulate a low-level 'Target Marker Bomb' long toss attack profile on Gibraltar.

The first Buccaneer S2 loss occurred on 9 June 1966 when XN979 crashed a few miles off The Lizard in Cornwall, whilst being operated by 801 NAS on HMS *Victorious*. Crash recovery teams managed to locate and salvage the wreckage from a depth of 360 feet, but investigations didn't provide a conclusive reason for the accident. Further investigations were made including more test flying, culminating in the loss of another S2 (XV153) immediately after launch on 10 October. Eventually, the cause was traced to a combination of underwing fuel tanks and stores which had not been evaluated in the launch configuration. Together, the stores produced a raised centre of drag which caused the aircraft to pitch up and stall. Blackburn subsequently modified the underwing tanks and revised the pre-launch tailplane setting, whilst also abandoning the accepted practice of selecting 'gear up' before launch which had been adopted by S1 crews. This allowed gear retraction to begin automatically once the wheels left the carrier deck, and helped to boost the S1's marginal take-off performance. For the S2 however, leaving the gear extended produced additional drag which reduced the aircraft's tendency to pitch up.

After settling into Naval service without any further problems, the Buccaneer S2 became a firm favourite with the Fleet Air Arm's pilots. Although the S1 remained in service, it was reassigned to second-line duties (predominantly with 736 NAS for conversion training, and 803 NAS for weapons trials) and by 1967 the Navy's front-line units had all re-equipped with the S2. It was also in 1967 that the Buccaneer's capabilities were first put to the test 'for real'. On 18 March an 118,000 ton supertanker (more properly referred to as a very large crude carrier, or VLCC) was sailing off Land's End, en route from the Persian Gulf to a British port. Just 16 miles from the Cornish coast, the *Torrey Canyon* went aground on the Seven Stones Reef. Potentially, all of the tanker's 100,000 tons of oil could have flowed onto British or French beaches, and repeated attempts were immediately made to pull the tanker clear of the reef. Unfortunately, the salvage attempts were unsuccessful, and there didn't seem to be any practical way in which the oil could be removed from the tanker. In a matter of a few days the tanker's hull had broken in two, and oil was beginning to spill into the sea. The Government was faced with an impending ecological disaster and the only viable solution at the time was to destroy the tanker in situ, and burn the huge cargo of crude oil.

Not surprisingly, the task of destroying the *Torrey Canyon* was initially allocated to the Fleet Air Arm, and No. 736 Naval Air Squadron was given orders to mount a strike on the tanker, early on 28 March. Operating from their home base at Lossiemouth, eight Buccaneers were quickly prepared for the mission, and loaded with 1,000lb bombs. In order to complete the attack before dark, the first two aircraft took-off as soon as they were armed (at 14:00), the remaining six aircraft following as soon as they were ready. At 15:30 the first aircraft arrived over the target, commanded by Lt-Cdr David Howard, CO of 736 NAS. Flying at 480 knots at an altitude of 2,500 feet, two 1,000lb HE bombs were dropped onto the tanker, but one failed to explode. Shortly afterwards, Lt-Cdr David Mears brought his Buccaneer over the target and delivered two more thousand-pounders, directly onto the centre section of the ship. A total of 42 bombs were dropped, and approximately 30 of them were deemed to be direct hits. The ship was burning and as the

A Buccaneer S2 on the production line at Brough. The aircraft illustrated is nearing completion, having already been painted dark grey with white undersides, and national insignia applied (still wet, according to the instructions on the port wing). The wing fold doors are visible, partly opened, and the engine bay doors are also open, revealing that the two Spey engines are installed.

Following the final attacks by Navy Buccaneers and Sea Vixens, a massed attack by RAF Hunters torched what was left of the tanker's superstructure, and by the following morning the Torrey Canyon *was gone. Important lessons were learned during this operation, not least the fact that high explosive bombs aren't always the ideal means of destroying a target, especially 'soft' targets like oil tankers.* (Photo via G. Pitchfork)

Buccaneers recovered to RNAS Brawdy to refuel, a huge column of smoke began to climb into the sky, eventually reaching 20,000 feet. Once the Buccaneers had successfully holed the tanker, oil began to flow from her tanks, and it was time for the RAF to join the operation, with Hunters from 229 OCU arriving from Chivenor, armed with fuel-filled drop tanks. The Hunters were responsible for burning the oil as it emerged from the tanker, and their fuel/air mix 'firebombs' quickly began to consume the *Torrey Canyon*'s poisonous cargo.

The next morning, much to the public's surprise, the *Torrey Canyon* was still very much intact, the relatively rough seas having quenched the fires overnight. With most of the smoke having cleared, it became clear that a considerable number of additional air strikes would be required, if the tanker's cargo was to be completely destroyed. The first of the day's air strikes was conducted by the RAF, with eight

Hunters arriving from West Raynham to join no less than 26 Hunters from 229 OCU, all delivering a mix of napalm tanks and 3-inch rockets. They were swiftly followed by a second attack by Lossiemouth's Buccaneers which, with more time in hand, had deployed to RNAS Brawdy to bomb-up, prior to mounting the attack (on the first mission, some Buccaneers had to 'buddy refuel' en-route to the target). During the mission, 736 Naval Air Squadron's Lt J. Todd managed to place one 1,000lb bomb straight down the *Torrey Canyon*'s funnel, earning himself the distinction of having achieved what must surely have been the 'best shot' of the operation. His observer (Flt Lt G. Pitchfork) later remarked that he was unsure if they would be able to quickly locate the target off Land's End, but as their aircraft passed Bristol, they could already see the huge column of smoke ahead of them. The Buccaneers returned later in the day, in company with a quartet of firebomb-

Buddy-buddy refuelling was part of the Buccaneer design concept right from the beginning. The system gave the Navy's aircraft great flexibility, especially when operating from carriers, many miles away from RAF tanker support. This Blackburn publicity photograph shows an unusual S2 and S1 combine demonstrating the refuelling technique. When the refuelling pod was carried (always on the starboard inner pylon) an external fuel tank was attached to the port pylon both to carry additional 'give-away' fuel, and to act as an aerodynamic counter balance.

armed Sea Vixens. Once again, the tanker was left to burn through the night and the next morning, the *Torrey Canyon* was again found intact, with more oil still inside her hull. Another concerted effort to hole (but not sink) the ship was made, and the eight Buccaneers were back in business again, joined by nine Sea Vixens. The RAF finally finished off the *Torrey Canyon* with 30 Hunters delivering kerosene-filled tanks and incendiary bombs, plus more 3-inch rockets. By the early evening the tanker was virtually destroyed and little more than a few patches of unburned oil remained on the surface of the sea. After three days, 165 thousand-pounders and an estimated 40,000 gallons of kerosene,

An unusual photograph taken by Blackburn for publicity purposes, showing the Buccaneer S1 and S2 in flight together. XN935 at the rear was assigned to No. 801 NAS shortly after this photograph was taken, while XK527 (foreground) remained with the manufacturers for flight trials and developmental work. The photograph emphasises the stark contrast between the S1's engine intakes, and the huge intakes of the S2's Spey.

the *Torrey Canyon* had finally succumbed to the military onslaught. The operation had certainly been a great success, as despite the public's belief (encouraged by the media) that the Navy and RAF were unsuccessfully trying to sink the tanker, their aim had been to open the tanker's hull, to enable the oil to spill out, at which stage it could then be burned. Unfortunately, marine experts had not anticipated the way in which the oil mixed with sea water, which made the task of burning all of the oil virtually impossible. From the Navy's point of view, the operation had certainly demonstrated that the Buccaneer was an outstanding 'iron bomber'.

Carrier operations were, of course, what the Buccaneer was designed for, and while the land-based units at Lossiemouth continued their training duties, the operational squadrons were busy sailing the world's oceans on board *Victorious*, *Hermes*, *Eagle* and *Ark Royal*. Although a variety of mission profiles were undertaken by the Navy's Buccaneers, the main role remained unchanged throughout the aircraft's many years of service with the Navy (a rare occurrence for any combat aircraft), namely Maritime Strike, and as the term 'Strike' indicates, the role remained both nuclear and conventional. A typical training sortie would begin a couple of hours before the scheduled launch time, with both the pilot and observer preparing the appropriate high-level and low-level maps required for the flight. Unlike modern computer-orientated cockpits, the Buccaneer crews relied solely on traditional navigation methods, rather than using them as a back up. After completing the pre-flight briefing, the crew would then kit-up with suitable flying gear, which almost always included a heavy and very cumbersome rubber immersion suit, intended for use in 'cold water areas'. In practice, the sea

736 Naval Air Squadron assembled a four-ship formation display team during 1967, operating a mix of Buccaneer S1 and S2 aircraft. As illustrated in this photograph dated 26 January 1967, the unit's pilots stretched the Buccaneer's 'aerobatic' envelope almost beyond the rule book. (Photo via G. Pitchfork)

temperature criteria applied to virtually the entire globe all year round and the 'goon suit' became something of a necessary evil. Some distance away, the crew's aircraft would now be on the flight deck, having been carefully towed from the confines of an uncomfortably small lower deck hangar, and onto the deck lift, a task which had to be carried out with extreme care and patience in view of the Buccaneer's size, which left just a few inches clearance between tail, nose, wing tips and the hangar walls. Once safely positioned, the aircraft would be prepared for flight and the weapons (if any) for the mission would be loaded into place. On most naval Buccaneer missions, the aircraft carried practice bomb carriers or external fuel tanks. Other regularly used options included rocket launchers (36 rockets housed in each pod) or inert 1,000lb bombs. Occasionally, Bullpup wire-guided anti-ship missiles were carried, but the Bullpup was never regarded as a primary weapon, and was only carried for rare firing exercises.

The Bullpup missile was to form a major part of the Buccaneer S1's armoury during the 1960s, and as such, it was tested extensively during carriage trials at Holme-on-Spalding Moor. In practice, the Bullpup wasn't a particularly reliable or accurate weapon, and its service use was fairly limited. Here, four missiles are attached to XK525 (two under each wing).

After completing their walk-round inspection of the aircraft, the crew would clamber into the cockpit, courtesy of two sturdy hook-on ladders attached to the starboard fuselage side. The cockpit checks and switch selections wouldn't provide any surprises for a sixties jet pilot, and in terms of complexity and layout, the Buccaneer's cockpit wasn't significantly different to that of the Phantom with which it shared the flight deck on HMS *Ark Royal* for many years. Most of the cockpit layout was fairly conventional, the only unusual feature being the airspeed indicator which was presented in the form of a sliding strip scale, rather than the usual dial instrument. One switch selection unique to carrier operations however, was 'Oxygen on 100 per cent', necessary in case the launch should fail, and the aircraft be forced to ditch. Naturally, a normal oxygen and air mix for the crew to breathe wouldn't be a good idea in these circumstances. With the engines started, the Blue Parrot radar could then be activated, a small amber-coloured light indicating when the unit is warming up. This process would take around five

minutes, but if the light didn't eventually go out, the radar would be declared unserviceable and the launch abandoned. Once satisfied that the aircraft's systems are all functioning correctly, and with just a few minutes to go before launch, the Buccaneer would be taxied from start-up position to the catapult, under the direction of the flight deck directors. Although the journey wasn't more than maybe 100 yards at most, the incredibly small amount of space on the flight deck (particularly on a British carrier) required a slow and careful taxy, with small applications of engine thrust and frequent stabs of brake pressure. Approaching the catapult loading chocks had to be performed very carefully and slowly in order to achieve a gentle contact. Lining-up the Buccaneer's nose with the catapult groove would then put the aircraft at the right angle, and the flight deck directors ensured that the aircraft was then brought smoothly and slowly over the retractable chocks. The flight deck engineering officers, referred to as 'Badgers' would then begin to scurry around the aircraft, attaching the catapult launch bridle to the Buccaneer's

The Buccaneer S2's huge air intakes created a great deal of airflow noise when the aircraft was operating at high speed. The cause was found to be airflow disturbance around the intake's intersection with the fuselage, and a variety of shaped fairings were assembled in an effort to cure the problem. The 'perfect' fairing risked engine airflow disturbance, and a 'compromise' shape was adopted which partially cured the problem, although cockpit noise became an accepted part of operations.

ATO (assisted take off) hooks under the fuselage, connecting the ship's inertial navigation system with the aircraft's master reference gyro (in order to align it), and attaching the hold-back bar to the Buccaneer's lower rear fuselage.

Meanwhile, 'Flyco' (the control tower crew) would notify the 'Badgers' of the aircraft's all-up weight, so that the appropriate amount of steam pressure could be selected on the catapult. The pilot selects the required tailplane angle based on the aircraft's take-off weight, the aircraft being set-up to fly before being launched, so that a 'hands-off' launch could be made, ensuring that the pilot could not over-rotate the aircraft into a stall. Once the correct setting had been set, a petty officer on deck would check the tailplane position against graduated marks painted on the tail fairing, displaying a card with the observed setting to the pilot, so that he could confirm that the aircraft was properly trimmed, as indicated by his cockpit instruments. Launches were made in the '45-25-25' configuration, meaning that the inboard flaps were set at 45 degrees, the ailerons drooped at 25 degrees and

the tailplane similarly set at 25 degrees. Once the catapult attachments were tensioned, the Buccaneer assumed the classic nose-up pre-launch pose with the aircraft's tail skid usually touching the deck. Care had to be taken to ensure that the aircraft's brakes were released as the catapult was tensioned, otherwise a slightly incorrect launch attitude could be adopted, and if the brakes were then released, a shock load would pass through the hold-back gear which was stressed to break at a load of 51,000lb. This premature 'break-out' would produce a hopelessly underpowered launch, resulting in the loss of the aircraft. However, assuming that the preparations had been made correctly, the deck crew would clear away from the aircraft and the pilot then runs-up both of the Buccaneer's engines to maximum power. At this stage, Buccaneer S1 crews would be busy establishing whether both Gyron engines were delivering full thrust, as even on a cool day with a good headwind, the aircraft's take-off performance was marginal. Sometimes there simply wasn't enough wind speed even with the carrier steaming at 25 knots, and the launch

Buccaneer S2 handling trials at Boscombe Down included a variety of test flights with various weapons fits. In order to fully explore the aircraft's performance envelope, an anti-spin parachute was fitted to the aircraft, as a safety measure. If the aircraft entered a spin, the 'chute could be deployed, slowing and stabilising the aircraft so that a safe recovery could be made. Even so, the Buccaneer was not intentionally spun, and the aircraft was only safely recovered from a spin on one occasion. The parachute was housed in a blister fairing attached to the air brake.

would be abandoned. Of course, the Buccaneer S2 didn't suffer from any such problems. The deck officer would raise a green flag which prompted the pilot to check the engine thrust, to check that boundary layer control blowing was functioning, and that the control surfaces were all properly set. Satisfied that everything was okay, the pilot would then push his head firmly back against his head rest (he would shake his head if there was a problem) and the deck officer would look to Flyco to check for the catapult's green 'go' lights and then lower his green flag. With the Buccaneer literally straining on the catapult at full power, the flight deck would vibrate to the urgent roar of the two Spey engines, but the launch procedure was never hurried. The POMEM (Petty Officer Marine Engineering Mechanic), lowering his hands from head height would finally

press the 'Fire' button to operate the catapult, and the Buccaneer's violent departure into the air would begin.

Some 340lb/sq in of pressure from a pair of 200ft cylinders below the flight deck instantly haul the Buccaneer along the catapult groove, and the pilot and observer are momentarily breathless as a force of 20g punches them back into their seats. In no more than a second the acceleration has reduced to a more tolerable 7g and the Buccaneer is travelling at 140 knots, rumbling off the flight deck with a thud, sinking a few feet towards the uninviting sea surface, before assuming a gentle climb. The pilot would then select 'undercarriage up' and turn on to the initial outbound heading to begin the mission. For Buccaneer S1 pilots, many such launches were made with a relatively small amount of fuel on board, in order to make the aircraft as light as possible. Take-off would be followed by a climb to a rendezvous with a Scimitar which would have launched from the carrier a few minutes ahead of the Buccaneer. Waiting with a refuelling drogue extended, the tanker would replenish the tanks of the lightweight Buccaneer, and then return to the carrier, leaving the Buccaneer crew to go about their business with their fuel tanks full. The Buccaneer S1's lack of engine thrust made such tasks very necessary in situations where there was a very high ambient air temperature, but in some respects, the S1 compensated for its shortcomings by being a very agile and streamlined aircraft which handled remarkably well. Certainly, once the aircraft was 'up to speed' it was only inferior to the S2 in terms of range.

After departure from the carrier, most training sorties would involve a series of attack profiles. Much of the Navy's early use of the Buccaneer centred on the development of dive bombing delivery, making use of the aircraft's computerised bombing system which enabled the crew to fly automated bomb release profiles, usually made on 20-degree dives at around 2,000 feet. Rockets were also an important part of Navy operations, and up to four pods could be carried, each containing 36 projectiles. These would be fired from a 10-degree dive, and were intended for operational use against fairly 'soft' targets such as fast patrol boats. Practice sorties often took advantage of 'splash' targets, towed behind Navy frigates. Night attacks often involved the use of rockets too, and a technique was devised whereby one

XN976 was the first Buccaneer S2 to join the Royal Navy. Pictured in the USA on 9 August 1965, the aircraft made a series of test launches at NAS Patuxent River, Maryland during a visit to what was (and still is) the US Navy's equivalent of Boscombe Down. In this illustration the aircraft is ready for launch, with the hold-back gear attached and the catapult sling attached to the aircraft's ATO (Assisted Take Off) hooks.

Illustrating the Buccaneer's roomy cockpit, the two ejection seats were staggered either side of the fuselage centreline in order to give the observer a better forward view. The observer's windscreen was fitted to all Buccaneers after trials (and one accident) revealed that airflow into the rear cockpit made escape virtually impossible, once the canopy was jettisoned. The windscreen redirected the airflow away from the rear cockpit, enabling a safe ejection to be made if the canopy was removed, although in practice, ejections were almost always made through the canopy after miniature detonating cords were fitted.

Buccaneer would approach the target at low level, before entering a 15-degree climb at which stage a series of 3-inch rockets would be fired, each containing a parachute-retarded flare. These 'gloworms' would illuminate the target for a couple of minutes, enabling two more Buccaneers to make their approach, diving in towards the target to release their rockets. In later years larger rockets housed in SNEB pods (18 projectiles per pod) became more common.

Buccaneer S2 XN974 made a series of catapult launches from the wooden deck of the USS Lexington *during hot weather trials in the USA. After completing the trials, the aircraft made a record-breaking non-stop flight of some 1,950 miles from Goose Bay to Lossiemouth, the first unrefuelled transatlantic crossing by a Royal Navy aircraft. This Buccaneer is now on display at the Yorkshire Air Museum at Elvington.*

Nuclear weapon delivery was, despite the relative destructive power of the Red Beard bomb, a fairly simple profile to practice, and so it wasn't flown as regularly as, for example, dive bombing attacks. The standard release method for the TMB was a toss manoeuvre, the Buccaneer approaching from low level and at a distance of approximately four miles from the target a steady 4g climb would be initiated, the bomb being released as the aircraft approached the vertical plane. After release, the pilot would continue pulling back on the control column, pulling the Buccaneer over the top of a loop, before rolling wings level into a steady descent at high speed, flying directly away from the bomb's impact point. The aim of the exercise was to get the aircraft as far away from the bomb as possible, before it exploded. Naturally, these 'long toss' deliveries were never extremely accurate, but of course a nuclear bomb didn't need to be delivered with any great precision. The more important part of the profile which did require practice, was the post-release escape manoeuvre which would be critical for the survival of the Buccaneer crew. For high-priority

targets which could not be easily identified on radar, a less-common TMB delivery technique was the 'over-the-shoulder' profile, the bomb being released as the Buccaneer went over the top of a loop. This enabled the bomb to be delivered accurately in a near vertical drop to the target, but it didn't offer any practical means of escape for the Buccaneer crew. Consequently, although it was practised, it was regarded as a last-resort 'suicide' manoeuvre.

After completing the objectives of the mission, the naval Buccaneer crews had to prepare for another critical task – the deck landing. After returning to the carrier's overhead position (and even this task could be difficult in bad visibility), the Buccaneer would break to port,

Six Buccaneers from No. 800 NAS on board HMS Eagle. *The Buccaneers were assigned to strike duties, with No. 899 Naval Air Squadron's Sea Vixens operating in the air defence role. Gannet AEW3s provided airborne early warning cover.*

turning downwind before extending the landing gear and drooping flaps, ailerons and tailplane to 45-25-25 configuration. Turning through 180 degrees, the aircraft was then brought on to final approach, usually on a fairly long descent in order to give the pilot plenty of time with which to line-up accurately. Approaching a very small carrier deck was naturally extremely difficult, not least because the deck would pitch and roll even on calm days. In order to provide additional forward speed for the pilot (and therefore lower the approach speed of the aircraft), the carrier would be steaming at full power which would create airflow vortices from the 'island' superstructure, and this would often lead to down-draughts just short of the touch-down point, making the final approach even more 'tricky'. Approach speed was normally made within three knots of the required 137kt airspeed on a 4-degree glide slope. In order to provide some assistance for the pilot, the Navy relied on the deck landing projector sight (DLPS) which was the naval equivalent of the civilian visual approach slope indicator (VASI). Flying above the glide slope produced a white light while a red light indicated that he was too low. The ideal slope produced a white light surrounded by a green bars, the infamous 'meatball' which every naval pilot would recognise. The Landing Safety Officer was also in direct radio contact with the pilot, and by using a hand-held sight marked with cross-hairs, he could give the pilot a steady talk-down. But even with such assistance, the final approach was always a nail-biting experience for observers, and no less exciting for the aircrew.

As the Buccaneer rapidly closed in on the tiny carrier deck, the pilot would hear a steady beeping noise through his helmet earphones. This tone was produced by the airstream direction detector (ADD) which was initially developed for the NA.39 test programme. So useful was the ADD that it was adopted for service use, giving the pilot a useful audio reminder of his approach attitude and speed. If the beeping was high-pitched, it signified that the approach was too fast, whereas a lower tone indicated a low speed. Airbrakes would be fully open by this stage, with the boundary layer control system switched on. Keeping an eye on the angle of attack indicator (which had remain below 24 units), the airspeed indicator and the DLPS while listening to the Landing Safety Officer and the ADD tone, Buccaneer pilots always had more than enough to keep them busy on final approach, although it is fair to say that the aircraft handled well, and with some practice, the approach wasn't quite as difficult as it sounds. Thundering-in over the wave tops, the Buccaneer was an awesome sight as the main wheels crashed onto the carrier deck, bouncing slightly as the tail hook brushed the 2-inch diameter arrester cables. It was by no means unusual to miss the cables completely, and the resulting 'bolter' required immediate application of full power before the Buccaneer rushed off the carrier deck back into the air. This was a particularly critical moment for the Buccaneer S1 which had to routinely take the cable at full power, as the Gyron's marginal thrust had to be ready to accelerate the aircraft off the deck if a 'bolter' was necessary. Indeed, an engine failure below 400 feet on final approach automatically required the crew to eject, as the S1 simply couldn't recover from that situation, on one engine with the landing gear extended. Things were less critical in the Buccaneer S2, but there were many heart-stopping moments when Buccaneers literally struggled back into the air as full power was applied just a little too late for comfort.

A successful landing was confirmed when the pilot and observer felt the brutal deceleration caused by the tail hook's engagement of the arrester cable, which would bring the aircraft to a standstill in a couple of seconds. It wasn't uncommon for new Buccaneer pilots to keep both throttles fully open until they were entirely sure that the aircraft had hooked the wire, often resulting in the impressive sight and sound of the Buccaneer at full power, restrained by its tail hook. Once safely at rest, a deck handler would indicate when the hook was disengaged from the cable, at which stage the Buccaneer could quickly taxy off the main deck area to make way for the next landing. Once safely 'spotted', the wings would be folded and locked, the engines shut down, and the aircraft 'lashed' to the deck with chains, while the aircrew removed themselves from the cockpit to begin a detailed de-briefing.

Although the Buccaneer enjoyed a long and successful career with the Royal Navy, even as the aircraft settled into Fleet Air Arm service, its demise was already being planned. In 1964 a new Labour government came into power and wasted no time in turning its attention to defence expenditure as a possible source of cost-cutting. Defence Minister Denis Healey presided over massive defence cuts on a hitherto unprecedented scale and much of his attention turned towards what he regarded as the last vestige of Britain's imperial past – the Royal Navy. The First Lord of the Admiralty resigned, followed by the First Sea Lord.

Deck tie-down picketing location drawing.

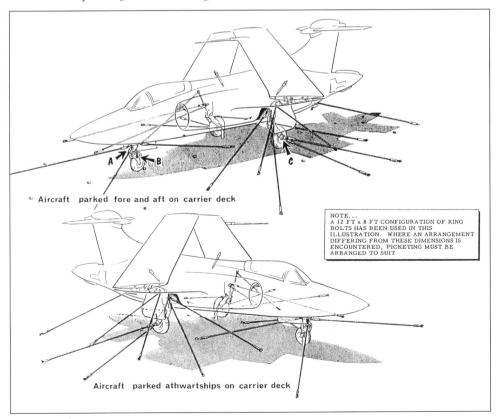

Aircraft parked fore and aft on carrier deck

NOTE...
A 12 FT x 8 FT CONFIGURATION OF RING BOLTS HAS BEEN USED IN THIS ILLUSTRATION. WHERE AN ARRANGEMENT DIFFERING FROM THESE DIMENSIONS IS ENCOUNTERED, PICKETING MUST BE ARRANGED TO SUIT

Aircraft parked athwartships on carrier deck

Not every Buccaneer landing went exactly as planned. XV353 veered off the deck after trapping the arrester cable on board HMS Eagle, on 25 April 1969. After some careful recovery work the aircraft was soon back in the air. Unusually, following transfer to the RAF in 1971, this aircraft was returned to the Navy in 1973 before being reassigned to the RAF in 1978.

Other high-ranking naval staff were replaced and after what seemed to be a remarkably short decision-making process, Healey announced that the Royal Navy was to completely disassociate itself with fixed-wing carrier operations. Ultimately this would mean the withdrawal of the Royal Navy's carrier fleet and the eventual removal of all Fleet Air Arm offensive and defensive aircraft. Despite a huge public and political outcry, the government would not be persuaded that countless years of global operations had demonstrated that the Navy's aircraft carriers were a vital national asset. The aircraft carriers would be withdrawn, and at a stroke the Buccaneer's fate was decided – or so it seemed. Until then, the Buccaneer was expected to continue operating for another 10-15 years, and attention was turned towards possible improvements which could be made to the aircraft to enable it to remain viable in the maritime

strike/attack role. Blackburn had already addressed such requirements as early as 1963, with a proposal for what was unofficially referred to as the Buccaneer Mk.3, for operation on board a new generation of aircraft carrier which Blackburn – and the Navy – then believed would be entering service in the not-too-distant future.

The Buccaneer Mk.3 was to have incorporated an inertial navigation system (using a Litton platform), a central digital computer, a high-definition dual band radar with search, ground mapping and attack modes, a separate terrain following radar, an optically-matched topographical map and radar display, and also a television sight display at the observer's station. It was also anticipated that airframe and engine improvements would be included. However, shortly after the design study had been completed, the Navy decided that it was too ambitious,

Buccaneer S2 XT276 wearing the markings of No. 736 NAS, pictured near Lossiemouth on 9 February 1967. After serving with Nos 801 and 800 Naval Air Squadrons, this aircraft was transferred to the RAF, serving with Nos 12, 15 and 16 Squadrons before being assigned to crash rescue training at Catterick in 1986.

no doubt after having realised that the long-term future of carrier air power was starting to look uncertain. Another study was commissioned in July 1964, again with the aim of improving the Buccaneer's weapons system, but this time with a firm limit on the scope and cost of the modifications. To avoid confusion with the earlier study, the new proposal was referred to as the Buccaneer 2*, the study being completed in March 1965. The main part of the proposal was the carriage of the Matra Martel missile which would be available in television-guided and anti-radar versions. A Ferranti inertial platform was again proposed but this time in analogue form rather than digital. The radar system was to be based on the Ferranti forward-looking radar which (in terrain following mode) was being developed for the TSR2, and was being test flown in a Buccaneer S1 from Ferranti's base in Edinburgh. Suitably modified to pick-up long range discrete targets at sea, the radar and inertial system would certainly have greatly improved the Buccaneer S2's capabilities. A head-up display would give the pilot all primary flight instrument information, and a pair of

'near-head-up displays' would be provided for the observer, one to give the Martel TV display or the TV optical sight which had been proposed previously, while the other would display a topographical map driven by the inertial platform, or the radar display, or possibly a combined display if it could be developed successfully.

Also proposed at this stage was the inclusion of rocket-assisted ejection seats to give the crew a zero-speed and zero-altitude escape capability. The actual shape of the cockpit would be changed too, the observer's seat being recessed into the fuselage bulkhead. The radar and optical sight would require a new nose profile while the inertial platform, navigation and weapon aiming computers and waveform generator would all be located below the cockpit. In order to carry Martel missiles, the wing pylons would have to be repositioned in order to accommodate the Martel's wing span. The existing stations were at 105 and 139.25 inches, and these would be changed to 118.5 and 166.5 inches respectively, and would enable a third pylon to be fitted at 142.5 inches, for carriage of additional bombs, etc. The original inboard station at 105 inches would be retained to carry wing tanks or the refuelling pod whenever necessary. With a weight increase of 800lb over the 'standard' S2, an in-service date of 1969 was offered for the 2*, but the proposal was dropped when the government abandoned the development of new aircraft carriers.

However, the short term future of the Buccaneer was assured, and in order to equip the aircraft for the rest of its anticipated service life, the concept of fitting the Buccaneers with Martel missiles seemed like a practical proposal. Blackburn's Roy Boot explains the background, "The pylons for wing-carried stores on the Buccaneer used single point suspension with a vertically-mounted ejector ram. They were therefore fairly deep. Attachment to the wing was by three bolted fittings, two side-by-side at the front and one at the rear. Modern stores were designed for two-point suspension, and for this the ejector ram lay horizontally in the pylon, operating from vertical rams via a linkage. The pylon was hence much shallower and attachment to the wing could be by two spigots on the centre line of the pylon. The main reason why the Martel couldn't be carried on the inner wing station when we proposed the 2* was the foul which would arise between the missile wings and the undercarriage door. The solution for carriage on the Mk.2 was a new station on the inner wing at 108.5 inches, which was

XV162 is seen on board HMS Hermes *on 2 February 1970. After service with No. 801 NAS, the aircraft was transferred to RAF charge in 1972, and went on to serve briefly with No. 12 Squadron before crashing into the North Sea near Bridlington on 13 June 1972.*

Proudly wearing the distinctive markings of No. 809 Naval Air Squadron, XT279 is depicted during a sortie from Lossiemouth on 26 February 1969. After serving with the Fleet Air Arm, this particular aircraft gained notoriety (after transferring to the RAF) as No. 16 Squadron's all-black John Player Special. *The aircraft made a few brief appearances, complete with the unit's saint and cross-keys markings, before being 'spotted' by the unit's CO, who ordered that the paint scheme be removed.*

sufficiently outboard to avoid the door foul. For a four-missile carriage capability, the outboard pylon would be positioned at 162.5 inches, moved inboard to 150 inches for a two-missile fit." One other problem which the missiles highlighted was the additional strain imposed on the wing fold mechanism, which was only just capable of functioning with a missile attached to the outer wing. The design changes for the proposed four-missile fit would enable the wing fold mechanism to be

changed to provide more power and reliability, but if the Navy opted for just the two missile fit, the wing fold would stay unmodified, although jack power could be improved slightly.

Not surprisingly, the Navy were attracted to the least expensive solution, even though Brough pointed-out that it would require five-sixths of the

With the mainwheels about to leave the deck, a Buccaneer from No. 800 NAS launches from HMS Eagle. A Wessex helicopter hovers nearby as 'plane guard' ready to provide rescue facilities if a launch fails. Visible under the fuselage is the catapult sling, about to fall away.

XT285 pictured over the Tain weapons range during April 1967, delivering 2-inch rockets to a banner target. After serving with 736 NAS and 809 NAS, the aircraft was transferred to the Ministry of Defence (Procurement Executive), and was assigned to the Tornado development programme. Fitted with a Texas Instruments radar unit in a Tornado GR1-style nose section, XT285 was operated until 5 July 1978 when it crashed during a sortie from West Freugh. (Photo via G. Pitchfork)

development time required for the four-missile option, and as other work would be done on the aircraft at the same time, the Navy would eventually get an inferior product at almost the same price. Roy Boot notes that, "Very much in our minds was the fact that with four new pylons and by using triple ejector racks, we could double the maximum bomb load which the Buccaneer could carry". A final meeting was arranged for the Admiralty to make a decision, and as Roy Boot recalls, "As professionals we arrived in good time. Just before the appointed hour a workman in overalls appeared through a large hole in the wall and announced that he was installing air conditioning ducting, and in a short time he would be making a noise which would render any meeting in the room impossible. We couldn't deflect him and neither could our important audience

when it arrived. After a somewhat chaotic delay, an alternative room was found and the audience reassembled. Meanwhile, one of the Admiralty people had folded the viewgraph and transported it to the new room, and set it up ready for operation. When we switched it on there was a flash and a bang, followed by a pall of smoke. By now it was lunch time and no alternative projector could be located, leaving the whole Martel conversion programme on the edge of disaster. As an act of desperation, I obtained a large sheet of paper, stuck it on the wall behind me, assembled those who were a combination of the most important and most unconvinced, and sat them centre front. Holding-up the transparencies to the sheet of paper, I then proceeded with the presentation. It worked, and we got the decision we had wanted, but it was a nerve shattering experience."

Associated with the Martel conversion, the Buccaneer's undercarriage would also be strengthened, in order to enable the aircraft to be deck landed with Martels attached to the wings. Although it was common practise to jettison bombs, the expensive Martels couldn't be dumped unnecessarily, and so the main gear was modified to incorporate a new fork and wheel, while the nose wheel was fitted with a liquid spring of increased travel, and a new fork. The only remaining obstacle to the Martel programme was the fitment of the television display which had to be placed inside the existing confines of the observer's cockpit. Ferranti suggested a display unit which featured a vertical cathode ray tube and an optical system which enabled the unit to be fitted behind the pilot's seat, but because a great deal of money had already been spent of Martel TV displays for both the (abandoned) F-111K and the Phantom, Brough were forced to adopt one of these designs. The Phantom's unit was a cumbersome L-shaped box which wouldn't fit into the Buccaneer, but the F-111K's display was capable of being slotted between the observer's legs, on the cockpit floor. It wasn't an ideal solution, but it was the best option available, and it was with some irony that the F-111's cockpit display eventually took to the air in the Buccaneer, and of course the proposal to fit Phantoms with Martel missiles was eventually dropped. Buccaneer S2 XK527 was assigned to handling, flutter and firing trials, flying for the first time early in 1968. XN974 and XV350 cleared existing armament on the new wing pylons, and then completed the Martel clearance programme in 1970. Deck trials took place on *Ark Royal* in 1972 and 1974, after which the Martel system was incorporated into regular service. *Ark Royal* was the last operational Royal Navy carrier, completing her last cruise in 1978 before being paid-off on 4

Series of motion picture frames showing an 809 NAS Buccaneer during the launch sequence on board HMS Ark Royal, *21 September 1971. The catapult tension is clearly seen being released, and the value of the retractable tail skid is self-evident. XT283 also served with 800 NAS before joining the RAF in 1974 after which the aircraft remained almost exclusively with No. 237 Operational Conversion Unit.*

December. A few days previously, during the morning of 27 November, the last 12 Fleet Air Arm Buccaneers belonging to No. 809 Naval Air Squadron were prepared for take-off, and on that cool and windy day in the Western Mediterranean, the last Buccaneer catapult launch took place, and the Royal

XV867 at RAF St Athan after returning from HMS Ark Royal, *following the completion of her last tour in 1978. This aircraft was transferred to RAF charge and served with Nos 12, 15 and 208 Squadrons, as well as with No. 237 OCU. Her last flight was in September 1993 when a hydraulic failure occurred after landing at RAF Leeming and the undercarriage collapsed. It was then grounded.*

Navy's association with its most potent warplane was at an end. The Buccaneers flew directly to St Athan in Glamorgan, where they were dismantled and overhauled, before emerging to begin a new lease of life, with the Royal Air Force.

Impressive 1960's picture of the Buccaneer S2, illustrating the variety of weapons carried by the aircraft whilst in service with the Fleet Air Arm. In addition to the various rockets and practice bombs, the 1,000lb HE bombs, Bullpup missiles and reconnaissance packs are joined by the huge Red Beard nuclear bomb, the Buccaneer's primary armament until the introduction of the WE177 bomb. Directly under the aircraft are external fuel tanks, a buddy refuelling pod, and an air starter unit.

CHAPTER FOUR

Export success

Despite the fact that the Buccaneer was immediately perceived as a success once it entered service with the Royal Navy, the Royal Air Force was completely disinterested in the aircraft, having decided to build its future offensive strategy around the TSR2. Not surprisingly, the RAF's refusal to adopt the aircraft tended to colour the opinions of potential overseas buyers who believed that if the Buccaneer was as good as Blackburn indicated, then surely the RAF would want it. In fact, RAF chiefs never seriously looked at the Buccaneer as an effective but cheaper alternative to the TSR2. From the outset, the Buccaneer was perceived as being a naval aircraft, and therefore almost by definition it couldn't (according to RAF thinking at

the time) be an effective land-based bomber. More importantly, the early 1960s were very uncertain times within the 'corridors of power' at Whitehall, and RAF chiefs certainly didn't want to pursue any pseudo-naval projects if there was even the slightest risk of any Treasury money being diverted away from the RAF. From both the military and political standpoint, the TSR2 was the Royal Air Force's best bet, and this attitude effectively destroyed any hopes of developing a Buccaneer derivative for the RAF.

With the chances of making substantial overseas sales already rather slight, the Buccaneer also suffered at the hands of British officials who were supposedly trying to sell the aircraft. Perhaps the

A SAAF Buccaneer S.Mk.50, carrying a pair of underwing fuel tanks, these being of significantly greater capacity than those carried by the S2. In exchange for the right to use base facilities at Simonstown, Britain agreed to supply 16 Buccaneers to South Africa, together with 10 Wasp helicopters (later extended to 17) and three frigates. Had politics not intervened, a significantly larger number of Buccaneers might have been sold to South Africa.

A close-up view of the Buccaneer S.50, illustrating the large capacity (430 gallon) fuel tank, and the Nord AS.30 air-to-surface missile. Also visible is the wing joint where British Buccaneers were fitted with hinges to enable the wings to retract inwards. Although the RAF retained this capability on their aircraft, the South African aircraft did not have a self-folding facility, although the wings could be hinged manually whenever necessary.

most serious interest was shown by West Germany, who required a new strike aircraft to replace a fleet of somewhat aged Armstrong Whitworth Sea Hawks. The Buccaneer seemed to be the ideal aircraft to supersede the Sea Hawk and the only practical alternative appeared to be the Lockheed F-104G Starfighter – a high-altitude interceptor which Lockheed had redesigned for ground attack operations. The German government spent three years evaluating the Buccaneer, but British efforts to provide detailed facts and figures were, to say the least, fairly half-hearted, especially when compared with the professional presentations made by Lockheed. Indeed, the only real enthusiasm seemed to come from the Royal Navy, who were keen to show the Germans what an excellent aircraft the Buccaneer was. One well-known story concerns a request for Buccaneer brochures which was made by the Chief of the German Naval Staff. The appropriate documents were faithfully prepared by Blackburn (which had become part of Hawker Siddeley), but because of their security-sensitive nature, they were transferred to the Ministry of Aviation and then on to Bonn by diplomatic bag. Weeks passed by without any brochures being received, and the German Naval Staff made another request for the material. An investigation revealed that the brochures had arrived in Bonn, but no British official had been tasked with delivering them to the German Navy. Consequently, the papers were eventually returned to London and once received by the Ministry of Aviation, they were filed away and forgotten. Because of incidents such as these, Germany was eventually persuaded by the more serious nature of the American offer, and decided to purchase the Starfighter, and with the benefit of hindsight, it's clear to see that the F-104 was hardly an ideal aircraft for low level strike missions.

Even more embarrassing was Britain's amateurish attempts to sell the Buccaneer to the United States Navy, who had already recognised the aircraft's potential during its development, thanks largely to the significant amount of equipment which was loaned to Blackburn as part of the US Mutual Weapons Development Program. The British sales team had only a very superficial knowledge of the Buccaneer's capabilities and engineering background, and one US Navy official later commented that he evidently already knew more about the Buccaneer than the sales team he had spoken to. Competing with Grumman, who were busy developing the A2F (which became the A-6 Intruder), the Buccaneer undoubtedly faced an uphill battle, but even when official governmental permission was given to sell the aircraft to America, the Buccaneer sales team really didn't have sufficient expertise with which to handle the job. Of course, the US Navy purchased the Intruder which was developed into a very potent attack aircraft, but one which was still inferior to the Buccaneer in some respects.

Only one country pursued the Buccaneer with sufficient interest to actually place an order, and that was South Africa, who were granted the opportunity to buy the aircraft as part of the Simonstown agreement, whereby Britain would be given base facilities at Simonstown (near Cape Town) in exchange for the supply of weaponry with which to defend the strategic sea lanes around the southern tip of Africa. Following the closure of the Suez Canal in 1956, this area had become vitally important to both Europe (including Britain) and the USA, and it seemed reasonable to allow South Africa to have aircraft with which to properly defend it, although it would appear that the British government turned a collective blind eye towards the Buccaneer's potential for

other uses. The Simonstown agreement covered the supply of (amongst other items) ten Wasp helicopters (which were augmented by a further seven a few years later), three 'Whitby' class frigates, and 16 Buccaneers, which would be of a similar standard to the Royal Navy's S2. The South African Air Force went about the purchase in a remarkably businesslike manner, listening to advice from Blackburn, whilst keeping a very firm opinion of what the SAAF actually required. The result was the Blackburn B.136, the Buccaneer S.Mk.50, which was essentially a standard S2 with a strengthened undercarriage and higher capacity wheel brakes, together with manually-folding wings. The SAAF specified that the aircraft should have an in-flight refuelling tanker and receiver capability and that longer range 430-gallon underwing tanks should be carried. Additionally, they showed some concern as to whether the Buccaneer would be able to operate from some of South Africa's high-altitude (and high-temperature) airfields, especially at the S.50's higher all-up weights which could be as high as 58,000lb. This led to the development of an assisted take-off mechanism.

The undersurfaces of the Buccaneer S.50 rear fuselage. Either side of the tail hook are retractable doors for the twin rocket engine installation. The rockets were designed to boost the aircraft's take-off performance, providing an additional thrust of 8,000lb for 30 seconds, which would have been valuable in 'hot and high' situations. In practice however, the SAAF Buccaneers were always operated from major SAAF bases which have relatively long runways, making the rocket packs redundant. They were never used operationally, and were only occasionally fired for demonstration purposes.

Blackburn proposed the installation of two Bristol Siddeley BS605 rocket engines which could provide the Buccaneer with a boost of power during take-off, ensuring that the aircraft could operate safely from fairly short runways. The rockets would be fitted towards the rear of each engine nacelle, directly under the jet pipe. Using hydrogen peroxide fuel mixed with kerosene drawn from the aircraft's reserves, the two rockets would provide a combined thrust of 8,000lb for approximately 30 seconds, using 1,100lb of hydrogen peroxide. The system was subsequently relocated, as Blackburn's Roy Boot recalls; "I conceived a retractable installation with the two motors positioned on either side of the arrester hook, with the peroxide tank in the bay above. With the installation adjacent to the fuel jettison line, kerosene was readily available to complete the package, and this was the arrangement which was finally adopted." There was some concern over the use of highly volatile peroxide fuel, but the development team produced a system which worked reliably, providing that it was kept scrupulously clean, with a healthy supply of water immediately on hand, ready to hose-down any spillage. Although the powered wing fold was deleted, the wings could still be folded manually by removing the latch pins, and the arrester hook was also retained, enabling the aircraft to take advantage of runway arrester cable systems, or even make deck landings on Royal Navy carriers during goodwill exchanges.

On 1 May 1965 No. 24 Squadron SAAF reformed at RAF Lossiemouth, initially using Buccaneer S1s 'borrowed' from other Navy units until new-build Buccaneer S.50s became available later in the year. The new SAAF unit continued to operate in conjunction with the Fleet Air Arm until an initial operational capability had been achieved, at which stage

The SAAF employed a rather crude but effective bomb aiming sight in the Buccaneer S.50, as seen in this example, visible just ahead of the windscreen framing. In all other respects the South African Buccaneers had cockpit layouts which were virtually identical to their RAF and FAA counterparts.

the first batch of eight Buccaneer S.50s departed directly from Lossiemouth, bound for South Africa, via a refuelling stopover at the Canaries, the first Buccaneer arriving at AFB Waterkloof just after 3pm on 3 November. Unfortunately, during the last leg of this ferry flight, one aircraft (serial No. 417) crashed into the sea off the African coast, after suffering a stall and double engine flame-out at high altitude, although the pilot and observer were located by one of their fellow Buccaneer crews, and picked up on a Dutch cargo vessel. As a direct consequence of this crash, it was decided that the remaining aircraft would be transported by sea, and so the next four aircraft were loaded onto the *Van der Stel* in Hull docks, suitably cocooned to enable them to be loaded as deck cargo, eventually arriving in Cape Town on 5 August 1966. The remaining four aircraft arrived on board the *Langkloof* on 17 October 1966, although it was something of a minor miracle that any of the aircraft had ever reached South Africa at all. During

1964, a new Labour government had come into power in Britain, and the new Prime Minister, Harold Wilson, was keen to pursue a proposed United Nations arms embargo against South Africa. Of course, the Buccaneer was the first casualty of this decision, but after lengthy protests from the South African government the delivery of the 16 aircraft was given the go-ahead, although the option on orders for a further 20 aircraft was immediately cancelled by Britain.

The arms embargo was enforced rigidly, and even the anticipated replacement of c/n 417 was prohibited, on the grounds that it (along with the other 15 aircraft) could potentially be used as part of South Africa's apartheid policy, operating attack missions against centres of population. Of course, the Buccaneer was hardly suited to this role, and the SAAF received aircraft which were designed specifically for counter-insurgency operations, as well as numerous troop-carrying helicopters. Surprisingly, the Wilson

Official badge of No. 24 Squadron, South African Air Force, the only SAAF unit to operate the Buccaneer. As the unit motto implies ('By Night By Day') the Buccaneer's were used in a variety of roles, although they were predominantly employed on ground attack duties.

government was strangely silent in condemning Italy and France who supplied the equipment, while steadfastly refusing to supply any further Buccaneers, much to the disappointment of Blackburn and thousands of aerospace workers. Sadly, as a dedicated bomber, the Buccaneer was in some respects a victim of its own success, as Roy Boot explains; "Those who wanted it were not allowed to have it, and those who would have been, didn't want it, having been influenced by the failure of the Royal Air Force to adopt it at the time. The political constraints are much greater for an aircraft which is essentially a bomber – and hence an aggressor – than they are for a fighter, essentially for the noble art of defence, but which of course are capable of offensive operations."

Having received a total of 15 Buccaneers, the SAAF soon began to appreciate the aircraft's excellent performance in terms of range, low level handling, and weapons carriage capability. Used primarily in the maritime role for which it was designed, the aircraft regularly participated in exercises with the South African Navy and Britain's Royal Navy. The Buccaneers were flown hard too, with some aircraft falling victim to flying accidents and by April 1978, no less than nine aircraft had already been destroyed, mostly as a result of the demanding environment in which they were being operated (in one particularly tragic accident, two Buccaneers collided during an attack exercise). Despite this, the SAAF continued to keep the dwindling fleet of Buccaneers in the air. The deteriorating political situation effectively ended any relationship with the United Kingdom, and joint exercises with the Royal Navy became increasingly rare, until they ended completely. Faced with isolation, South Africa pursued its own political agenda, and the internal disputes began to extend into 'external operations'

A traditional display of weaponry, in this instance a Buccaneer Mk.50, with a selection of rockets, rocket pods, free fall high explosive bombs, and air-to-surface missiles. Unlike British Buccaneers, the S.50s did not carry nuclear weapons (South Africa not being a nuclear power).

conducted in neighbouring countries. With a limited number of combat aircraft at its disposal, the SAAF was forced to use whatever aircraft were available in order to implement the policy of the South African government. Having been operated successfully on maritime training missions for more than a decade, the Buccaneer was recognised as being the SAAF's most valuable asset, and it was therefore no surprise when it was quickly 'called-up' for active duty in the growing 'Bush War'.

The first operational Buccaneer mission took place on 4 May 1978, when Operation Reindeer began. An attack was mounted on the small Angolan mining town of Cassinga, where a large Swapo garrison was known to exist. The Buccaneers were tasked with the 'softening-up' of the target in preparation for an assault by 278 paratroopers. The initial low level attack was made by Canberras which delivered a load of anti-personnel bombs. Six Buccaneers followed-up the Canberra attack, making dive attacks on the target, each aircraft carrying eight 1,000lb bombs, with delay and impact fuses. The attack was successful, and after returning to base, the Buccaneer crews

were tasked with a second mission, to attack insurgent bases at Chetequara, some distance to the south. During the flight to the target, the Buccaneer crews received news that an armoured convoy was approaching Cassinga, where South African troops were still waiting to be airlifted out of the area by helicopter. In order to stop the convoy, two Mirages were scrambled, but with only 30mm cannon to stop the tanks and APCs, they were unlikely to do much more than slow the convoy's progress. At this stage, Capt. Dries Marais (with his navigator Capt. Ernie Harvey) was diverted to Cassinga, as he recalls; "I rolled into my dive attack on the tanks which had by now reached the outskirts of Cassinga. In front of me, just settling into their attack were the two Mirages. The 30mm HE rounds of the first one exploded ineffectively on the lead tank and I called out to the second aircraft to leave the tanks alone and go for the personnel carriers. The pilot confirmed my request and the next moment I witnessed Major Joham Radloff take out three BTRs with a single burst from his twin cannon. Ernie gave me a selection of 12 rockets which also flew true, and then we had to break off violently to avoid

Although South Africa's Buccaneers were delivered wearing a very smart glossy paint scheme, they were eventually 'toned-down' like the aircraft of many other nations. Matt colours were substituted and national insignia were removed, leaving the aircraft with just a unit badge and serial codes. As is customary with matt paint, the effect of intense sunlight and strong airflow soon gives a weathered appearance, making the Buccaneers look distinctly 'battle-worn'.

flying through the debris from the exploding tank. Turning round for another pass, we could see the first tank burning like a furnace, and on this run the lead Mirage pilot destroyed no fewer than five BTRs with a long burst, running his shells in movie-like fashion right through them. Then our second salvo of 12 rockets, every third one with an armour piercing head, also struck home."

In just a few seconds, two tanks and 16 APCs had been completely destroyed, and the Mirages were down to their minimum combat fuel, and were forced to return to base, leaving the Buccaneer crew to 'mop-up'. The tanks were the main priority, but the BTRs were armed with twin-barrel 14.5mm anti-aircraft guns, some of which were now being trained on the Buccaneer, as Marais recalls; "Even one of the tanks was firing with its main weapon and I remember being amused at the gunner's optimism, hoping to hit a manoeuvring target travelling at 600 knots. Ernie, on the other hand, was far from amused as he was aware of several AA positions firing at us. He was even less impressed at my dismissal of the problem, but my whole system was now charged to take out the remaining tanks. As we turned in again,

these two tanks left the road and disappeared into the bush. We destroyed another BTR, but decided to save our ammunition for the tanks. Flying around trying to locate them, I became annoyed with one AA site which kept a steady stream of tracer in our direction, and I decided to take it out. It was in fact the gun which had been towed by the BTR we had just destroyed, so I only have respect for the discipline and courage of the gun crew and some of the troops who kept up their firing – even with their small arms – until my rockets exploded amongst them, killing the lot and destroying the gun." He continued, "As I broke off from this attack, the huge gaggle of helicopters passed under us and landed in the pre-planned area to pick up the troops. By this time I had learned that the Chief of the Army, Lt-Col. Viljoen was on the ground with them, and there was grave concern for his safety. Then as the helicopters were landing, the remaining two tanks reappeared on the road, and started shelling the landing area which was in a shallow depression. Because of this, and the inability of that particular type of tank to lower its gun far enough, they were overshooting by some 300 yards."

"We were in a perfect position for an attack from the rear on the front tank, and calculating that we had 12 rockets left, I asked Ernie to give me only six, leaving another salvo for the other tank. Timing was critical as the tanks were beginning to find their range. I realised that they had to be stopped. It was a text-book low angle attack, and the Buccaneer was steady as a rock in the dive, but when I pulled the trigger nothing happened – no rockets, not even one. I jerked the aircraft around, almost in agony, cursing Ernie for having selected the wrong switches. He was adamant that he had selected the switches correctly so we went in for another attack, but with the same heart-stopping result. Without really thinking about it, I opened the throttles and kept the aircraft in a dive, levelling off at the last moment, flying over the tank very low and doing nearly Mach One. Turning, we went in again from the front, this time doing the same thing with the tank shooting at us once more. I assumed that the crew would have no idea that were were out of ammunition, and hoping to intimidate them, we continued to make fast, head-on low level mock attacks. The Buccaneer from close-up is an intimidating aircraft. Flying low, it makes a terrific amount of noise compressed into a single instant as a shock wave, and if it was being amplified inside the tank, then its crew would have to be well-trained to stay with it!" Eventually the tank crews were sufficiently concerned to head back into the cover of the bush, enabling the helicopters to recover the troops from the area. When the Buccaneer returned to Grootfontein, a total of 17 hits were counted on the airframe, including a 37mm AA hit through the port flap, and several hits through the engine bays. Dries was awarded the Honoris Crux (silver) for his brave actions, while Ernie Harvey received the Chief of the Defence Force's Commendation Medal, for his commendable actions. The raid on Cassinga demonstrated the Buccaneer's long range capability. The aircraft were bombed-up with 1,000lb bombs at Waterkloof, 24 Squadron's home base, before being flown on their outbound leg which took some 1 hour 30 minutes. The target at Cassinga was 150 miles from the Angolan border, and the Buccaneer's return leg of 300 miles took the Buccaneers to Grootfontein, where they refuelled prior to returning to home base.

On these attacks, two aircraft (Nos 416 and 412) were hit by 45mm ground fire, but they survived without any serious

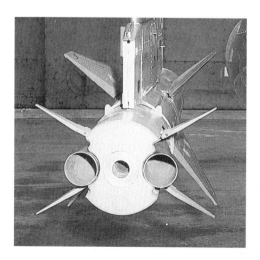

The Nord AS.30 was a French air-to-surface missile, designed for maritime operations. In essence it was a less-sophisticated unguided version of the Martel. The decision to sink the tanker Wafra *in March 1971 gave SAAF Buccaneer pilots an opportunity to test their skills with the missile, and they were successfully fired at the tanker from 3,000 feet. Depth charges dropped by Shackletons eventually sealed the fate of the* Wafra.

An impressive Blackburn publicity photograph showing a Buccaneer S.50 streaking past the company's cameraman at little more than 100 feet over Holme-on-Spalding Moor. With four Nord AS.30 missiles under her wings, the aircraft looks every inch the potent beast that it was. In SAAF service the missiles were rarely used however, not least because of their cost.

damage. The operations were deemed to be a great success, and from then onwards the Buccaneers were regularly tasked with attack missions. The next operation (over south-west Zambia) involved a series of dive attacks, delivering 1,000lb bombs, the total flight time of the sortie being 3hr 15min. Another significant operation took place in March 1979, when No. 24 Squadron conducted the first night attacks. For each of these missions, four Buccaneers would take off and settle into a radar trail, with each aircraft separated by three miles. The trailing aircraft also staggered their altitude, with each aircraft 500ft lower than its predecessor, so that their radars would be continually pointing upwards where they would be unlikely to be detected from the ground. The target was plotted by ground radar with co-ordinates being passed to the Buccaneer crews. From a total of 32 x 1,000lb bombs dropped, no less than 22 fell within the target area, despite total cloud cover which forced the crews to bomb 'blind'. The first night attack (by aircraft Nos 414, 422, 413 and 416) was judged to be another great success, leading to more nocturnal raids in the future. The next mission took place on 14 March 1979, three aircraft taking part after one aircraft went unser-

viceable just before take-off. A long-range 'strategic' target, the weather conditions were very poor, and the three aircraft had to fly at altitudes of around 100ft in order to remain in visual contact with the ground. As with many of these missions, the raid was conducted in co-operation with No. 12 Squadron's Canberras, which dropped anti-personnel 'Alpha' bombs. On the second mission which was launched later the same day, one Canberra was lost after the pilot was hit (and killed) by small arms fire. This prompted the SAAF to rethink the tactics which were being employed to fly these attack, and as a result it was decided that the Buccaneers should abandon level dive bombing in favour of medium-level toss delivery techniques.

The next operational mission took place on 5 July 1979, and this was the first raid on which the Buccaneers flew toss deliveries. The crews perfected the technique so that the 1,000lb bombs were often laid in parallel sticks, approximately 800 yards long and 500 yards wide, and with a delivery accuracy better than 100 yards. On this particular mission, two of the Buccaneers were unserviceable, and only two aircraft actually took part, flying as part of a strike package with Mirage F1AZ fighter-bombers. Interestingly, the

A Buccaneer S.50 photographed during rocket-assisted take-off trials at RAF Elvington.

two Buccaneers carried the same bomb load as seven of the Mirages, flying exactly the same mission profile. By the end of 1979 the raids over Angola and Zambia were becoming more difficult for the Buccaneer crews, as radar-guided weapons systems were beginning to be employed, and an extensive search radar network was being put into place. Worse still, only six Buccaneers remained operational, and of these, just four were assigned to active duty, while the fifth was undergoing servicing and the sixth was designated as a reserve aircraft. No. 24 Squadron continued to develop techniques however, and on 24 May 1980 the unit used night illumination for the first time. Equipped with 6,000,000 candle-power flares. One aircraft ran-in at low level to toss the flare which then descended by parachute, while the remaining three aircraft also approached at low level to pitch-up for a dive attack. The flare dropper would then tuck-in behind the other three to make its own

bomb delivery. On 7 June, another attack was launched, with four Buccaneers running in behind 16 Mirage F1AZ fighter-bombers. Two of the Mirages were fired upon by SAM-2 and SAM-3 weapons, and both aircraft were damaged quite extensively, although both managed to return safely, making a high speed and a dead-stick landing respectively. The aircrew were called off the target, the SAAF having decided that it was too well defended to risk the use of its dwindling number of operational Buccaneers.

Area targets which couldn't be pinpointed with great accuracy, were subjected to high-altitude level bombing, flown in 'Mother Goose' fashion. A Canberra (equipped for level bombing) would lead a Buccaneer and two Mirages in a four-aircraft cluster, with each aircraft dropping its bomb load in unison, often as part of a 16-aircraft package. The Buccaneers would, as usual, carry 1,000lb bombs, the Mirages carrying 500-pounders, and the Canberra carrying

2,000lb bombs and 500-pounders. Because of the increasing sophistication of the defences, the SAAF began to launch more reconnaissance sorties in order to try to locate radar sites and anti-aircraft missiles, etc. The reconnaissance Canberas were not equipped with any form of electronic warfare equipment, and so Buccaneers usually acted as escorts for the Canberras, because of their fairly sophisticated EW fit. The conflict gradually intensified, and No. 24 Squadron gradually assumed responsibility for more pinpoint attacks on radar and other defensive sites. The Nord AS.30 air-to-ground missile was ideal for this kind of mission, and the Buccaneer crews trained intensively to develop a good capability with the weapon. Delivered in a 30-degree dive (in order to maintain good separation from ground fire) the AS.30 was

Top: A SAAF Buccaneer Mk.50 carrying a heavy load of free-fall bombs. Note the low-vis camouflage scheme (no national insignia on the wings) and aerial fit, compared with an earlier image, above, of 412 which shows the early-style full-colour insignia, and lack of aerial/chaff additions to the fuselage underside.

normally carried by all four aircraft, each flying in trail, and launching the missile at about 13km from the target, pulling off from the approach at 5km while controlling the missile via a radio link. Taking just 25 seconds to reach the target, the missile impacted at a speed of around Mach Two, with its 30kg warhead giving the same effect as a 1,000lb bomb. Eventually, some 33 AS.30 missiles had been fired, of which 30 arrived on target and as usual, the Buccaneers were used as effectively as possible, with four 1,000lb bombs being carried in the bomb bay. The combined weapon load enabled the crews to attack three different targets each, on every mission (two AS.30 targets and one bomb target). In order to deliver the weapons as accurately as possible, crews were normally assigned to specific aircraft, and every effort was made to keep the same crew with the same Buccaneer, so that the small handling differences between each aircraft would become familiar to the crews.

The Buccaneers continued to fly operational missions through subsequent years, culminating in an intensified period

A close-up of the terrain warning radar (TWR) antennae on the Buccaneer S.50.

of operations late in 1987. All of these attacks were made using 1,000lb bombs or AS.30 missiles, together with some 'occasional fits' required for specific targets. Additionally, Buccaneers also flew reconnaissance missions when necessary, using a camera system developed in South Africa specifically for the aircraft. Camera crates were delivered with the Buccaneers in 1965, but these were lost in subsequent crashes. Consequently, the SAAF was faced with a requirement for a tactical reconnaissance system, and so a long range oblique camera pod was developed, which could be fitted in the Buccaneer's bomb bay. Capable of photographing targets from a distance of up to 10km, the Buccaneer would run in to the target at low level (at over 500kt), pitch-up into a climb at 10km, before making a 30-second photo run at 20,000 feet. The aircraft would then be rolled inverted and

pulled into a dive, running out from the target area at low level. Because the reconnaissance system was derived from the equipment fitted to SAAF Mirage RZ aircraft, the aiming system came directly from the Mirage and was custom-fitted to the Buccaneer. Likewise, other South African-built equipment was progressively fitted to the Buccaneers, including TWR (threat warning receiver) sensors which were fitted under the nose, to give the crew information on the range, location and type of threat. Chaff/flare dispensers were attached to the aircraft too, positioned either side of the aircraft's Doppler radar, fixed under the rear fuselage, and not surprisingly, they were used regularly during the Buccaneer's many operational missions.

Because of the increasing sophistication of Angolan defences (supplied by the Soviet Union) and the demands being placed upon the remaining six Buccaneers (and an ever-decreasing supply of spare parts), operations gradually wound-down, and the last operational Buccaneer sortie over Angola took place on 6 February 1988. Peace talks began in May and on 22 December a peace settlement was signed, and this formally ended the conflict between South Africa and Angola. Of course, No. 24 Squadron's Buccaneers also main-

A chaff/flare dispenser, as fitted during SAAF service.

A Buccaneer S.Mk.50 wearing the markings of No. 24 Squadron, SAAF. The colour scheme appears to be an 'intermediate' style between the original post-delivery scheme, and the final low-vis arrangement.

tained their maritime strike capability throughout the many years of the Angolan conflict. In 1971, SAAF Buccaneers were called upon to perform a mission which was remarkably similar to the Royal Navy's destruction of the tanker *Torrey Canyon*. On 27 February that year, the Liberian tanker *Wafra* sent a mayday message, stating that its engine room was flooding. With a full load of 60,000 tons of crude oil en route from the Persian Gulf to the Caltex oil refinery near Cape Town, the tanker was quickly assisted by the crew of a Soviet tanker which was sailing nearby. They attempted to take the tanker in tow, but after a couple of hours the tow cable snapped, leaving the *Wafra* stranded. Eventually a South African coaster made a second attempt to tow the tanker, but increasingly heavy seas gradually pushed *Wafra* closer and closer towards the coast. The anchor was finally dropped, but even this didn't prevent a gradual drift inshore, and the crew were ordered to abandon ship shortly before she ran aground at Cape Agulhas, and began leaking oil. The next day, attempts to tow the tanker clear began, but after a

few days, it began to look like an impossible task. The tanker was badly damaged and its owners wrote her off, having decided that the prospect of pumping oil out of the tanks would now be far too dangerous. The only option left was to tow *Wafra* out to sea and then sink her. On 9 March the tanker was finally pulled clear, but the journey 200 miles out to sea was made progressively more difficult by the deteriorating condition of the tanker and poor weather. The South African government decided to act quickly and sink the tanker as swiftly as possible, instructing the SAAF to create as little oil pollution as possible.

This left a range of options, including the use of torpedoes and depth charges, but it was decided that the best approach would be to use AS.30 missiles fired from Buccaneers. These could hole the tanker below the water line and sink her intact, without allowing much of the oil cargo to spill out. On 10 March, two Buccaneers took-off from Waterkloof and headed directly for the *Wafra*. The AS.30 attack was made in poor light and bad weather, but from the four missiles which were fired, one was a direct hit. Unfortunately, it had little effect upon the tanker and so a repeat attack was scheduled for the next day. This time, four Buccaneers arrived over the target, delivering eight missiles of which six were direct hits. By the end of the day the ship's cargo was burning fiercely, although the tanker was still intact, as had been planned. By 7pm it was agreed that the oil fumes surrounding the ship had been largely consumed, and a SAAF Shackleton was called in to drop depth charges. Because of the growing darkness, a second attack was postponed until the next morning and the Shackleton went into a long cruise through the night, remaining within the vicinity of the tanker. At first light the following morning another depth charge drop was made by the Shackleton crew and the *Wafra* was set completely ablaze, sinking below the wave tops within an hour. Rear Admiral J. Johnson who masterminded the sinking of the ship, recalls; "We certainly could have done the job much faster using 1,000lb bombs, but they would simply have broken the *Wafra* up and internationally we could have picked up quite a few complications. The whole idea was to sink her with as little pollution as possible. To bomb her the

conventional way would not necessarily sink her, and if she just broke up, you would have the dangerous possibility of huge pieces of wreckage – possibly as big as tugs – floating around in one of the world's busiest shipping lanes."

Johnson continues; "It was decided to give the Air Force pilots a chance at this live target with their AS.30 missiles. These were fairly new at the time and it was desired that pilots should test them for accuracy and power. Torpedoes would have been far more costly than the missiles. A torpedo is like a hand-made Swiss watch on a very much larger scale, a precision instrument and very costly. On the first sortie, two Buccaneers went in. There was a very good hit and a large explosion. Had this been a wartime operation, that strike would have been sufficient to cause the crew to abandon ship. The fact that there was no fire can be explained by the fact that it was a ballast tank that had been hit. The Second World War showed again and again that you can tear a tanker almost in half and the chances are her buoyancy tanks will still keep her afloat. We were trying to sink *Wafra* with the least possible inconvenience to everyone." Some time after the incident, South Africa's Mr Botha commented that he hoped Harold Wilson took note of Operation *Wafra*, and the way in which the Buccaneers had been used, referring to the infamous *Torrey Canyon* affair.

Buccaneers being loaded on to a container ship at Hull Docks, ready for their long journey to South Africa. In order to protect the aircraft from the salty, and therefore corrosive, sea air, they were sealed in plastic wrapping for the trip.

XV350 retained its 1970's-style colour scheme throughout its flying career, which ended with British Aerospace at Scampton during the early 1990s. It is now preserved at the East Midlands Aero Park.

Buccaneer in colour

The farewell line-up of Buccaneers for a media gathering at Lossiemouth. XV168 in the foreground enjoyed an appropriate fate, returning to her birthplace on 15 October 1993 to become 'gate guardian' at British Aerospace's Brough factory.

A No. 12 Squadron Buccaneer breaks left over RAF Lossiemouth. No. 208 Squadron's shelter complex can be seen to the left of the picture, with No. 12 Squadron's shelters in the far distance.

A nostalgic view of XN974, the first production Buccaneer S2 which also earned the distinction of being the first Fleet Air Arm aircraft to cross the Atlantic, unrefuelled, non-stop.

XX895 was one of a few Buccaneers to serve with No. 216 Squadron, prior to the unit's premature disbandment. After receiving a wing transplant in 1980, the aircraft later saw service in the Gulf War, flying seven operational missions. After retirement it was sold to a civilian buyer at Enstone, Oxfordshire.

Of the few S1 survivors, XN957 is certainly the best, and is currently with the Fleet Air Arm Museum, resplendent in the markings of No. 736 Flight, with which the aircraft served, and coded '630'.

A beautiful four-ship formation of Buccaneers from Nos 12 and 208 Squadrons, shortly before the type was withdrawn from RAF service. The standard grey/green camouflage was progressively being replaced with the light grey scheme at the time of withdrawal.

This unusual view of a No. 208 Squadron Buccaneer with 'everything down' illustrates the type's wing upper surfaces and the wing fold doors which were often permanently removed in order to afford swift inspection of the internal mechanism.

During the 1980s the Lossiemouth Buccaneer squadrons adopted a twin letter tail code system, as illustrated by XV869 at St Mawgan, one of No. 12 Squadron's Forward Operating Bases. This aircraft was placed in long term storage at Shawbury in 1990, before being scrapped in 1994.

XV868 at low level over the Orkneys, passing the Old Man of Hoy with refuelling drogue extended. The aircraft was one of two Buccaneers deployed to the Falkland Islands during 1993 as part of a rapid reinforcement exercise.

No. 208 Squadron's XT287 in a hardened aircraft shelter at Lossiemouth. Named MacRobert's Reply *in 1980, the aircraft was eventually scrapped on site at Lossiemouth in May 1992.*

Doing what Buccaneers do best, a No. 12 Squadron machine gets smartly airborne from St Mawgan, with the landing gear retracting as soon as the wheels lift from the runway.

XX894 carried special markings to celebrate No. 12 Squadron's 75th anniversary in 1980. After serving in the Gulf War, the aircraft was painted in Fleet Air Arm markings in 1993 as part of the Buccaneer's retirement celebrations. Ironically, it had never actually seen service with the Royal Navy.

Pictured taking on fuel from a VC10 tanker, XV168 is now on permanent display outside the British Aerospace factory at Brough, on the banks of the River Humber.

One of the Defence Research Agency's fleet of trials aircraft, XV344, was responsible for the flight trials of the TIALD pod which had now entered service with the Royal Air Force. During the trials the aircraft was named Nightbird and painted with appropriate artwork.

XW988 wearing her unusual high-visibility yellow/green colour scheme, prior to retirement in 1995.

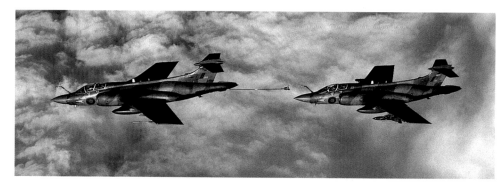

Buccaneer-to-Buccaneer 'buddy' tanking in progress, high over the North Sea during October 1987.

Having spent virtually her entire service life at Lossiemouth, XV165 was scrapped at RAF Shawbury during February 1994. The cockpit section was sold to a civilian buyer.

History was to repeat itself yet again on 20 April 1972, when the Liberian tanker *Silver Castle* collided with the *SA Pioneer*, six miles from the mouth of Bushman's River. Suffering serious damage and with fires burning, the rescue crews tried desperately to prevent the disabled *Silver Castle* from drifting ashore. Thankfully, they managed to transfer the tanker's oil cargo onto another ship, and the *Silver Castle* was towed out to sea, where it was decided that the tanker was beyond economical repair and would best be scuttled. Once again, the maritime Strike Buccaneers were ideally suited to the task, but because the tanker's oil had been removed, there was no need to carefully hole the tanker with missiles. For this exercise, 1,000lb bombs could be used to destroy the ship as quickly and effectively as possible. On 13 May, five Buccaneers arrived over the tanker which was now 170 miles off Port Elizabeth. Flying from Waterkloof to a forward base at Langebaan, the aircraft 'buddy' refuelled en route to the target from a sixth aircraft. Carrying 1,000lb bombs, the aircraft quickly engulfed the tanker in smoke and flames, and the crew of a circling Shackleton were able to watch the tanker on radar, as she rapidly took-on water and sank. In little more than ten minutes since the attack began, the *Silver Castle* was gone, with just small pieces of wreckage and the slightest trace of oil remaining on the sea surface. The operation had certainly been much easier than *Wafra*, simply because the oil cargo had been removed, making all-out destruction a viable option. It was also a perfect opportunity for No. 24 Squadron to demonstrate that above all else, the Buccaneer was perfectly designed for the ship-sinking business.

The Buccaneer Mk.50 pilot's cockpit.

The Buccaneer Mk.50 rear cockpit.

The South African Air Force's association with the Buccaneer ended in 1991, when the last flight was made on 10 April by aircraft No. 416 which was delivered to its final resting place at the SAAF Museum at Ysterplaat. By the beginning of 1991, just four Buccaneers were still operational with No. 24 Squadron, another two having been lost in accidents. Clearly, even with the best will in the world, four aircraft could not serve any practical purpose, especially when the aircraft were becoming increasingly unserviceable and dependent upon spares which couldn't be obtained. Even so, the SAAF pilots were reluctant to say goodbye to a much-respected aeroplane. Undoubtedly, the decision to buy the Buccaneer had been a good one, and the only real regret was that more aircraft had not been ordered and delivered before the UN arms embargo was enforced. As for the aircraft which were purchased, the SAAF only regretted the deletion of the powered wing fold (which simply wasted time and effort) and the inclusion of the rocket assisted take-off motors. In practice, the rockets were only ever used four times, for demonstrations at air shows. The logistic support required to supply and load the peroxide fuel created long turn-round times which made the system impractical. In any case, many of the SAAF runways were 12,000ft long, enabling Buccaneers to get airborne with full weapons and fuel loads on all but the hottest days, and even in those circumstances, the Buccaneer's buddy refuelling capability was a much more practical way of getting heavy Buccaneers out of the hot and high airfields. With hindsight, the rocket assisted take-off facility was a waste of money, but the Buccaneers themselves were without doubt one of the most cost-effective purchases that the South African Air Force ever made.

CHAPTER FIVE

The Royal Air Force

It is particularly ironic that the Buccaneer's export success was damaged by the Royal Air Force's reluctance to adopt the aircraft, when history now records that it later became one of the most successful and effective aircraft ever to have served with the RAF. Because the Royal Air Force was firmly committed to the TSR2, any suggestion that the Buccaneer should be developed into a land-based bomber was regularly dismissed by service chiefs. Despite this attitude, Blackburn continued to produce design studies in the hope that the RAF would eventually show some interest. Even as the original requirement (OR339) was issued in 1957 for a Canberra replacement, Blackburn had produced a design based around the NA.39, which would have met the RAF's needs (albeit with further development), but the naval origins of the design effectively discouraged the RAF from seriously considering the concept. Of course, the TSR2 programme finally fell victim to cost over-runs and a Labour government which was determined to abandon the aircraft. When the final announcement came that the TSR2 was to be scrapped, it was simultaneously announced that an option had been secured to buy the General Dynamics F-111 which (at that time) was expected to

become the US Navy's and the US Air Force's standard fighter-bomber. Defence Minister Denis Healey also commented that, "We must see if TSR2's strike role can be carried out by sea, or land-based Buccaneers". Healey's suggestion wasn't taken too seriously in Whitehall however, but in 1968 the Air Staff did ask Hawker Siddeley to produce a proposal for a supersonic version of the Buccaneer, using a reheated version of the Spey engine. As Blackburn's Roy Boot comments; "One must assume that the intended role was strike interdiction, which until then had been scheduled for the F-111. Not for us to reason why, but to meet the requests of the customer to the best of one's ability."

This supersonic Buccaneer (the P.150) had an extended rear fuselage which eliminated the need for the area ruled bulge, and the centre fuselage was stretched by two feet, with a further extension added to the rear cockpit. The wing was non-folding and because of different aerodynamic loading, a new tail unit was also incorporated. Much heavier than earlier designs (7,000lb heavier than the S2), the P.150 also featured a bogie undercarriage. Engines were to be Spey 25Rs (later fitted to RAF Phantoms) but with a transition pipe passing through the spar rings, and a thrust reverser fitted ahead of the reheat

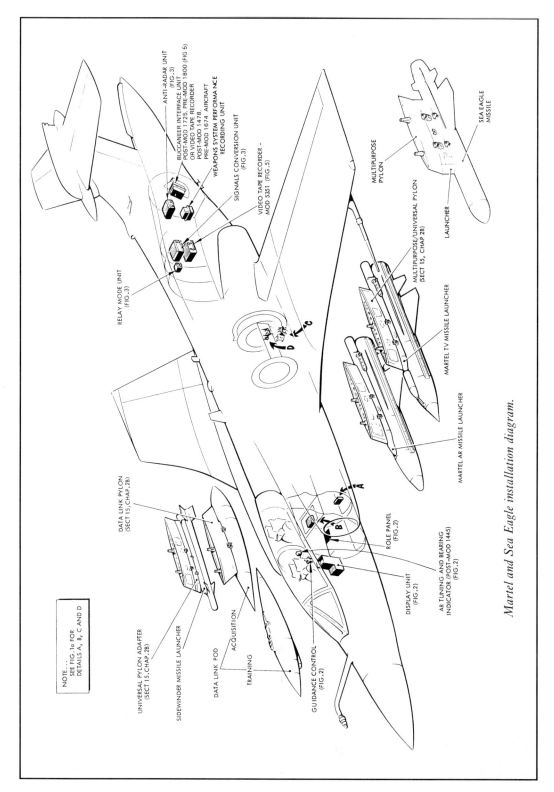

Martel and Sea Eagle installation diagram.

XV350 was initially delivered to the Royal Navy in 1967, but on 1 January 1969 it was transferred to RAF charge, and joined 'A' Squadron at Boscombe Down, where it was employed on a variety of trials connected with RAF weaponry destined for service with the RAF Buccaneer squadrons. It continued to operate as a trials aircraft with British Aerospace until its withdrawal in November 1988, when it was retired to the East Midlands Aero Park, still wearing its glossy camouflage and full-colour national insignia.

pipe. Maximum speed was estimated to be Mach 1.8, and an in-service date of 1975 was offered. Roy Boot adds that; "We considered this to be a paper exercise and this indeed proved to be the case". Two years previously, immediately following the cancellation of TSR2, Hawker Siddeley had produced another proposal for a new Buccaneer variant – the P.145 which featured the rocket assisted take-off provision incorporated into the Mk.50, together with the capability to carry Martel anti-ship missiles and long-range 430-gallon underwing fuel tanks. In order

History in the marking at RAF Honington in Suffolk as the RAF's first two Buccaneers arrive on 1 October 1969. Led by Wing Commander G. Davies, the aircraft formed the nucleus of No. 12 Squadron. At this stage, the Buccaneer's custom-made access ladders had evidently yet to arrive at Honington, and a traditional step ladder is about to be brought in.

to minimise changes to the design of the forward fuselage, a new inertial platform was to be mounted in the radio bay, and a mirror system would be fixed under the fuselage to harmonise it with the existing nose-mounted equipment. Cost savings would be made by using navigation and weapon release computers which were already being developed by Ferranti. Other new innovations would include a head-up display and a new bogie under-carriage. Also proposed for the P.145 was a new reconnaissance pack which would fit into the aircraft's bomb bay (whilst still leaving the wing stations free to carry stores), comprising of a range of cameras, an infrared linescan system and a sideways looking radar. The P.145 had an estimated take-off weight of 62,000lb, and could carry 4,000lb of bombs over a 1,400 mile radius. Alternatively it could carry a 10,000lb bomb load over an 800 mile radius, or a maximum load of 16,000lb over a radius of 400 miles. Take-off distance was estimated to be a very respectable 4,000 feet. Other weapons options were examined, but precise details would be dependent upon customer requirements, and as no customer had been identified, the design was effectively frozen at this stage. The P.145 obviously had export potential, but most importantly it was hoped that the RAF would be interested in it. Of course, the Air Staff had shifted its attention towards the F-111. The government believed that when compared with the TSR2, the F-111K would be an effective and much cheaper means of providing the RAF with a new strike aircraft, but as time progressed, it became increasingly obvious that the F-111K was not going to be the 'ideal' aircraft which it had once seemed to be, not least in terms of the price tag which continued to rise until it began to assume the same proportions as the TSR2's budget. It was hardly surprising therefore, that the F-111K – once described by Harold Wilson as a 'bargain' – was also eventually abandoned.

Buccaneer S2 XV350 pictured during manufacturer's trials at Holme-on-Spalding Moor, carrying a standard maritime strike fit, as used by No. 12 Squadron. Three underwing hardpoints are occupied by television-guided Martel missiles, while the fourth pylon carries the missile data link pod. The bomb bay remains empty and in service, it could be used to carry more fuel or an additional load of bombs if necessary.

No. 15 Squadron's initial complement of eight Buccaneer S2s at RAF Laarbruch, 3 May 1972. Assigned to the overland strike role, the unit's aircraft trained to deliver 1,000lb free-fall and retarded HE bombs, and the WE177 tactical nuclear bomb which could be delivered in a lay-down or toss mode. Both Nos 15 and 16 Squadrons at Laarbruch maintained RAF Germany's QRA (Quick Reaction Alert) capability, with aircraft kept on standby at all times, armed with WE.177s.

When the F-111 order was cancelled in January 1968, it was announced that a fleet of McDonnell Douglas F-4M Phantoms would be purchased for the RAF and that they would be operated as offensive (rather than defensive 'fighter') aircraft. Once again, it looked as if the Buccaneer wasn't going to be considered for RAF service and that the RAF was going to be denied its much-needed long-range strike aircraft. Then, on 10 July 1968, the government finally announced that the Buccaneer was to be purchased for the Royal Air Force, as a replacement for the abandoned F-111K. With complete disregard for the way in which the Buccaneer had been looked upon as 'inappropriate' for so many years, RAF chiefs were now warmly embracing a Fleet Air Arm aircraft. Indeed, they would literally be operating naval aircraft, as the remaining Buccaneers assigned to the Fleet Air Arm would also be transferred to the RAF, to join a batch of 26 new-build airframes and a further order for 17 aircraft which was subse-quently made. Air Vice Marshal Sir Peter Fletcher, Vice-Chief of the Air Staff said that, "the additional bomb door fuel tank we are fitting to our aircraft will increase the capacity by some 425 gallons. This, coupled with the favourable specific fuel consumption of the Spey at both medium and low levels, will extend the Buccaneer's range to meet our target requirements. The aircraft's extended radius of action will enable us to fight the sea battle in all relevant areas of the North Atlantic and Mediterranean. The Buccaneer should be a most valuable means of long-range attack in both the maritime and land roles for some time to come." In retrospect, Sir Peter seemed to be suggesting that the increase in the Buccaneer's range was the reason why, after so long, the aircraft was being adopted by the RAF. In reality, the situation was probably rather different, and it is reasonable to assume that after having lost both the TSR2 and F-111, the Buccaneer was perceived to be the only available solution to the RAF's requirements, and of course the government had already announced its intention to shift the Navy's carrier-borne strike capability to land-based units. There could be no better way (or at least no cheaper way) to do this than by simply transferring the Navy's aircraft to the RAF.

The Blackburn (Hawker Siddeley) staff were naturally delighted that at long last, the Buccaneer was to be built for the Royal Air Force, but in some respects their excitement must have been tempered by regrets that, despite having proposed a number of variants specifically geared towards RAF requirements, the final choice would be the S2, essentially the same aircraft as the Navy's. Indeed, the first ten aircraft were to be produced from partially completed airframes which had been intended for Fleet Air Arm service, but which had been cancelled following the loss of HMS *Victorious* (which was written-off by a huge fire during refit). Without any carrier limitations on weight, the RAF's Buccaneer S2 could be fitted with South African-style 430-gallon underwing fuel tanks and the Mk.50's wheels and brakes. A reconnaissance capability was specified, and Brough suggested the bomb bay package which had been proposed for the

P.145. After a great deal of discussion, the RAF settled for the same Blue Parrot radar, but with the addition of monopulse enhancement as had been previously proposed. In just a few months the Air Staff Requirement was issued and the flight test programme was drawn-up. In order to maintain commonality with the Royal Navy airframes (and to save additional design and manufacturing expense) the same powered wing folding was retained for the RAF machines, together with the arrester hook. A wide range of weaponry was proposed, including the Martel system used by the Fleet Air Arm. However, unlike the Navy machines, the RAF's Buccaneer S2s would not be configured to carry the Red Beard bomb (which was now decommissioned), and would feature a tandem installation for two WE177s in a fairing which could be fitted into the bomb bay. Also proposed was a triple ejector rack for three 1,000lb HE bombs for each underwing pylon. Sadly, this feature was dropped on cost grounds after having been designed and (successfully) test flown up to a full load of 16 bombs. Another casualty was the new reconnaissance pack which was dropped in favour of the older

Buccaneer XT270 pictured early in its service career with No. 12 Squadron, firing a pair of SNEB rocket pods for a publicity photograph. The rocket pods were phased out during the 1970s and Martel missiles became the main means of attack for No. 12 Squadron, assigned to the maritime strike role.

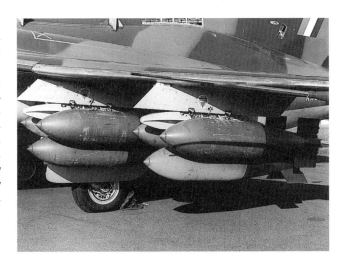

Trials aircraft XV350 carried a variety of weapons, and during October 1971 the aircraft was fitted with triple ejector racks, each carrying three 1,000lb bombs, providing the Buccaneer with a total bomb load of no less than 16 x 1,000lb bombs, albeit at the expense of a considerably lengthened take-off run. The RAF chiefs however, decided not to proceed with the proposal to equip the Buccaneer fleet with TER's.

Naval camera crate. Likewise, the 430-gallon underwing fuel tanks were also later abandoned, after flight testing. Although the tanks handled well in flight (which was no surprise after having introduced them into regular SAAF service some years previously), the trials test pilot reported a significantly longer take-off run before the aircraft would comfortably unstick. The cause was eventually traced to a shift in the Buccaneer's centre of gravity, the SAAF Mk.50s having rocket motor gear in the rear fuselage to balance the additional forward weight of the larger fuel tanks. Although the RAF's S2s could have been suitably modified to handle the larger tanks, the development of the bomb door fuel tank meant that additional fuel could now be carried internally, and so the 430-gallon underwing tanks were no longer required.

The first of the RAF's Buccaneers was XV350, a former Royal Navy machine which first flew in its new configuration on 11 February 1969. The first Royal Air Force squadron was No. 12, which reformed at Honington on 1 October 1969. Honington had been subjected to an extensive modification programme in anticipation of the first F-111K squadron, and so it was a logical base for

the Buccaneers, not only those belonging to the RAF, but also the Navy's, as No. 809 NAS was to use this Lincolnshire base as their headquarters. No. 12 Squadron reformed as the first of two planned maritime strike squadrons, reviving a capability which the RAF had not exercised since the days of the Banff Strike Wing, at the end of World War Two. In essence, the RAF was now tasked with the provision of Fleet support, both in terms of air defence (Phantoms) and strike/attack, all of these aircraft being assigned to CINCFLEET, as part of a concept known as Land Air Support and Maritime Operations (LASMO). The Buccaneers were tasked with the destruction of major naval targets, in effect, the Soviet's capital ships. Wing Commander G. Pitchfork (who flew as a navigator in Buccaneers both with the Navy and RAF) recalls that; "It was back to the *Bismark* days in a way, and we hadn't done that sort of thing since the Second World War, so the guys on 12 Squadron set about getting into this new job. The Navy had lots of restrictions of course, for example, you could only fly wherever the carrier actually was at any given time, whereas we had much more flexibility. As long as there was an air base we could use, we could operate anywhere. We had

An unusual photograph showing a Buccaneer in formation with one of a small fleet of Hunters which were equipped with Buccaneer cockpit instrumentation. Because there was never a dual-control version of the Buccaneer (another legacy from its naval ancestry), the Hunter enabled students to familiarise themselves with the Buccaneer's instruments in company with an instructor, before 'going it alone' in the real thing.

a much longer range too, with lots of tanker support, so we perfected the maritime strike business, both by day and night. We were brought into maritime exercises which had been going for many years, things like Northern Wedding, and they'd never really had an effective attack element before. We were so good at our job of attacking ships that in lots of these exercises, we had to be the enemy, a real nuisance for us, but of course our warships wanted lots of practice against aircraft like the Buccaneer, as we gave them the most realistic opposition. So did the fighter guys, as they always wanted to be up against the Buccaneers.

Buccaneers from Nos 12 and 208 Squadrons at RAF Akrotiri, Cyprus, during Operation Pulsator. The Buccaneers made two flights over (or possibly 'through') Beirut on 13 September 1983, racing over rooftops at high speed and an extremely low altitude. The British forces in Beirut were certainly comforted by the presence of the Buccaneers, and their spirited arrival impressed everyone, including French and American forces in the area.

It was a bit frustrating, but we often had to fly a profile which was for the 'Orange' role, but something typically enemy. We weren't getting much training value out of it, but we did get to fly the 'Blue' friendly role too. We regularly used our Forward Operating Bases at Lossiemouth, Stornoway, St Mawgan and so on, and we were in and out of Lossie all the time. We'd often deploy there at full squadron strength, especially for the big autumn exercises. So we sometimes wondered why on Earth we ended up at Honington, but of course it was a big base, completely refurbished for the F-111."

The first Buccaneer to arrive at Honington was XV155, designated as a Buccaneer S.Mk.2A, the 'A' denoting its origins as former Fleet Air Arm machine. New-build RAF Buccaneers were designated S.Mk.2B, and when the Martel missile was introduced into FAA and RAF service, the non-Martel RAF machines were designated S.Mk.2A and the Naval equivalent as the S.Mk.2C. Likewise, the RAF's Martel aircraft were designated S.Mk.2B, and the Navy's became the S.Mk.2D. Following the withdrawal of the last FAA machines in 1978, the 'C' and 'D' suffixes were dropped. Even before the Martel was introduced, No. 12 Squadron had become an important part of the RAF's offensive capability, as Wing Commander Pitchfork explains; "We had a great aeroplane which worked well both in daylight and at night. The radar altimeter, the Radalt, was probably the most important piece of kit in the aircraft. The radar was optimised for maritime operations, and we developed some very good tactics, some very skilful, complex and co-ordinated tactics which would confuse the enemy. At sea we were cleared down to 100 feet altitude, and really you wouldn't want to be any lower for long, particularly if you were flying a laydown attack. Laydown wasn't something we did against ships as it would have been like a suicide attack. The ships had immensely powerful air defence systems, and you wouldn't want to be going straight over them. We didn't go after the small fry, we were after the big ones, and we only wanted to be at 100 feet to reduce the warning time that we gave the enemy. The aim was to come into the radar lobe of the enemy search radar at the minimum range of around 25 miles, but we'd come in on co-ordinated attacks from different levels, some at low level, some going into toss deliveries, the idea being to suppress the defences. We had a phrase which went, 'Poke him in the eye before you knee him in the balls'. Just the sort of thing we did in World War Two, but we were just using different weapons. For example, we would toss bombs which were delay timed to go off at 100 feet, and the shrapnel would wipe out the aerials and radar. You could blind the enemy, and then the other lads would come in at 100 feet, to launch their Martels. You could also fire the anti-radar Martels and that would blind your enemy, after which the TV Martels could be used to make a precision attack to punch a hole in the ship. We had some doubts about the anti-radar Martel though, as we couldn't be sure that an enemy radar would stay on long enough for the missile to home in, but the TV-guided Martel was very good, and during the 1970s it was something we hadn't had before, so it was certainly a good missile at the time".

Even through this period, the Buccaneer's tactical nuclear delivery capability was retained and regularly practised, not only to maintain crew standards, but to demonstrate the role as a visible deterrent. It remained an option, albeit an increasingly unlikely one, as Wing Commander Pitchfork explains; "The scenarios we trained for on 12 Squadron rarely required tactical nuclear

Formed on 1 July 1979, No. 216 Squadron (a former Comet transport unit) enjoyed only a brief association with the Buccaneer. Intended to take-on Buccaneers which had been withdrawn from Fleet Air Arm service in 1978, the squadron had barely begun operational flying when the entire Buccaneer fleet was grounded, following the loss of an aircraft in the USA. When the much-reduced Buccaneer fleet resumed flying, there were insufficient numbers available to re-equip all of the squadrons, and so No. 216 was disbanded again thereby releasing more Buccaneers for the other squadrons.

bombs, but that's not to say that we couldn't do it. It was always a deterrent, and they knew that in extremes, we could come and nuke 'em". In fact, the WE177A tactical nuclear bomb was to become the primary armament of the next RAF squadron to reform on the Buccaneer, this being No. 15 which reformed on 1 October 1970 at Honington, prior to moving to its permanent base at Laarbruch the following year. It was joined by No. 16 Squadron which reformed on 16 January 1973. Unlike other Buccaneer units which were dedicated to maritime operations, both of these squadrons were assigned to over-land strike/attack duties, and maintained a round-the-clock QRA (Quick Reaction Alert) commitment to NATO, their 'Battle Flight' Buccaneers fuelled and fully prepared for flight, armed with a pair of WE.177As. In essence, the Buccaneers of Nos 15 and 16 Squadrons were pure bombers, following in the traditions of the V-Force, and the bomber squadrons of World War Two. Their targets, although still classified, were likely to have been air bases, command and control centres, and troop concentrations beyond East Germany and into Czechoslovakia and Poland, possibly even as far as the USSR itself. Following the departure of No. 15 Squadron to Laarbruch, its place at Honington was taken by No. 237 Operational Conversion Unit, which formed on 1 March 1971. Tasked with the training of RAF pilots and navigators, the unit also assumed the training task performed by No. 736 NAS, when that unit disbanded on 25 February 1972. In effect, this reversed the situation which had prevailed for the past couple of years, during which time RAF crews had been trained by No. 736 NAS at Lossiemouth. Now that the Navy had only a small (and decreasing) requirement for Buccaneer crews, the task could easily be absorbed into the OCU's activities. Unusually, the first aircraft assigned to the OCU were not Buccaneers. They were in fact Hunters, equipped with Buccaneer cockpit instrumentation. Without a dual-control version of the Buccaneer on which to convert students (a situation created largely by Naval tradition), the Hunters provided an opportunity for fledgling pilots to familiarise themselves with the Buccaneer's instruments and characteristics, aided by the physical presence of an experienced instructor, before getting airborne in the real thing. Interestingly, although the lack of 'twin-stick' Buccaneers might seem to be a classic example of the proverbial 'accident waiting to happen', history records that throughout the Buccaneer's FAA and RAF service, only one aircraft loss was ever regarded as being conceivably due to a lack of dual controls.

As the Buccaneer settled into RAF service, discussions were already underway concerning improvements to the aircraft's weapons systems. Many of the ideas put forward by the RAF had in fact been anticipated by the design team at Brough, and in March 1969 they had produced a proposal for the P.149. This Buccaneer variant included a new navigation system using a Ferranti inertial platform installed in the rear fuselage, using digital computing for navigation and weapon aiming. Ferranti were working on a ground mapping spinner which could be fitted in a chin fairing, under the Buccaneer's radome, and this would have given

the aircraft search, ranging, and terrain following modes. As a cheaper alternative, it was suggested that the TFR fitted to the RAF's Vulcans could be refitted on the Buccaneer, once the Vulcan force began to wind down. Because the terrain following radar would require the pilot to fly the aircraft manually based on its signals, a head-up display would also be necessary. Alternatively, an automatic terrain-following capability could be provided, but the state-of-the-art systems which were available at the time wouldn't be sufficiently reliable, so Boulton-Paul suggested a triplex system, with a cut-out designed to operate if a disparity was sensed between the two primary systems. Other 'goodies' on offer included a reconnaissance pack, and an RB162 lift engine which would be

An artistic image of a Buccaneer S2 wearing the distinctive eagle marking of No.216 Squadron. In the foreground is the head of a Pave Spike laser designation pod. The Paveway system was to have been the unit's primary armament, but operations were very short-lived.

An attractive pose for the cameraman as a No. 12 Squadron Buccaneer passes by one of Scotland's majestic country residences during a sortie from Lossiemouth. Carrying practice bomb carriers under each wing, the aircraft is otherwise 'clean'. Although underwing tanks were almost a standard fit on all Buccaneers in the 1970s, they were progressively removed towards the end of the Buccaneer's service life, largely because of the increasing amount of weaponry (such as the Pave Spike designator, laser-guided bombs, ECM pods and Sidewinder missiles) which needed to be carried on the underwing hardpoints.

fitted in place of the S.50's rocket motor, to produce a 25 per cent reduction in take-off run. Sadly, the proposal wasn't adopted by the RAF, although the inertial navigation system was seriously considered. However, one part of the P.145 was adopted, this being the bomb door fuel tank.

Roy Boot recalls the background to the bomb door tank's development; "The dimensions of the cross section of the internal weapons bay were not necessarily determined by the stores carried, but by the arc swept by the corners of the door whilst it was rotating. If this arc swept over the outside of the door, with front and rear of the resultant shape faired off, the door itself, even allowing for stores and carrier mountings, could become an integral fuel tank. A check on the possible capacity showed that this arrangement could hold 70 per cent of the fuel carried by the pallet which had been previously proposed, and with a less draggy installation it appeared to be a very good proposition." The concept was not seriously considered for some time however, but it

reappeared during the development phase of the RAF's Buccaneers, when the 430-gallon underwing fuel tank was proposed, as Roy Boot explains; "At a Ministry of Defence meeting finalising the specification for the RAF's Buccaneers, I was asked if any difficulties were likely to arise. I confidently answered in the negative, but I was wrong. The increase in the 430-gallon wing tank's capacity was obtained largely by a longer nose. When we came to test the aircraft with the large tanks, we found that the take-off was being impeded by the inability to raise the nosewheel at the desired speed. This wasn't helped by the fact which we discovered much later, that for some totally inexplicable reason, the particular Buccaneer we had used for the test required a 10 knots higher nosewheel raise speed than any other Buccaneer we'd tested. We'd failed to appreciate that without the rocket motor at the rear of the aircraft, the centre of gravity would be somewhat further forward. It was then that we recalled the bomb door tank, and realised that with

Returning to their roots, aircraft from No. 208 Squadron fly over the most famous landmarks in Egypt. No. 208 Squadron was first formed in Egypt, and as part of a Far East exercise, the unit took advantage of a rare opportunity to make a return visit to the country. The second aircraft in the formation is wearing the final camouflage scheme applied to RAF Buccaneers, an overall light grey which rendered the aircraft less visible in the maritime environment.

this and the existing wing tanks, the Buccaneer would have more range than with the larger tanks alone. Additionally, the bomb door tank could be filled, leaving all four wing stations free for the carriage of offensive stores. A dummy tank was flown and the drag increase with the door closed was found to be less than 2 per cent of the basic aircraft."

The proposal to fit the bomb door tank was met with usual British bureaucracy. There was no Operational Requirement for the fit, and it wasn't in the RAF's Specification. It would cost money too, although some would admittedly be saved by not building 430-gallon tanks. Thankfully, some key members of the Air Staff knew a good thing when they saw it, and they encouraged a suitably sympathetic member of the Procurement Executive to press for the proposal to be adopted, and after several meetings the bomb door was accepted to become a standard fit on all RAF Buccaneers. Such was its success that it also found its way to South Africa, to be fitted on Buccaneers which already carried the ill-fated 430-gallon underwing tanks. Because of the Brough team's efforts to have the bomb

door adopted at an early stage in the Buccaneer's RAF career, money was saved by avoiding the production of conventional bomb doors for the new-build RAF airframes, although Hawker Siddeley had to provide temporary funding for the project, while formal discussions were still being completed.

The next RAF Buccaneer unit to form at Honington (on 1 July 1974) was No. 208 Squadron, dedicated to the overland strike/attack role, but remaining as a UK-based unit, unlike Nos 15 and 16 Squadrons which became part of RAF Germany. Without any requirement for Martel missiles, 208 Squadron initially received No. 12 Squadron's Buccaneer S2As, until deliveries of S2Bs made more 'new-build' aircraft available. After reaching operational status on the Buccaneer, 208 Squadron was privileged to become the first RAF unit to be invited to participate in the US Air Force's 'Red Flag' exercise at Nellis AFB, Nevada, and during August 1977 the unit despached ten Buccaneers on the long transatlantic flight from Honington to Nellis, via Goose Bay. Of these ten aircraft, four were painted in a temporary two-tone brown 'desert'

Shortly before withdrawal, a new camouflage scheme was devised for the Buccaneer, comprising an overall light/medium grey paint together with pink/light blue national insignia and white serials. Intended primarily to render the aircraft less conspicuous over the sea, it probably had more to do with the ongoing 'fashion' for grey paint schemes than any operational value. Even more peculiar was the way in which the colour scheme was slowly being adopted even though the aircraft were being retired.

colour scheme, which was intended to render the aircraft less visible at low level over the barren Nevada landscape. In fact, 208 Squadron needn't have bothered with special paint schemes, as the Buccaneers took everybody by complete surprise (apart from 208 Squadron themselves, of course) and proceeded to out-fly every other unit in the exercise. Flying at high speed, at altitudes which never seemed to exceed 100 feet, the Buccaneers battled their way across the desert, leaving numerous USAF chiefs open-jawed. One memorable quote came from a USAF air traffic controller, watching the approaching Buccaneers; "Hey you guys, come outside if you wanna see something really good!" They were indeed, really good, as Wing Commander Pitchfork recalls; "The Americans just couldn't believe it, the Buccaneers really surprised them, although they didn't surprise us much, of course, as we did that kind of flying all the time. They were so impressed that they immediately invited us back, but 208 Squadron's Buccaneers pioneered the RAF's participation in the Flag exercises.

We were in big demand after that, simply because we flew low and fast. We were very low too, and we were cleared to 100 feet over land, and we were perfectly capable of doing that in the Buccaneer because the aircraft was such a smooth ride, and very stable. Fighters just can't get you at 100 feet and 580 knots, so we became very popular, both at Red Flag and back in the UK, where there was hardly ever a trip where we didn't have fighters wanting to fight with us. It became known as 'Dial-a-Fighter' because the Lightning and Phantom guys always wanted to fight Buccaneers as we always gave them a good run for their money. No. 208 Squadron also pioneered the introduction of the Buccaneer's radar warning receiver in 1975 which was fitted in the tail bullet, and that gave us an even greater capability which made the fighter guys want to work with us even more."

Despite the punishing nature of the high speed and low level environment in which the Buccaneer was being operated, the Royal Air Force never showed any great concern over the structural integrity

During the 1980s, the Buccaneer was afforded a self-defence capability, courtesy of an AIM-9L Sidewinder air-to-air missile which could be fitted to the port outer hardpoint. Until then, the Buccaneer crews had been forced to rely on evasive manoeuvring for defence, although the carriage of retarded 1,000lb HE bombs did offer the possibility of - to use the pilot's phrase - 'dropping one's knickers'. The term was derived from the perforated parachute attached to the bomb, which would certainly spoil the aim of any enemy fighter pilot if it was dropped in front of him.

of the aircraft. Bearing in mind that the Buccaneer was designed to withstand manoeuvres of up to 12g at an all-up weight of 37,000lb, and had a primary structure manufactured from 80 ton steel, it was hardly surprising that the RAF had great faith in the Buccaneer's robust construction, even though some aircraft were lost due to structural failures. In every case, the cause of the failure was found to have been a manoeuvre which overloaded the aircraft's limits, therefore the basic strength of the Buccaneer wasn't in question. However, on 12 July 1979 No.

15 Squadron's Buccaneer XW526 crashed near Osnabruck after having lost its starboard wing during a relatively gentle 3g turn. The entire Buccaneer fleet was temporarily grounded pending an investigation into the accident, and it was quickly revealed that the forward latch pin (which transmitted the front spar loading from the outer wing to the inner wing) had suffered a fatigue failure, despite being more than two inches in diameter and produced from solid steel. A detailed examination of the entire Buccaneer fleet revealed that fatigue cracks were only

present in a handful of pins, and even these were so small as to render them fairly insignificant. XW526's port pin did have a crack of critical size however, and so it seemed reasonable to assume that the starboard pin had failed, leading to the loss of the entire wing. Having inspected the fleet, the Buccaneers were returned to service and the incident was consigned to history, although much more attention was now to be paid to the Buccaneer's structural integrity.

Early in 1980, Nos 15 and 16 Squadrons deployed more Buccaneers to Nellis, to participate in another Red Flag exercise. On 7 February, XV345 was being flown by a 15 Squadron crew, as part of an eight aircraft attack profile on simulated targets in the Nevada desert. Just 40 minutes into the sortie, the aircraft entered a gentle turn which, according to other pilots in the vicinity, suddenly developed into a roll. At this instant, the other pilots realised that XV345's starboard wing was missing, and within seconds the Buccaneer had rolled sharply to the right and crashed onto the desert floor, killing the crew. Once again, Buccaneer operations were immediately suspended, while British Aerospace engineers and Air Investigation Branch officers flew in from the UK. It was quickly established that the starboard wing had separated at the root in the plane of rib No. 80, and that the tailplane had separated from the top of the fin. A severe fatigue crack was found in the front spar bottom boom lower aft corner, between the two lower aft lugs which secure the spar to wing rib 80. At this point the boom is approximately 3 inches by 2 inches in section. The separation was in the plane of this fatigue crack, and the main failure was apparently a simple overload. The tailplane failure was a simple overload of the attachment bolts, due to an up-loading with a strong rolling moment to port (whereas the Buccaneer

would normally have a tail down-loading of approximately 10,000lb in the prevailing conditions). XV345 was carrying a modified accident data recorder which was configured to record fin root bending moment, as part of ongoing investigations into the aircraft's fatigue life based on general squadron usage. This helped the investigators to piece-together a detailed analysis of the aircraft's last few seconds. A Buccaneer model with a missing starboard wing was tested in Brough's wind tunnel and the crash investigators were surprised to find that the aircraft yawed away from the remaining wing, rather than towards it, as might be expected. Brough aerodynamicists believed that this was due to a sidewash being created across the fin, which yawed the aircraft away from the port wing. The combined evidence of the eyewitness accounts, instrumentation data, and the wind tunnel model encouraged British Aerospace to support the theory that the wing broke away due to the fatigue fracture in the wing spar, and that the tailplane was either hit by the wing as it fell away, or it was broken by the local airflow, disturbed by the wing as it broke free.

The Accident Investigation Branch didn't immediately reach any firm conclusions, but the same wing off first solution was regarded as the most likely. Boscombe Down also reached the same conclusion, although there was no evidence to explain why XV345's starboard wing had already sustained a 3.5g turn earlier in the flight, and some 5g manoeuvres in recent flights, but failed during a 2.5g turn. It was suggested that there may have been an instrumentation error in the flight data recorder, or that there may have been some other physical influence on the wing, such as a bird strike, a severe gust or even contact with the ground. However, there was also the possibility that the fatigue crack was

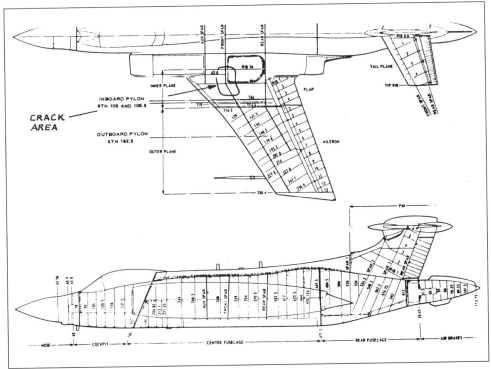

Structural station diagram, illustrating the location of the fatal crack which developed in XV345, leading to the aircraft's destruction during a Red Flag exercise in 1980.

Drawing of XV345's inner wing spar, illustrating the location of the fatigue crack.

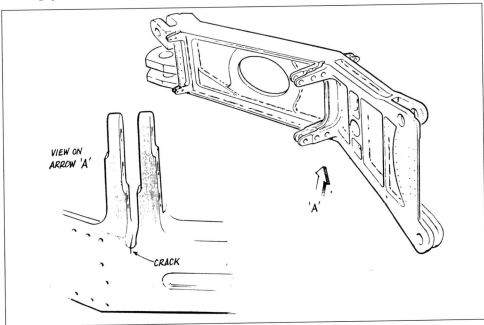

worse than it appeared, or that there had been a fast crack growth during the final flight. Whatever the true cause, the most important consideration was that there were fatigue cracks in the Buccaneer's wing spars, and an inspection of the RAF's fleet revealed that roughly two-thirds of the Buccaneers had similar cracks in the same location, either in one or both wings. The worst crack was 1.5 inches long, with several in the 0.5-1.0 inch range, compared with the 0.6 inch crack found in XV345. Strangely, Brough's Fatigue Test Specimen (FTS) had been tested to some six times the calculated fatigue index (FI) of the fleet leader, and yet it showed no signs of any cracks. Following the loss of XW526, the FTS's test procedure was already being reappraised, and the crash of XV345 prompted British Aerospace to look at the Buccaneer's fatigue testing even more closely.

One of the MoD(PE)'s Buccaneer aircraft was fitted with strain gauges and associated instrumentation, to record loads within the airframe structure. Simultaneously, the FTS airframe at Brough was fitted with the same instrumentation, to provide a direct comparison between the test model and the real thing. It was found that the local stress levels in the area of the failure were much higher than expected, and were beyond the yield point of the steel from which the front spar forging was manufactured. The MoD Buccaneer's stress levels were found to be higher than those experienced by the FTS, and the reason for the discrepancy was found some distance away, at the wing tip. In order to extend the Buccaneers range, the wing tip fairing had been extended on the S2 variant, and this had been expected to create an additional 2-3 per cent stress (which was of no significance) at the attachment point between the front spar and the engine rings. Nobody had expected stress

to be created in the area of the rib 80 lugs, and this had been the ultimate cause of the accident. The FTS testing was revised to produce new fatigue indices for the Buccaneer fleet, and British Aerospace drew up a schedule of structurally sensitive areas which would have to be inspected at regular intervals throughout the remaining life of the structure. As for repair possibilities, there was only one area where damage could not be restored, and this was the front spar at the rib 80 area. It was at this stage that the Buccaneer's inherent strength once again proved to be invaluable. Computer analysis indicated that up to 0.1 inches of metal could be shaved from the throat of the rib 80 lugs without unacceptably affecting the structure's safety. Further physical testing indicated that up to 0.2 inches of metal could be removed, and this enabled a significant number of aircraft to be repaired, by shaving-out the crack.

Throughout the investigation, the Buccaneer fleet remained grounded, and in order to keep the crews 'current' on aircraft of some sort, a fleet of 34 Hunters was assembled, some aircraft coming out of storage while others were borrowed from the Tactical Weapons Units, the Fleet Requirements & Air Direction Unit, and MoD establishments. As the crash investigation progressed, the length of the Buccaneer's grounding began to run into months, and many of the Hunters began to be adopted by the various Buccaneer squadrons, receiving appropriate unit markings. The Red Flag aircraft remained on the ramp at Nellis AFB, and Laarbruch's 'Battle Flight' Buccaneers stayed inside their shelters, although their alert status continued and the aircraft would have been launched if necessary, despite the grounding order. Indeed, at least two Buccaneers were seen flying in the vicinity of Laarbruch during this period, for reasons which remain unknown. Buccaneer attack profiles were flown in the Hunters, and one aircraft (T.Mk.7 XF310) was fitted with practice bomb carriers. Naturally, Paveway, Martel and ECM training couldn't be continued, and conversion training was also impossible, resulting in the suspension of No. 237 OCU's activities. Meanwhile, two Buccaneers (XV340 and XW538) were dismantled at Brough for detailed examination to establish whether any other areas of the airframe structure might have been damaged by fatigue stress. XV340 was the 'fleet leader' (the aircraft with the highest usage) and XW538 was the aircraft which had revealed the largest rib 80 crack, therefore they represented the two 'worst cases' which ought to reveal any other problems – if indeed there were any. After careful examination (during which XV340 was literally tested to destruction) it was concluded that both aircraft were in excellent condition,

but that there were various structurally-sensitive areas which were prone to fatigue, and these would have to be inspected regularly.

After a long six months of inactivity, Buccaneer operations were slowly resumed, and the Hunters were gradually withdrawn as Buccaneers returned to flight status. The Buccaneers at Nellis were flown home, with the exception of XV864 and XW538 which were deemed to be in need of immediate repair, and they were eventually shipped back to Hull. The entire Buccaneer fleet was categorised, and aircraft were either returned to operations without modifications, repaired as necessary, or withdrawn from use, depending on the severity of any fatigue problems which were found. A new batch of front spars was manufactured by British Aerospace to enable 'transplants' to be conducted on some aircraft, while many others were subject to the previously-described 'shaving'

Sea Witch Debbie (XV863) had the distinction of flying No. 237 Operational Conversion Unit's last sortie, with Wing Commander Dave Ray at the controls. Originally a Fleet Air Arm aircraft, XV863 also flew with Nos 16 and 12 Squadrons, and flew six operational missions during the Gulf War. Following her retirement, the aircraft was placed on display as Gate Guardian at RAF Lossiemouth.

XW547, affectionately named Pauline *during her deployment to the Gulf, flew 11 operational missions as a Paveway laser-guided bomber, during operation Desert Storm (or Operation Granby as the RAF contribution was code named). After serving with Nos 15, 12 and 216 Squadrons as well as No. 237 OCU, the aircraft made its last flight on 20th January 1993 to the RAF Museum at Cosford, where the aircraft is now on show. Incredibly, the bare-breasted nose artwork was subsequently 'dressed' after the aircraft returned to the UK.*

process which effectively cut away the offending cracks. It was also suggested that the S2's larger wing tip fairings be replaced by the shorter S1-style tip, in order to remove the source of additional stress, and some aircraft were suitably modified, but not by any means the entire fleet. As a result of the earlier pin failure on XW526, the wing fold doors were progressively removed from most Buccaneers to enable regular and easy inspection of the wing fold mechanism, and the small rectangular holes on the upper wings became a familiar sight throughout the remainder of the Buccaneer's service life. British Aerospace received XN982 to become the basis for a new (recalibrated) Fatigue

Test Specimen, and it was quickly positioned in the Brough factory to begin testing at a rate which would enable it to catch up and eventually pass the fatigue rate of the active squadron aircraft. In retrospect, the Red Flag incident had more to do with the inability to predict and detect small fatigue cracks rather than any real problem with the Buccaneer's structural integrity.

Another unfortunate result of the Red Flag accident was the extremely short history of No. 216 Squadron's association with the Buccaneer. Following the decommissioning of HMS *Ark Royal* and the disbandment of the last Naval Buccaneer squadron (809 NAS), their aircraft were now available for RAF operations, and No. 216 Squadron was reformed at Honington on 2 December 1978, ready to take advantage of the availability of more Buccaneers as they emerged from refurbishment. Assigned to the maritime strike/attack role with a fleet of Buccaneers and at least one suitably-marked Hunter T7, 216 Squadron was to become No. 12 Squadron's 'sister' unit, but just a few weeks after the squadron was declared operational, the fateful crash near Nellis grounded the whole Buccaneer fleet. When the aircraft returned to active duty, a significant number of Buccaneers were found to be beyond economical repair, while others were placed in long-term storage at Shawbury, pending their possible repair in the future, if funds or circumstances permitted. The reduced Buccaneer fleet effectively forced the RAF to decommission one squadron so that the remaining Buccaneers could be distributed amongst the other units. As the most recent unit to have been formed, No. 216 Squadron was of course the ideal candidate for disbandment. Wing Commander Pitchfork recalls that; "My own squadron – 208 – was looking a bit dodgy with just eight aircraft initially and then ten, but we just didn't have the aircraft and it was crucial that we kept the two strike squadrons up to strength in Germany, and that the only maritime squadron was also fully equipped. Then there was the OCU which got the less capable airframes, because they just wanted them for flying, rather than for operational missions, but for quite a while 208 Squadron struggled on with eight aircraft. After the crash, the only real difference was that there was a closer monitoring of the aircraft's fatigue index, but it didn't stop us doing what we wanted to do. When we got the Buccaneers back we had the utmost confidence in them. 208 was still operational as we had six single-seat Hunters on strength, so we were back in business in no time at all, and we flew the Buccaneers as hard as ever. In many ways we were even more confident because we knew they'd been thoroughly inspected and worked on by the engineers."

Throughout the first decade of RAF operations, the Buccaneer had proved itself as an immensely valuable asset, and in many respects it had become the

Because of the need for initial familiarisation, the Hunter became a common sight at all three RAF Buccaneer bases (Honington, Lossiemouth and Laarbruch). When the entire Buccaneer fleet was grounded in 1980 following the crash of a Buccaneer in the USA during a Red Flag exercise, Hunters were loaned from other RAF and RN units to enable the Buccaneer pilots to maintain their minimum number of flying hours. They remained active for more than six months until suitably-repaired Buccaneers were reintroduced into service.

A January 1991 picture of a No. 208 Squadron Buccaneer in its protective hardened aircraft shelter at Lossiemouth. In keeping with RAF policy in the 1980s, Lossiemouth's operational squadrons were dispersed from the flight lines into clusters spread around the airfield perimeter. No. 208 Squadron was assigned to a shelter complex on the southeastern side of the airfield, with No. 12 Squadron in an identical complex on the western side. The OCU Buccaneers continued to operate from the former naval flight line in front of the base hangars.

'perfect' strike/attack platform that the Royal Air Force had wanted. However, after ten successful years, a replacement was on the horizon and by 1983 the Panavia Tornado was beginning to enter RAF service, signifying the gradual wind-down of the RAF's Buccaneer force. On 1 July 1983, No. 15 Squadron reformed on Tornado GR1s, followed by No. 16 Squadron on 29 February 1984. No. 208 Squadron relinquished its overland role in July 1983 and moved north to Lossiemouth to join No. 12 Squadron and No. 237 OCU which moved there from Honington in October 1984, effectively ending that base's association with the Buccaneer. The type's historical links were renewed with Lossiemouth, where the two remaining operational units would be operating exclusively in the maritime role. However, the Buccaneer's story was far from over, and during the course of 1983, six aircraft from Nos 12 and 208 Squadrons were deployed to

RAF Akrotiri in Cyprus, as part of the British government's reaction to the deteriorating situation in the Lebanon. United Nations peace-keeping forces in and around Beirut were being subjected to continual attacks from Druze forces and other Palestinian-backed guerillas in the area, and the British contingent of 100 British troops was perceived to be at some risk. In order to provide close air support for the forces, should it be required, the Buccaneer would be deployed to the nearest RAF base, this being Akrotiri. Although Nos 12 and 208 Squadrons were now dedicated maritime units, No. 208 had only recently switched from the overland role, and many Buccaneer pilots were still very familiar with this type of operation. As part of Operation Pulsator, the Buccaneers would be placed on standby at Akrotiri, ready to go into action with their Paveway laser-guided weapons system.

Of course, the task wasn't as simple as

XV332 was designated as a reserve aircraft for Gulf War operations, and as such, the aircraft was painted in desert sand camouflage and received the customary nose artwork, in this instance Dirty Harriet. Depicted flying over Lossiemouth shortly before retirement, XV332 enjoyed the distinction of flying the last RAF Buccaneer sortie on 5 April 1994, when the aircraft was delivered from RAF Cottesmore to RAF Marham, where, at the time of writing, it resides as a battle damage repair training airframe.

it may have seemed, not least because the Buccaneer crews had trained to unleash their laser-guided bombs at large naval targets, rather than small armoured targets tucked away in the middle of a city. There were various ways in which a precision attack could be made, and the best option was to have the target/s laser designated by troops on the ground, but the concept was deemed to be too risky, not only for the Forward Air Controller who would designate the target, but also for civilians in the area who might be injured if radio communications between the FAC and the Buccaneers were lost. Designating and bombing from a medium altitude of around 15,000 feet would make precision targeting very difficult, whereas a low-level attack would create the same problem. Bombing at any height lower than 15,000 feet would run the risk of damage from anti-aircraft guns and missiles which were deployed in the area. Consequently, the Buccaneer crews began training for all three kinds of mission. The preferred option was to use a FAC on the ground near the target/s, and so the Buccaneer crews devised a system whereby a series of six initial points were established, which were easily identifiable by both the FAC and the Buccaneer crews. The FAC would then be able to give a precise direction and time-to-target from the IP's, using laser-designation to pinpoint the precise location of the target. This created an efficient and simple system which was likely to achieve the best results if the Buccaneers were called in to destroy any targets. RAF Phantoms were also deployed to Akrotiri to provide fighter cover for the Buccaneers, not least because the reaction of Syrian forces was difficult to predict, indeed, on several 'feints' and training missions from Akrotiri, the Buccaneers were tracked on Syrian radar and their aircraft did react. The Pulsator Buccaneers were each

fitted with an AIM-9L Sidewinder AAM for self-protection (less-capable AIM-9Gs were normally assigned to Buccaneers), 11 aircraft being suitably modified, while 12 aircraft were fitted with AN/ALE-40 chaff dispensers. Each aircraft would also carry an ALQ-101 ECM pod which, together with the chaff, missiles and Phantom fighter cover, would provide the Buccaneers with an impressive array of defensive options. As the situation in Beirut grew even worse, the possibility of the RAF being called on to operate in anger began to look very likely. By way of an 'interim' measure, on 11 September, two Buccaneers were tasked with a low level flight over Beirut, which wouldn't require the release of any weapons, but would serve to indicate the RAF's capability and intentions. At 09:00 local time, two Buccaneers duly appeared, 100 feet over the water, dashing towards Beirut on a heading of 041 degrees, climbing slightly as they crossed the coast, passing just south of the international airport, heading for the British base at Hadeth before turning onto 344 degrees to depart to the northeast. Manoeuvring at high speed and an astonishingly low level, the two Buccaneers wheeled around the city skyline before disappearing as quickly as they had arrived. After turning on to 176 degrees back to Hadeth, the Buccaneers returned, flying even lower and more aggressively. Many locals abandoned their cars and dived for cover, fearing that an attack was about to begin. Local observers remarked that the aircraft appeared to be within a few feet of the rooftop television aerials, while others are convinced that one Buccaneer departed between a group of buildings, rather than over them.

Armed with just a Sidewinder and an ECM fit, the Buccaneer crews never intended to deliver any weapons, but their overflight, together with a repeat performance made two hours later, certainly gave everyone something to think about. The flights also surprised the French and American pilots who had been overflying Beirut at medium altitude, never expecting to see the Buccaneers seemingly weaving in and out of the city streets. In fact, the Buccaneer navigators were using such unique 'close-up' navigational features as street corners and roundabouts! Two days later, another mission was launched, covering the same route, after which no further overflights were made, although the Buccaneers remained at Akrotiri until the British UN contingent was withdrawn in March 1984. As Lt-Col David Roberts (Commanding Officer of the British troops in Lebanon) said at the time; "It is a tremendous boost for morale. It is a comforting thought for us all to know that now we have a squadron of air support aircraft that can appear within ten minutes should we come under attack". The overflights were certainly successful, and they helped to suppress the threat to British forces to the extent that 'live' missions were not needed. This may well have been a blessing for both the Buccaneer crews and people in Beirut, as even with precision-guided munitions and an excellent aircraft such as the Buccaneer, the crews were under no illusions as to the difficulty of performing 'surgical strikes' in a city. Ironically, seven years later, they were called upon do just that.

As a direct result of Operation Pulsator, No. 237 OCU was given a wartime reserve role as a designating force for the Jaguar and Tornado squadrons, as neither type was Paveway-capable. As part of their training for this role, OCU instructors regularly deployed to a designated Forward Operating Base (FOB) at Laarbruch from where they operated with Tornados and Jaguars. In a wartime scenario each Buccaneer would be armed with an ALQ-101 jamming pod and an AIM-9G Sidewinder, together with four 1,000lb bombs carried in the aircraft's bomb bay, to provide an additional stick of unguided bombs for employment against whatever target was being attacked by the combined 'package'. By the beginning of the 1990s however, the Buccaneer was nearing the end of its operational career. Substantial reductions in defence expenditure were releasing Tornado GR1s from the overland strike/attack role, and the Ministry of Defence decided that it would make financial sense to use these 'surplus' aircraft to replace the two existing maritime Buccaneer squadrons. Although the Buccaneer was still performing well, the cost savings made by removing an aircraft type from the RAF's inventory would be substantial and so, almost by default, the Buccaneer's withdrawal schedule was established. However, as the OCU's training commitments began to dwindle, events in the Middle East were developing, and as 1990 drew to a close, there was little doubt that the Royal Air Force was about to become heavily involved in a 'shooting war'.

When Operation Granby (the British contribution to Desert Storm) began in 1990, it was made clear right from the outset that the RAF's Buccaneers would not be required to participate in any way. The RAF's low level attack missions over Iraq would be conducted by Tornado GR1s, with other targets being assigned to Jaguars. When the first airfield attacks were made in January, it quickly became clear that although the Tornado's JP.233 airfield denial munitions pod was a very effective weapon, the need to release the weapon at low level left the Tornado crews at the mercy of Iraq's deadly anti-aircraft defences. Despite the fact that RAF losses were much lower than defence chiefs had expected, future bombing missions over Iraq would be better conducted from medium level, once air superiority over the area had been established. Consequently, the first 'dumb' bombing raids were launched, and they were certainly successful in terms of the crew's survivability, but less than successful in terms of bombing accuracy; 1,000lb unguided bombs can't be delivered with much precision from 20,000 feet. On 23 January, Lossiemouth was asked to quickly assemble a force of six Buccaneers together with experienced crews, for immediate deployment to the Gulf, to act as laser designators for the Tornado detachments. In just three days, six aircraft were fitted with Have Quick II secure radios, Mk.XII Mode 4 IFF, and painted in desert camouflage, ready for the long ferry flight to Muharraq, Bahrain. Back at Lossiemouth, the AN-ALE-40 chaff/flare dispenser system was reintroduced and AIM-9Ls were delivered to Muharraq to replace the AIM-9Gs normally carried by the Buccaneers in the European theatre.

Fitted with the Westinghouse AN/ASQ-153 Pave Spike designation system, the Buccaneers quickly restored the Tornado's bombing accuracy, but from an altitude of 20,000 feet, safely above the Iraqi anti-aircraft missiles and guns. Carrying a Sidewinder and an AN/ALQ-101 ECM jamming pod, each Buccaneer was also able to carry additional fuel in the bomb bay, so that only one refuelling rendezvous was necessary, this being on the outbound leg of each mission. By comparison, the Tornados usually required three 'prods'. Although the Tornado crews had never dropped laser-guided bombs until now, the Buccaneer crews from 12 and 208 Squadrons (and the OCU) quickly provided sufficient training for the first operational mission to take place on 2 February. Four Tornados departed from Muharraq in company with two

Buccaneers, tasked with the destruction of a road bridge across the Euphrates at As Samawah. A cell of two Tornados and one designating Buccaneer was assigned to each end of the bridge, and it was destroyed with devastating accuracy, with little or no damage to any surroundings. On this first mission the Buccaneers returned to Muharraq with the Tornados, transiting at 37,000 feet, way above the Tornado's normal cruising height. More successful missions followed, and from 5 February the Dahran-based Tornados also began to operate with the Buccaneers. For each mission the same twin-cell concept was used, with a minimum separation of 45 seconds to enable the first stick of bombs to impact before the second target point was illuminated (if it was illuminated too early, the first bombs may have homed-in on the second impact point). The system worked well, but because the Pave Spike system relies on a monochrome TV for location, it was often difficult to pinpoint targets at slant angles, through dust and humidity. Consequently, the crews elected to lock the Pave Spike designator straight ahead, and dive to 15,000 feet, using the pilot's head-up display to acquire the target. When the navigator had pinpointed the target on his TV screen the Pave Spike's pod would be rotated onto it and the Buccaneer would climb away, while still illuminating the impact point.

The Buccaneers eventually released 169 laser-guided bombs to destroy a total of 24 bridges, although the last sortie, conducted on 13 February saw three bombs failing to glide to the target, and one of the bombs landed in a market place, killing a number of civilians. By this stage however, attacks on other targets had begun, and by the previous day the Buccaneer crews had begun turning their attention to airfields, initially destroying hardened aircraft shelters, followed by runways and, from 16

XW527 never flew with No. 16 Squadron, but when the unit reformed as the shadow designation for No. 226 OCU, the opportunity was taken to temporarily repaint this No. 12 Squadron aircraft in representative markings for a photographic rendezvous with a No. 16(R) Squadron Jaguar.

February, command bunkers and ammunition storage areas. On 14 February, a 'double mission' was launched with four Buccaneers (from a total of 12 which had been at Muharraq since 8 February) and eight Tornados. Attacking Al Taqaddum, one Tornado was shot down by a pair of SA-2 SAMs, and this contributed to the decision to abandon any future 'double missions' which were perceived to be too complicated. On 21 February, the Buccaneers relinquished their Sidewinders, as they were deemed to be unnecessary, the Allies having clearly secured the airspace over Iraq. With additional space now available, the Buccaneers could carry two 1,000lb LGBs to add to each raid. Following the Tornados' bomb drop, the Buccaneers would dive in from 25,000 feet at an angle of 40 degrees, delivering their bombs into the 'basket' which was being illuminated by their own designator pod. Such was the success of this concept that a total of 48 LGBs were dropped from Buccaneers, prior to the cessation of hostilities. Having destroyed numerous bridges, airfields, command centres and even aircraft (a pair of Antonov An-12s were bombed on 27 February during an airfield attack on Shayka Mayhar), the Buccaneers flew a total of 216 sorties – not bad for an aircraft which wasn't even intended to participate in Desert Storm.

March 26, 1994 and RAF Lossiemouth paid farewell to the Buccaneer in style, with a formation flypast over the airfield, and a display of aircraft specially painted in the markings of every RAF Buccaneer squadron. In recognition of the Fleet Air Arm's association with the aircraft, XX894 received very authentic 809 NAS markings and camouflage. Unfortunately, this particular aircraft never actually served with the Royal Navy and it is perhaps something of a pity that a former FAA airframe wasn't repainted in its original colours.

CHAPTER SIX

From the cockpit

The Buccaneer began its military service at Lossiemouth and it was appropriate that some 33 years later, the type should end its operational career on the same base. Although the aircraft's withdrawal had been planned since 1992, Buccaneer crews certainly didn't sit around, twiddling their proverbial thumbs until the last squadron (No. 208) disbanded. Indeed, the Buccaneer remained very much in business up until the last day of March 1994 when, at midnight, the Royal Air Force's maritime strike commitment effectively transferred completely to the Tornado GR1B. Over the next few days the remaining aircraft departed for their final destinations, some flying out to other RAF stations to serve as battle damage repair or crash rescue trainers, while a few survivors joined museum collections around the country. Sadly, many Buccaneers never flew again, and were simply dismantled on site before being destroyed in a nearby scrap yard. It is also sad to reflect upon the Civil Aviation Authority's ruling on the operation of 'warbirds' which prohibits civilian owners from flying Buccaneers because of their 'complexity'. Unless the CAA changes this lamentable attitude, the Buccaneer's distinctive whine is doomed to be gone from Britain forever, and it would surely be a great shame if we all forgot just what an impressive beast the Buccaneer was. So what was it like to fly in the Buccaneer? Few civilians were ever afforded the privilege of finding out for themselves, but the author was extremely lucky to have been offered such an opportunity, and by way of a conclusion to this book, the following account provides an interesting insight – from an enthusiast's point of view – into how the Buccaneer was operated, and what it really was like inside the cockpit of the very last, and certainly one of the best British Bombers.

RAF Lossiemouth is a relatively large military base, originally developed for the Fleet Air Arm, but now a very significant part of the modern Royal Air Force. Situated on the shores of the Moray Firth, 'Lossie' is a remote airfield which often sulks under a veil of mist or cloud. Even on crisp, sunny days, it is usually either cold or breezy, or both. The airfield is, by present standards, remarkably busy with two resident maritime strike squadrons (operating Tornado GR1Bs), the Jaguar Operational Conversion Unit, a Sea King Search and Rescue detachment, and a regular stream of visiting NATO aircraft. Not too long ago it was even busier, when the airfield was also the home to No. 8 Squadron's venerable Shackletons. The faithful old 'Shacks' shared the airfield with three Buccaneer units, these being No. 237 Operational Conversion Unit (whose aircraft graced the apron in front of the base hangars), and Nos 12 and 208 Squadrons, which were dispersed to hardened aircraft shelter (HAS) complexes on the opposite side of the airfield.

No. 208 Squadron occupied the southern HAS complex, the shelters and administration buildings being surrounded by a (guarded) barbed wire fence, and without a suitable pass, nobody could get in or out of the squadron's concrete citadel. The journey from the main base and the shelter complex required a drive of around five minutes, along the airfield perimeter road past the secondary runway threshold, but for an aspiring Buccaneer passenger, the journey was much longer. The first part of the journey was a visit to the Station Medical Officer, who is tasked with signing the last in a series of papers to enable a journalist to climb into the back seat of a Royal Air Force bomber. Needless to say, he doesn't sign the paper without first satisfying himself that the eager passenger is going to survive the experience. One simple demonstration flight might sound like a relatively safe proposition, but wiser counsel will readily remind any naive writer that combat aircraft are not simply smaller versions of the kind of aeroplane one might encounter on a package holiday. Military aircraft, particularly those which the RAF refer to as 'high performance' types are very different machines, and they have to be treated with the greatest of respect. Even before arriving at Lossiemouth, an RAF medical lecturer explained in detail to the author (and a captivated if not slightly terrified audi-

ence of student pilots) just a few of the ways in which a Buccaneer – like any other combat aircraft – could quickly and easily kill the unwary.

Pronounced as being 'fit to fly', the next stop was the Buccaneer simulator building, which was used by both operational squadrons together with the OCU. Lacking the full motion generated by the latest equipment, Lossiemouth's simulator was geared towards the reproduction of the Buccaneer's instrument readings, so that pilots and navigators could explore a seemingly infinite number of ways in which systems could work as advertised or, as was often the case in a simulator 'flight', fail at the most inconvenient moment. For a would-be passenger, the simulator provided a perfectly safe and very realistic reproduction of a real Buccaneer cockpit, in which one could familiarise oneself with a bewildering array of switches, dials and knobs. Because Blackburn never produced a dual-control variant of the Buccaneer, anyone destined to occupy the aircraft's rear cockpit had to be well acquainted with the equipment at his disposal, and not surprisingly, it took quite some time to fully understand what some of the more obscure switch panels were for. The most important item to remember was a bank of switches on the port side of the cockpit which controlled the fuel flow for the external fuel tanks, the bomb bay tank (if one was fitted) and the bomb door tank. Without any duplicated controls in the front cockpit, the back seater – whoever it was – would have to know what to do with them, and when to do it. Apart from the obvious risk of running out of fuel, the wrong switch selection could disrupt the lubrication system provided by the fuel, resulting in overheating and possibly a fire. On the other side of the cockpit, more switches are of immediate interest, these being for the IFF (identification, friend or foe) and

No. 208 Squadron Buccaneers in their element, at low level, surrounded by hillsides. The unit was declared to NATO and regularly deployed to its designated wartime operational area in Norway, where many sorties were flown over (and through) the countless fjords. The unit's overland role was finally given up and the squadron joined No. 12 Squadron at Lossiemouth as a maritime strike unit. Following the demise of the Buccaneer, No. 208 is now a reserve squadron within No. 4 FTS, flying Hawk T1As.

SSR (secondary surveillance radar) equipment. Like most modern aircraft, the Buccaneer used SSR and often required Buccaneers to 'squawk' their radar information. This was another task which the navigator had to perform, as was the selection of the bomb switches, which activated the various weapons stations, enabling whatever stores which might be carried to be dropped. Less important from a safety point of view, the prominent radar scope was certainly of interest, but learning to understand how a seemingly meaningless radar picture could be properly interpreted into useful information would have taken more than a few minutes, so in order to provide the author with a means of at least being able to use the scope, its controls had to be explored and memorised. After a couple of hours, the Buccaneer's rear cockpit looks much less frightening, but just in case anything hasn't been properly digested, there is a list of 'homework' to study for that evening.

Early the next morning, an MT minibus collects a handful of aircrew from the Officer's Mess and transports them (together with one civilian) to No. 208 Squadron's shelter complex. The cold, damp October gloom isn't exactly 'flying weather' but the Met man has already offered some promise of better conditions later in the day, and so the mission is still 'go'. Inside the squadron's administration offices (part of the 'soft' complex which is used during day-to-day training), the atmosphere is much brighter, with pilots, navigators and administration officers taking a break in the crew room, where a healthy supply of tea, coffee, biscuits and other goodies are on hand, together with a scattering of morning newspapers to accompany the television news which some of the aircrew are watching. Walking back outside, just a few feet away is the entrance to the squadron's hardened accommodation where the serious business of conducting the day's flying operations is already underway. During exercises or if East-West tensions had seriously deteriorated, No. 208 squadron (along with every other RAF front-line unit) would transfer all operations into the concrete bunker,

sealing off the outside world to protect against 'NBC' conditions, that is, nuclear, biological or chemical warfare. The hub of the squadron's activity is the operations room, where personnel keep a tally of which aircraft are serviceable, which are flying, what armament is carried, which pilots are flying which machines, at what time, with how much fuel and so on. From this small room, No. 208 Squadron's 'War Exec' conducts every mission.

In an adjoining (planning) room, aircrew are busy preparing maps for their sorties, laying out their charts on two large tables in the centre of the room. Although the Buccaneers were very

A No. 12 Squadron Buccaneer at low level, revealing the positioning of upper surface camouflage and walkway markings. The forward wing fold doors are not fitted, and following the Red Flag accident, most surviving Buccaneers regularly flew without them, mainly to enable the ground crew to inspect the locking mechanism more easily.

much part of modern warfare, they did not possess any of the computerised equipment available to state-of-the-art machines such as the Tornado, and so every tiny detail of the sortie had to be properly plotted in the usual time-honoured way, with pens, rulers, and calculators. For today's mission, the maps are both high level and low level, reflecting the varied nature of the sortie, and the navigators are busy examining new information which is posted on the walls, showing the day's special airspace restrictions, avoidance areas, and other items which might affect mission routing. Otherwise, the low level charts already show fixed locations which must be avoided, and larger areas (such as cities) which must be overflown at altitudes above the usual low-level height of 250 feet. To some extent, the Buccaneer navigators have a degree of flexibility in planning their routes, as the open sea contains few restrictions, but like many Buccaneer missions, today's will include an overland section which must be planned carefully.

A call from the nearby briefing room indicates that it is time to begin the pre-flight briefing. Once settled inside, the leader of today's mission begins his briefing, aided by an overhead projector through which he displays relevant figures. "Okay, good morning gentlemen, the aim of today's sortie is for two aircraft to go off and deliver some weaponry, and to do some low level navigation, but with the main aim of doing some Buccaneer-to-Buccaneer air-to-air refuelling. We have a VC10 tanker as a bonus, but everything will be aimed at making a rendezvous with the Buccaneer tanker. Write down all the details please and look up when you're ready." The crew quickly scribble down the relevant details, onto a plastic kneepad. The morning's weather details have already been discussed, and so the mission details can now be explored in detail. "Okay, I'll carry on

now. The crews are myself and Mike leading with the Boss and Tim flying as number two. Call-sign will be 'Skull One' and 'Two', and the HASs for our aircraft are XV168 in HAS 24 and '287 in HAS 22. We have the SX stores fit and you have the SE. Your load is two inerts, probably on wing station three, and two flares on station four. Drop the inerts please. We have our standard stuff, namely three KGs. Fuel is 18K for ourselves and 19K for you Boss." Although the pace of the presentation is swift, the facts are all covered. The 'Boss' is a much-used term for a squadron Commanding Officer, who in this case, will be flying the second Buccaneer. Having established what shelters our aircraft are in, what weapons they're carrying and how much fuel, the briefing continues.

"Weather at Lossie is quite nice now, looking out of the door. We'll taxy out to whatever runway is in use, it's one-zero at the moment, and we'll line-up on the runway as per the wing in a 20-second stream . . . I'll be going blown, then you chase after me to catch up. Join at whatever kind of position you require and if you need any photographs of us Tim, just tell the Boss what you need. I'll try to go for an arrow formation, but if you want to come in close Boss, please make sure that I know so that I don't rack on the bank too much. However, it's whatever you like, arrow or battle formation Tim, but clear it through the Boss so that I don't do anything silly and bash into you. When we've completed the sortie, we'll come back here for a pair approach, on one-zero that'll be a surveillance radar approach, and that'll be a precision approach radar to runway two-eight, although we may just do it visually if the weather's good enough. Make sure you're upwind of us Boss, and we'll use hand signals. We'll overshoot the pairs approach at 400 feet and I'll put the

A Buccaneer at night during a deployment to Gibraltar where the type continued to exercise right up until their retirement. The relatively short runway at Gibraltar ensured that every Buccaneer take-off was an eye-catching spectacle, and the sight of a stream of Buccaneers roaring off over the sea was a familiar one to personnel serving 'on the Rock'.

airbrake in, after which there will be a pause. Then when the airbrake's travelled, I'll bring the power up, so the airbrake will be your signal that I'm about to start overshooting. We'll try to keep it nice and tight, and whoever is towards the downwind leg will turn downwind away from the other guy, a positive turn to get us into the airfield circuit. Landing separation is 20 seconds minimum, and remember there will be other people in the circuit too. All through the exercise, if we go unserviceable you will have to wait for us to get another aeroplane. If you go unserviceable, we'll wait for you."

The reference to 'going blown' refers to the Buccaneer's boundary layer control system, which wasn't normally employed for take-off at Lossiemouth, there being more than enough room for a conven-

tional departure on the 8,393ft runway. However, on this occasion Lossiemouth's main runway was closed for major resurfacing work, and so the shorter 6,023ft runway was in use, requiring the use of the Buccaneer's high-lift device. Back to the briefing . . . "Time check, and a look at the Royal Flights, the only one being to the south of us, so we've had to sign for it but it doesn't affect our route. Danger areas, there are two of them, the first being 809 South which is active to 8,000 feet so we'll transit above that on our way north, and then there's 609 which we need to keep clear of. Safety altitude we can use is five point five throughout this part of the high ground, and please remember that there are big lumps of rock sticking out of the ground around there. Notams, there aren't any that affect us, although there is a late warning that I'll point out later, which refers to a crop sprayer in our area. As for airways, we'll be transmitting over the advisory routes but we'll be getting a radar service from Scottish Radar. If our internal chatter is too much, I'll ask for a frequency they don't mind us blathering about on. Coming back at low level, we should be under all those airways. Pressures, we'll take them when we walk out. Fuel is 'Bingo One' at ten, and probably the same after tanking so that we know after all the different tanking events going on where we start from. 'Bingo Two' of five-point-five is a fuel from round about the Orkneys, to come back low level through the Pentland Firth, a fairly straight re-covery." This part of the briefing covers the areas of airspace which must be avoided, especially Royal Flights, and also Notams, or notices to airmen, which outline unusual occurrences which temporarily affect routings or timings on any given day. Fuel information deals primarily with 'Bingo' calls, which advise the crews when a pre-briefed amount of fuel is remaining on board the aircraft, signifying that the return leg of the sortie has to begin.

Continuing with the briefing, the main elements of the mission are now explored. "Okay, the plan then. If it's runway two-eight, it'll be a big right turn, or if it's one-zero it's straight ahead heading 090 out towards Rosehearty. It's five minutes from abeam the lighthouse here, so we'll be in at the target at 420 knots. We'll go in battle formation with you on the left, and when we're abeam we'll turn downwind and increase to 500 knots, squawking 4320. There are heli-copters around there Tim, so keep your eyes open, and if you see anything, tell us about it. Okay, we're in there for two passes, probably visual laydowns, and we'll rendezvous at Troup Head off the second pass, although you'll probably be

fairly close behind us in any case, so you can call us to turn, jink or whatever. Then we'll set off around this low level nav route. We'll try and fly this route, and feel free to move around us to get a good angle for your photographs Tim. The only thing to beware of on this leg is Balmoral, out here to the right. Okay, that'll take us out to Montrose and we go under this airway here, so if there's weather down there, the base area level is six-five. Then on to Montrose, measur-ing the heading, and it looks like 080 from Montrose, climbing up to 230 initially, and we'll go across to Scottish Radar then on 2484 . . . we'll call when clear. Rendezvous with the tanker, call-sign 'India India eight-five'. We'll climb out heading up into the towline talking to Scottish, and then we'll hand over to Buchan. Then we'll endeavour to do the tanking, and you can do whatever photographs you want Tim, and we can manoeuvre as you like. The VC10 guys are very flexible and they'll probably be able to do whatever we ask for. We'll wait with them until the Buccaneer tanker turns up, callsign 'India Echo Uniform three-three', arriving from his Tornado tasking, okay? He'll be aiming to get there between 15:00 and 15:30, so he should be able to join us on the towline and he'll probably take a bit of fuel from the VC10 as well, so we can watch that, and then we'll set off to Duncansby Head, to do our Buccaneer-to-Buccaneer tanking."

Continuing with the briefing; "We'll try to get a quiet frequency and do our tanking on that leg. The tanker will then go home and we'll let down to low level, heading north from around the Pentland Firth area. Then we'll look at a tactic, and we'll do half of a Delta attack, which Simon will brief. Then we'll follow around the Orkneys as much as we can depending on how much fuel we have left. There are light aircraft in that area so please keep a look out. Then it's back to Lossiemouth, through the Pentland Firth, past the oil rigs and back here. We'll commence recovery on the 'Bingo Two' call. Any questions"? At this stage, the lead navigator completes his briefing, and hands over to his pilot, who examines the mission from his viewpoint; "First task then, is off to Rosehearty to drop our bombs. Now, you've already been shown the bomb distributor Tim, and there aren't too many switches to worry about, apart from the Start, Stop and the Singles switches, and I'll cover those with you again at the end of the briefing. We'll do two passes with the 28 inerts and the 3kgs for us. Rosehearty Range is the call-sign and the frequency is Stud 17. We'll use Target Two which is a small orange raft which sits out there in the middle of the water. Sometimes you can see it easily and sometimes you can't. Sea level and the danger area are Standard Operating Practice, and what we're looking for is to put the bomb close to the target so that we don't bomb any fishing boats in the area. The bomb ought to drop between a thousand foot over or a thousand foot short. The Boss will make quite sure that the bomb's not going to hit anything else and then he'll call 'Singles', which is your cue Tim, to make the final safety switch selection from 'off', and it should already be set at 'Start Three' and 'Stop Three', okay? That's providing that the inerts are on station three, and they should be, but we'll check that in the book when we get out to the aircraft."

"Boss, it's 251 for the heading that we're dropping the bombs on, and that's what the range will give you the score off. We'll go for a visual split, and please make sure that you're a good 20 seconds behind us, and then we'll RV again off Troup Head. Once you're aboard, call us and we'll head off on our route. The wind we've got is a slight southerly drift of 15 knots, but at the bombing height it's about plus ten, and your own speed is 504 knots, and we'll work our own out. Tim, you want five-point-one set to allow for the weight and the type of attack you're doing, and the Boss will offset for wind velocity, laying about 40 feet into the wind for every ten knots. The raft is 30ft long as a good guide and we're looking to get the bombs inside 140 feet. Once you're complete on the range Tim, make the switches safe and we'll make a call to remind everyone. Okay, the low level nav bit. Remember everyone that there are solid centres to those clouds, so if we have an emergency, get away from low level. You know how to squawk emergency Tim. Okay, we then go up to the tanker, and he's planning to be at flight level 250, and we'll join with an RV Charlie using full RT. If you spot the tanker before us Boss, then try and get our eyes onto it. If we need the airbrake I'll take it, and I won't call it. We'll join on the port in arrow formation initially and we'll refuel in the order One and Two, and we'll take 2K each. Have you been up to a VC10 before, Boss? Okay, if we have a half-hour slot it might be worth taking a few dry prods as well. After that, we'll depart to Duncansby. We will have refuelled before the Buccaneer tanker, so we'll sit off to starboard and wait for him to refuel from the VC10. When he's complete, we'll move out into a tight battle formation so that he can move up on the inside and then it's off back to Scotland . . . oops, hopefully not that dramatically!" The magnetic aircraft symbol he's using to illustrate the mission objectives, drops from the wall board amid hoots of laughter. The briefing is almost always a lighthearted affair, even though vital information necessary for the forthcoming mission is being discussed in detail.

"On to Duncansby then, probably at around flight level 250. We'll try to do the tanking as quietly as we can, so as not to

Proudly wearing the crossed sword markings of No. 237 Operational Conversion Unit, this close-up view of the Buccaneer reveals some interesting details, not least the attitude indicator markings on the refuelling probe, and hydraulic fluid leaking out over the bomb door.

clutter the Scottish frequency. We'll tank from the Buccaneer in the order One and Two, initially for 1K but if you want us to take dry prods Tim, or change headings to get the sun in the right place for your photographs, just tell us as we'll have plenty of gas at that stage. Once we're complete we will be on the starboard, and we'll clear to low level. Emergencies at any stage are SOP, and we can divert to Leuchars, otherwise it's back here to Lossie. If you have a problem Boss, we'll come with you and drop you off somewhere, but if we're with the tanker, we'll let him take you home. As for the VC10, remember Boss that the aircraft has lots of dihedral which can be quite disorientating, especially if there's any cloud around, but otherwise it's quite a smooth affair, with a nice big basket which tends to wobble a bit. If you sustain any damage during the tanking, it's a diversion into Leuchars. Now, let's look at the tactic. To make it nice and simple we'll do a Delta Two Experimental with One and Two in the 1,500 yards swept position. We'll use 200 feet to get us away from the sea, and please watch the weather around there. If it's poor, then try to get into close formation and ease away from the water, otherwise just pull up, call our heading and you take us through. Escape manoeuvre is SOP, and use instruments in the toss recovery. Once you're happily back on the horizon, get me visual and follow me out. Follow me up using 4g."

In order to clarify what is going to happen, the lead navigator explains; "To give you an idea of what we're talking about Tim, we're going to simulate

attacking a ship which is probably unde-
fended, so we're going to dash in and toss
a bomb at it from a distance of about 3½
nautical miles. So, what we'll do is, at 30
miles we'll accelerate up to 550 knots, to
get us there quickly once we've popped
up over the enemy's horizon. At 15 miles
we'll call 'Bananas', a ridiculous thing to
say, but it signifies that the target is at 15
miles, on the nose. Then we'll race in,
and at 3½ miles we'll pull up. You'll hear
us say 'standby, standby, now' and then
you'll hear a beep which is us going up.
The Boss will start his stopwatch five
seconds later and follow us. After four
seconds in a 4g climb, the bombs would
come off and begin to fall towards the
target. The Spikers, the guys down at the
back, would begin illuminating the target
with their pods. We'll recover in the
opposite direction and then go on with
the rest of the sortie. Looking at cockpit
management, you've already covered the
fuel Tim, and when we're on the tanker,
you must switch the overloads off. You
can use the radar at any stage during the
sortie, but put it on standby while we're
tanking, so that we don't irradiate the
poor guys in the tanker. When you get
back on the ground, make sure that
you've put all the pins back into their
locations before you unstrap. There's no
rush to do anything unless the aircraft's
on fire, in which case you can run like
hell! Generally speaking, you're taking
cameras with you, so be careful where
you put them and make sure that you can
reach the ejection handle at all times. If
the Boss takes a bird in the face at low
level and he can't speak to you, then you
need to get out of there pretty quickly,
otherwise he'd brief you on what's going
to happen if you need to get out of the
aircraft. As for disorientation, tell the
Boss if you don't know which way up you
are, and he'll tell you what's going on . . .
hopefully. Okay, any points to add? Let's
do it then."

The briefing complete, the crew leave
the room to gather at the ops room
window, where they make a last-minute
check of the aircraft status and look at
any other information which might need
to be incorporated before leaving for the
aircraft, a process known as 'out-brief-
ing'. As for the intrepid passenger, it's
time to complete the kitting-up process
in the adjoining clothing area. Having
already donned a pair of fairly unglam-
orous 'long johns', a pair of anti-g
trousers and a heavy, smelly and cumbersome rubber immersion suit, together
with a pair of standard-issue leather
flying boots, the remaining equipment is
gathered from a locker. First addition to
one's attire is the life jacket – not the
simple inflatable that you might see on an
airliner, but something much sturdier
and heavier, which is carefully buttoned
into place. Inside the 'Mae West', there is
a radio homing beacon which will automatically transmit on a distress
frequency, after ejection from the
aircraft, enabling Search and Rescue
helicopter crews to quickly locate the
wearer. There's also a set of small flares
which can also be used to attract the
attention of a rescue crew. After the life
jacket, the next items are the leg restraint
garters, which are strapped into place
around one's calves. The garters include
buckles through which the ejection seat's
leg restraints are threaded, before being
plugged into the base of the seat. If the
ejection sequence is initiated, the leg
restraints quickly retract and snap the
wearer's legs firmly against the seat, to
avoid the very real possibility of losing
one's kneecaps or lower legs on the cockpit panels, as the seat leaves the aircraft.
Finally, in addition to a pair of fire-retar-
dent flying gloves, a tough (but surprisingly heavy) flying helmet completes the
outfit. Although the resulting sight is
familiar to all RAF aircrew, an 'occasional' flyer can't help feeling somewhat

A striking photograph of the Buccaneer in belligerent pose, with a Martel anti-radar missile under each wing, together with a practice bomb carrier and an AN/ALQ-101 electronic counter measures pod. This view also illustrates how the Buccaneer S2's engine exhausts were keyed outwards to provide additional directional stability, and how the bolt-on refuelling probe was offset to starboard.

self-conscious in such alien clothing, but every item is essential for fast-jet operations, and the whole outfit is treated simply as routine by the other aircrew. Ready to walk, the crew assemble and make their way out of the clothing area, and out through the PBF door, crossing a metal grille under which a pit is filled with fuller's earth. This provides a decontamination area for aircrew returning from missions in NBC conditions, when their clothing could well be covered in radioactive fallout. Closing the huge metal door behind us, we leave the dark and slightly sinister world of the PBF building behind us, and take a minibus to our designated hardened aircraft shelters.

A couple of minutes later, we've crossed the puddle-marked taxiways and arrived at HAS number 22, where the overcast conditions are brightened by a row of bright spotlights attached to the shelter roof. Through the shelter's open doors, the imposing shape of a Buccaneer is visible, with two members of the ground crew completing last-minute inspections of the aircraft's exterior. This particular Buccaneer is S.Mk.2B XT287, a former FAA machine which joined the RAF in 1971. Unusually, after flying with No. 237 OCU for some time, the aircraft was transferred back to the Royal Navy in 1973 before re-joining the RAF in 1978. After spending some time with Nos 15 and 16 Squadrons in Germany as an overland nuclear bomber, '287 returned to Lossie and joined No. 208 Squadron. Inside the HAS, the Buccaneer looks particularly large and menacing, the grey/green camouflage, bulged area-ruled fuselage and deep belly tank adding to the effect. Two access ladders are attached to the starboard side of the fuselage, and after climbing up to the rear cockpit, one is able to carefully thread one's legs down into the floor space ahead of the ejection seat, before slowly lowering oneself down onto the seat, whilst holding onto the windscreen frame. Safely settled into the seat, the blue leg restraints are threaded through their respective buckles and into place at the base of the ejection seat. Then the PSP (personal survival pack) is attached, so that the seat occupant is physically connected to the inflatable dingy, packed into the seat pan. Next, come the seat straps, two of which are pulled up from between one's legs, with another two being pulled down over the shoulders. These are routed into a QRB (quick release box) positioned over the wearer's crotch. They are then each pulled tight, almost to the point of discomfort, until it's virtually impossible to move one's body. This done, the PEC (personnel equipment connector) is attached, connecting the wearer with the aircraft's oxygen system, and the air pressure supply for the g-suit. After dialing-in an appropriate weight on the ejection seat's trajectory-adjustment control, the large, heavy and uncomfortable flying helmet is squeezed into place, tightly gripping one's head and ears – the helmet has to fit tightly in order to avoid movement during ejection. With helmet suitably adjusted and oxygen mask clipped and clamped into position, the 'strapping-in' sequence is more or less complete.

It takes approximately ten minutes for an inexperienced passenger to settle into the Buccaneer's rear seat, even with much of the cockpit already 'set-up' prior to entry, and while the process is being completed, the Boss is busy looking at the aircraft's exterior, checking for hydraulic leaks, pieces of stray equipment, damage, or any other items which may have accidentally been overlooked by the ground crew. Once satisfied that the aircraft is ready for flight, he also climbs into the Buccaneer, quickly straps in, and begins setting up his cockpit, while his passenger has a few minutes to look at what will be his surroundings for the next three hours. Although relatively spacious, the Buccaneer's cockpit is crammed with equipment, switches and dials. Inside the HAS, it's also dark and rather claustrophobic, with a distinctive odour of kerosene, oil and sweat which only partially disappears once both crew are breathing an air and oxygen mix through their masks. The navigator's ejection seat is positioned a couple of inches to the right of the fuselage centreline, the pilot's being just to the left, which enables the back-seater to see something of the activity taking place in the 'front office'. A Palouste air starter unit is attached to the Buccaneer's port engine and in response to the Boss's signal, the ground crew wind up the unit to full power; muffling the Palouste's noise, the bulky flying helmet doesn't seem to be such an inconvenience after all. The port engine starter button is pressed and almost imperceptibly, the Spey turbofan begins to turn, causing little more than a vague vibration through the airframe, and surprisingly little noise. With good RPM and TGT readings, the starboard engine is started, and by pulling the lower portion of one's helmet outwards, the crescendo of noise circulating around the HAS can be heard, confirming that the two Speys really are running. Although the ground crew have kindly removed some of the ejection seat safety pins, two have been left in place, but they too are now removed and placed in their stowage points on the cockpit wall and panel coaming. A quick check that all 11 pins are there means that the ejection seat is now fully operational, and ready for use. The Boss is busy flexing the aircraft's control surfaces, the ground crew (standing in front of the aircraft) confirming by RT connection that his inputs are having the appropriate effect. Suddenly, 'Skull One' checks-in to confirm that they are ready to taxy from their HAS. The Boss replies and confirms that he is also ready to roll, and with permission to taxy obtained from Lossiemouth's control tower, it's time to go.

As one member of the ground crew pulls away the wheel chocks, another signals for our aircraft to move forward. The two throttles are nudged forwards slightly and the Speys give out a gentle rumble, and the Buccaneer rolls forward, stopping in a neat curtsy as the Boss stabs the wheel brakes to check for brake pressure. Another little surge of power and we're off again, rolling out into daylight as 'Skull One' taxies past ahead of us, the pilot and navigator giving us a friendly wave. Turning smoothly onto the taxiway, the canopy is slid forward and locked into place and we begin a fairly long journey around the perimeter track towards the holding point just short of runway 10's threshold. The ride is fairly smooth and the Buccaneer's sturdy landing gear rides effortlessly over the taxiway's intersection bumps and paving cracks, gently pitching in a rather amusing (and appropriate) nautical fashion, with just an occasional squeeze of brake pressure as the Boss keeps the aircraft's speed under control. A few minutes later we come to rest at runway 10's holding point, ready to make the final pre-take-off checks. First check is the trim settings, followed by the airbrake position, bomb door position, fuel contents, flaps, aileron and tailplane position, blow selector, electrical

system, flight instruments, ADD, engine temperatures, and eventually the final check for the seat safety pins and a good tug on the seat harness to ensure that everything is tight and secure. ATC gives us permission to take-off, and 'Skull One' rolls onto the 'piano key' threshold markings, taking the left-hand side of the centreline, as we position to the right. Turning onto the runway, the overcast conditions contrast starkly with the blaze of runway lights stretching ahead of us towards a horizontal row of red lights in the distance, marking the end of the runway. The red lights seem to be uncomfortably close, but the Boss comments that we're taking Lossiemouth's short runway, while resurfacing work continues on the main strip. With boundary layer blowing, there would be just enough runway for us, although as a safety measure the OCU Buccaneers with their student pilots would be operating from nearby Kinloss. To our left, 'Skull One' throttles up to full power and a trail of thick brown smoke begins to spew from the engine exhausts. Our engines also wind-up and the aircraft begins to tremble and rock as the power increases. 'Skull One' begins to roll, and is quickly enveloped in a cloud of smoke and water vapour, the exhaust from the two Speys buffeting our aircraft as we prepare to begin our take-off run. Brakes off and our engines go up to full power, the distinctive Spey 'whistle' filling the cockpit as we begin to roll, gently accelerating as 'Skull One' climbs away ahead of us. The 1,000ft runway markers sweep by more rapidly now, and the approaching runway threshold appears to be getting uncomfortably close while we power on down the runway. The take-off roll certainly doesn't compare with the breathtaking acceleration of a Phantom or a Lightning, but it's exciting nonetheless. With just a few hundred feet of runway remaining, we gently rotate and ease smoothly into the air, the landing gear thumping into its retracted position as we sweep over the boundary hedge at little more than 50 feet; take-off on Lossie's short runway in a Buccaneer is never boring.

Once comfortably settled into our climb-out, we turn left to skirt Lossiemouth's neat rows of houses and head out over the Moray Firth, already at a very respectable speed of 420 knots. Despite the speed, the ride is very comfortable and the Buccaneer's reputation as a rock-steady low-level performer is immediately apparent. In most high performance jets, a combination of 420 knots and 500 feet would produce a ride which felt similar to a 747 in turbulence, but in the Buccaneer, conditions are remarkably unexciting. Turning towards the Rosehearty weapons range, our 'playmate' 'Skull One' is just visible ahead of us, low down over the sea, rushing in towards the splash target. We also begin to accelerate and quickly notch-up 500 knots, whilst edging carefully down to just 200 feet. The wave tops merge into a grey blur as the Boss calls for the final bomb switch selections to be made. He makes a verbal count-down to bomb release, and at 'zero' the brightly-painted splash target zips past under our nose. The Boss immediately hauls XT287 into a fairly tight (4g) turn to port, and for the first time on the flight, the g-suit inflates, creating the customary clench around one's legs and stomach. Round the range circuit and back for a second pass, we achieve two good bomb scores and depart from the range, joining up with XV168 ('Skull One') to head inland, climbing briefly to avoid disturbance to the small coastal towns and villages, before descending to 250 feet, out in the wilds of the Scottish Highlands.

On a heading of 225 degrees at a speed of 420 knots, the low level route takes us to the first turning point at Huntly,

north-west of Aberdeen. At a height of 250 feet, the hillsides rush by at an alarming rate and without some prompting from the Boss in the front seat, it would be impossible to connect the rapidly-unfolding panorama with the route outlined on the map. The Boss insists that low level and high speed navigation isn't too difficult once you've practised, but it's hard to believe him when every identifiable landmark flashes by at nearly 500 mph and it's difficult to even work-out where we've been, let alone where we are or where we're going. As we approach Huntly, the pre-plotted 1:500,000 scale map comes into use, with a line marked with one-minute intervals to show precisely where we should be, if we're on track. Sure enough, the larger-scale map does confirm that the Boss is right on track as we rush past Huntly and turn hard on to 196 degrees. The weather is starting to deteriorate as we head out into bleak countryside, and 'Skull One' closes in on us slightly in order to maintain visual separation with us. Even the Buccaneer can't produce a smooth ride in these conditions, and the turbulent 'lumps and bumps' gradually increase as the hills get bigger and the weather gets worse. Ahead of us there appears to be a solid wall of grey cloud, and remembering the briefing which mentioned how Scottish clouds often have solid centres, we're forced to move off our intended track to manoeuvre around the cloud. The Boss opts to turn right and hauls the aircraft into a gut-wrenching 6g turn, while XV168 flips smartly onto her back and heads into a valley, to fly down to the left of the weather, a long stream of condensation trailing from her wing tips. A few seconds later we're round the weather, and we turn smartly back towards our original course, closing-in to maintain a loose formation on 'Skull One'. Another turn on to 080 degrees and we're 200 yards behind XV168 as we close-in on Montrose, thundering across the fields as sheep, telephone polls and hedges flash under our nose. It looks cold and miserable outside, but in the Buccaneer's cockpit it is, not surprisingly, hot and sticky. At Montrose we complete our low level overland route and begin a gentle ascent as the first houses come into view. It's been 30 minutes since take-off but the journey seemed to last forever. Low level flying over Scotland is exciting, but it's also very demanding on both pilot and navigator, and a 20-minute leg is more than enough for practical training purposes. Certainly, it's enough to demonstrate that the Buccaneer's naval ancestry didn't prevent it from performing surprisingly well over land too, and of course RAF Germany's Buccaneers were assigned exclusively to the overland role with both conventional and nuclear weapons.

The climb from Montrose takes ten minutes, after which we arrive in one of the North Sea's refuelling areas, some 30 miles off the Scottish coast. 'Skull One' makes initial contact with the VC10 tanker which is already waiting for us, flying a long racetrack circuit inside the refuelling 'box'. The Boss spots the tanker and we slowly close-in to position off the tanker's port wing, some 25,000 feet over the North Sea. High above the clouds in crisp sunshine, the majestic tail of the VC10 towers over the cockpit of XV168 as it edges in to take a gentle stab at the tanker's starboard refuelling basket. We then manoeuvre into position behind the port basket and the Boss slowly and carefully nudges XT287 forwards until we make a reassuring 'clunk' as the Buccaneer's nose probe makes contact with the VC10 refuelling basket. Fuel immediately begins to flow and we take on 2,000lb of jet fuel. It looks deceptively easy to do, but keeping formation with the VC10 and especially the initial basket contact, requires some

very skilful flying. As we complete our refuelling, a third Buccaneer comes into view, this being XV868 which is configured as a 'buddy tanker' with a refuelling pod attached under her starboard wing. The crew had just completed a rendezvous with some RAF Tornado GR1s and having refuelled them, it was time for the tanker to be replenished from the VC10. Once the task is completed, the three Buccaneers are ready to depart from the refuelling area, leaving the VC10 captain to take his aircraft back to Brize Norton. Descending on a heading of 314 degrees under the control of Scottish Radar, the next leg of the sortie takes us out towards the Orkneys, and provides an opportunity to refuel from the Buccaneer tanker. XV868 slowly extends her refuelling drogue from the Mk.20 refuelling pod, and both 'Skull One' and 'Skull Two' each take a fuel load of 1,000lb at 16,000ft, and 280 knots (the drogue's limiting speed is 290 knots). Refuelling complete, the hose is wound back into its pod, but refuses to completely retract. The pilot of XV868 tries some careful jinking to try to persuade the hose to move, but without success. Finally, after losing some airspeed, the wing flaps are deployed and these disturb the airflow around the hose sufficiently for the basket to finally slip back into place.

Just off the north-east tip of the Scottish coast, the three Buccaneers finish their descent at 250 feet, sweeping in loose formation past John O'Groats en route for the Orkneys. The Buccaneer tanker has some fuel in reserve, and we decide to trail the refuelling hose once more in order to capture a few images of the tanker at low level. The refuelling system's lowest operating altitude is 2,000 feet, so a 'prod' is out of the question, but the hose can be trailed at lower altitudes even though it does bob about rather dramatically. Passing the Old Man of Hoy and a few fulmars which hadn't expected three Buccaneers to disturb their afternoon, the formation makes a gentle turn back south, passing Scapa Flow and heading out towards the Pentland Firth to prepare for the final part of the sortie. The plan is to fly a Delta Two attack demonstration, showing how two aircraft would use the Paveway laser-guided weapons system. Used with great success during the Gulf War, the Buccaneers dropped bombs from medium altitude with superb accuracy. However, dropping bombs from altitude was a luxury which could only be afforded in an area where air supremacy had been established, and it was always more customary to deliver Paveway bombs from low level, using a toss delivery to literally throw the bombs at their target. Of course, the same toss technique was also used by Buccaneer crews to deliver Red Beard and WE177 nuclear bombs.

For today's demonstration, no live weapons would actually be dropped, but the manoeuvre would be flown as if they were. On a 'real' attack, more Buccaneers or Tornado GR1s would be trailing our aircraft at about 5,000 yards, illuminating the target with Pave Spike laser designation pods. Accelerating to 550 knots, the Boss allows us to descend to just 200 feet and the Buccaneer begins to contradict its 'smooth ride' reputation. At this speed and this altitude, the Buccaneer's huge bulk is literally roaring towards the target area, puffs of condensation occasionally forming over the wings, the tips of which can be seen to waggle in the turbulent air. The two Speys are whistling loudly and airflow is thundering over the cockpit canopy. Forty miles from the target, with the tanker having departed for Lossiemouth, 'Skull One' and 'Two' break left and right, and settle into a widely separated line-abreast position, in which each aircraft can keep a watch on

the other's six-o'clock position. Because the 'spikers' are so well separated, it wasn't uncommon during exercises for an 'enemy' fighter to close-in on the lead Buccaneer, only to find himself sandwiched in front of another Buccaneer, armed with an AIM-9G Sidewinder missile. At about 25 miles from the target, one aircraft would normally pop-up from low level to locate and nominate the target on radar, before quickly descending to 200 feet or lower. In practice, 100 feet was the minimum altitude for a peacetime 'spike attack', but 50 feet would be more likely in a real combat situation, at least for the final few miles towards the target. If a Nimrod happens to be at altitude nearby, a VASTAC (Vector Assisted TACtic) is performed, the Nimrod crew passing target details to the Buccaneers so that they don't need to pop-up from low level and risk radar detection.

Fifteen miles from the target and the leader calls 'Bananas' and 'Skull One' and 'Two' break left and right into hard turns, before pulling sharply into 4g climbs, huge clouds of condensation streaming over the aircraft's canopy, fuselage and wings. Continuing upwards, we reach the point at which the bombs would be released, after which they would slowly curve into a long descent, homing-in on the illuminated target. For a nuclear toss delivery, the bomb would follow the same trajectory but continue unguided to its destination. With 'bombs gone', we continue over the top of a loop, pulling sharply back down towards the horizon, with more g-forces winding on. Rolling wings level, we're back at low level again in a few seconds, flying directly away from the target, making good our escape, with 'Skull One' just visible a couple of miles ahead of us.

The Paveway system does require the designator aircraft to approach fairly close to its target, and this makes the system less than ideal for heavily defended targets. The Buccaneer's main anti-ship weapon was the Sea Eagle missile, which replaced the TV-guided and radar-homing versions of Martel. Essentially a 'fire-and-forget' missile, Sea Eagle could be launched at around 60-70 miles from the target, leaving the Buccaneer to turn through 180 degrees, and away to safety, while the missiles continued on their deadly trajectory. For a heavily-defended target such as a 'Kirov' class cruiser, up to six Buccaneers might be launched, each carrying four Sea Eagle missiles. Launched from a distance of nearly 70 miles at a height of just 100 feet, the missiles would be closing-in on their target at supersonic speed before they were even detected, their launch aircraft having never even been

A rare picture of the Buccaneer carrying four Sea Eagle missiles during a training flight from Lossiemouth. The Sea Eagle is a true 'fire and forget' missile, which would have enabled the Buccaneer to continue in the maritime strike role, possibly into the next century, had an airframe life extension programme been implemented. Unfortunately, the cost effectiveness of operating Tornado GR1s in the maritime role meant that the Buccaneer could no longer be afforded.

seen on radar. Even a 'Kirov' cruiser can't pick-off a battery of 24 missiles all at once. In order to demonstrate what a Sea Eagle attack would be like from the Buccaneer navigator's viewpoint, the Boss descends from 200 feet to an even lower altitude. The precise height is questionable, but the wave tops seem to be lapping around the cockpit canopy and this really is as low as you can possibly get. Despite some heavy 'lumps' of turbulence, the tough old Buccaneer still roars on, riding out most of the rough air with ease, and even in these conditions the ride still couldn't be described as uncomfortable. There are no real tactics to demonstrate as such, simply because the Sea Eagle doesn't require any, but Buccaneer crews regularly simulated the missile itself, for the benefit of naval radar and gun operators, who valued these ASMD (anti-ship missile defence) attacks. Pretending to be a Sea Eagle missile, the Buccaneers would press-home their attack at high speed and low level, streaking over the target ship at 100 feet or less. On the radar screen inside the ship, it looked just as terrifying as the real thing.

Climbing up to 2,000 feet, we make radio contact with Lossiemouth to obtain the airfield weather status, while XV168 slows and pulls into tight formation off our port wing tip. The extension of the airbrakes is, as promised, very impressive, and from a transit speed of 420 knots, we're down to an approach speed of 180 knots in a few seconds. The Boss had said that the sensation would be like 'flying into a brick wall' and he was right. Back over the Scottish coast, the Boss extends the aircraft's landing gear and settles on to a long approach behind XV168. The boundary layer system is blowing and the control surfaces are set at their 45:25:25 positions. We're now in what the crews euphemistically describe as 'marginally stable flight', meaning that

the Buccaneer is not the easiest of aircraft to handle in approach configuration. With 'everything down' the Buccaneer doesn't handle too well if an engine fails, but thankfully that's not something which happens very often. The Boss comments that, "the Speys are remarkably reliable. They eat birds and don't even splutter." Making a steady descent back to the airfield, the runway lights are clearly visible ahead of us as we make our final approach, the two Speys changing their pitch as the Boss makes small adjustments to our speed and height. The ADD (airstream direction detector) beep changes to a low tone as we sweep over the runway threshold and thump firmly back onto the concrete, some three hours after we had left. Holding the nose high, our forward speed quickly decays and we're travelling at a comfortable taxying speed long before we reach the end of the runway, where we turn right and head back towards the shelter complex. The ground crew are already waiting for us, and a marshaller guides us back into position in front of the shelter, so that the aircraft can be winched back inside once we've vacated it. The canopy slides back and a very welcome rush of Scottish air floods into the cockpit. The seat safety pins are placed back into their respective sockets and the two Speys slowly wind down, while the Boss and his passenger begin to remove themselves from the various straps and buckles which attach them to the aircraft. Three exciting and action-packed hours have passed quickly, and the mission is almost complete; all that has to be done now is to return to the PBF to conduct a detailed de-briefing, looking at the mission from start to finish, examining what went right, what went wrong, and what lessons can be learned for the next flight. For the author it was the end of a long and thoroughly fascinating afternoon, bombing in a Buccaneer.

CHAPTER SEVEN

Conclusion

The final years of Royal Air Force Buccaneer operations effectively began when No. 12 Squadron moved from Honington to Lossiemouth, followed by 208 Squadron in July 1983. The move was made to enable the squadrons to operate closer to the Norwegian Sea and Faroes-Iceland gap, the most likely wartime areas of interest for the Buccaneer force. As more Tornado GR1s were brought into RAF service, No. 208 Squadron's overland strike role was less important, and the unit was reassigned to the maritime role, joining 12 Squadron, and replacing what was to have originally been the RAF's second maritime strike unit, No. 216 Squadron. Equipped with the Paveway laser-guided weapon system, 208 Squadron also used the anti-radar version of the Martel anti-ship missile, while 12 Squadron used both this and the TV-guided variant of the same weapon. When 237 OCU moved to Lossiemouth in October 1984, the entire RAF Buccaneer force was finally concentrated at one base (Nos 15 and 16 Squadrons re-equipping with Tornado GR1s).

Good though Martel was, the missile was a 1960s-technology weapon which had some disadvantages. The anti-radar version relied upon radar transmissions in order to home-in on its target, but there was never any guarantee that any

enemy radar would remain switched-on long enough for the missile to find it. The television-guided version was more reliable in this respect, but it required the operator (the navigator) to steer the missile onto its target with a small joystick control situated between his knees in the Buccaneer's rear cockpit. Until the missile had impacted, the launch aircraft had to remain fairly close to the target which it was attacking in order to maintain the TV link, and this obviously placed the aircraft at some risk from enemy defences. Worse still, only one TV Martel could be fired at any one time, which made it a fairly easy target for enemy anti-missile gunners. Although, technically-speaking, the Buccaneer could carry four Martels, this only applied to the anti-radar version, as the TV-guided weapon required a suitable data link pod to be carried on one of the wing hardpoints, so that three missiles was the maximum load.

This shortfall in weapon capability was addressed by Air Staff Target (AST) 1012, an £80 million programme to update the RAF's Buccaneer fleet. From an original fleet of 26 aircraft, the RAF received a further 62 Buccaneers from the Fleet Air Arm, together with another 19 aircraft which were later ordered. From these, a small number of aircraft had been lost in flying accidents, while a more substantial number of airframes had been lost following the Red Flag crash. Some had been scrapped, while others had been placed in long term storage, and were effectively withdrawn from use. Consequently, a batch of 36 aircraft was established as a suitable figure for the update programme which would upgrade the aircraft for operations into the late 1990s. The core of the programme was an improved weapon system, centred around the British Aerospace Dynamics Sea Eagle missile. Although remarkably similar to Martel in terms of size and shape, the new missile represented a quantum leap in performance when compared with Martel. Most importantly, Sea Eagle was (and is) a 'fire-and-forget' missile which doesn't require any guidance from the launch aircraft once it is released. Approaching over the wave tops at 100 feet, the Buccaneers could evade enemy radar until the very last moment, with just one aircraft briefly 'popping-up' to around 5,000 feet to make a swift radar sweep of the area, to pinpoint the target. Then, the missiles could be sent on their way while the Buccaneers head for home. With four missiles carried by each Buccaneer, the Sea Eagle was the weapon around which the Buccaneer Force would build its operational tactics for the next ten to 15 years.

However, AST 1012 also included some other fairly significant improvements to the Buccaneer. Using synthetic aperture technology, the Blue Parrot radar would be updated to incorporate the single-sweep 'freeze-frame' capability which would be necessary for the 'pop-up' prior to a Sea Eagle attack. The pilot's cockpit would be fitted with a head-up display (HUD) while a new Ferranti inertial navigation system, new ECM and ESM equipment and a new Plessey radio would also be fitted, as well as chaff and flare dispensers. In essence,

the upgrade would tailor the Buccaneer to suit the maritime strike role for which it had been originally designed. As is often the case with such programmes, the estimated cost began to rise, and by January 1985 the upgrade was to apply to 60 aircraft at a cost of £150 million. It was also proposed that 14 aircraft which were in storage at RAF Shawbury could be refurbished and modified to act as defence suppression aircraft, a sort of 'Wild Weasel' version of the Buccaneer. At a time when defence expenditure cuts were being made almost on a weekly basis, the Buccaneers were unlikely to be immune from attention, and eventually the number of aircraft in the programme dropped again to 42, and the proposal to produce defence-suppression aircraft was abandoned. Air Staff Requirement (ASR) 1012 specified that the 42 Buccaneers would receive an upgraded radar, a Ferranti FIN1063 INS (a derivative of the INS carried by the Jaguar), a Sky Guardian passive detection system, and Tracor AN/ALE-40 chaff and flare dispensers, together with a Plessey radar to integrate the Buccaneer with other RAF aircraft. At the heart of the programme remained the Sea Eagle missile, but the HUD would not now be included, nor would other (smaller) improvements. Although something rather less than the RAF had originally hoped for, the programme would enable the Buccaneer to remain viable as an anti-ship weapons system well into the 1990s and possibly beyond 2000. The modification work would, by necessity, have to be carried-out by British Aerospace's Brough division but as ever, the Buccaneer could not safely be operated from Brough's tiny runway, and the former test airfield at Holme-on-Spalding Moor had finally closed on 12 December 1983. Consequently, the programme was assigned to the Woodford factory, with workers from

XT272 was one of two aircraft fitted with the Tornado GR1's radar unit during the aircraft's trials programme. Operated from Warton, the aircraft's naval-style grey colour scheme was livened-up considerably by the application of Day-Glo orange patches. Subsequently, the whole airframe was painted in the current MoD(PE) 'raspberry ripple' paint scheme.

Brough being ferried to the site near Manchester, as and when required. The first updated aircraft (XW529) was completed at Brough, and transported to Woodford from where it made its first flight in modified form, remaining there for flight trials, while subsequent aircraft were flown directly to Woodford for conversion. A batch of ten Buccaneers were modified to carry Sea Eagle during their second-line maintenance at Lossiemouth between December 1984 and April 1986. Another ten aircraft were suitably modified at St Athan during major servicing between April 1985 and September 1986. The remaining aircraft were upgraded to carry Sea Eagle as part of the update programme at Woodford.

By the end of 1986 No. 208 Squadron was operational with Sea Eagle and with Paveway as a secondary option. No. 12 Squadron continued to operate Martel, although they too were gradually incorporating Sea Eagle into their operations. The Buccaneer upgrade programme was completed in 1989, but by this time the Buccaneer's future had virtually been established. Instead of continuing in service for another ten or even 15 years, the availability of surplus Tornado GR1s would enable the RAF to equip two maritime strike squadrons with suitably modified Tornados, which would carry two Sea Eagle missiles under the fuselage. Although the Tornado couldn't match the Buccaneer's unrefuelled range, maritime Tornados would allow the entire Buccaneer fleet (together with an extensive support structure) to be withdrawn from service, and the financial considerations of this move outweighed any operational considerations. The first indication of the Buccaneer's demise was the disbandment of No. 237 Operational Conversion Unit on 1 October 1991. By this stage, there was no longer any significant requirement for Buccaneer crew conversion, and the small amount of training which was still required could be absorbed by the two remaining squadrons. Little more than one year later, on 1 January 1993, No. 12 Squadron ended Buccaneer operations and converted on to the Tornado GR1B, many of their 'new' aircraft coming from the recently-disbanded No. 27 Squadron at Marham. Finally, the last RAF Buccaneer unit, No. 208 Squadron, disbanded at Lossiemouth on 31 March 1994, making way for a new maritime Tornado unit in the shape of the reformed No. 617 Squadron. The remaining Buccaneers at Lossiemouth were removed either by air (to various RAF station fire dumps or to museums) or by road to collectors or scrap merchants, while a few airframes were simply cut-up on the airfield prior to being removed. The very last RAF Buccaneer flight was made by XV332 on 5 April 1994, when the aircraft was transferred from Cottesmore (to where it had previously been delivered from Lossiemouth) to RAF Marham, where it was initially used for battle damage repair training, but has subsequently been moved into a hangar, its future unknown. Some time previously, on 15 October, XV168 was flown to British Aerospace's Brough factory, making the first and last Buccaneer landing at the former Blackburn company airfield before being placed on display at the factory's entrance, in recognition of the countless individuals who worked-on or flew in, Blackburn's final (and greatest) achievement.

The Buccaneer's story was not complete however, as the Defence Research Agency (DRA) formerly the RAE, was still operating the Buccaneer as part of ongoing research and test programmes. Throughout the Buccaneer's history, various examples have been assigned on either long or short-term loan to the many defence research establishments scattered around the UK. Most of these detachments were connected with the Buccaneer's weapons systems, but a small number of Buccaneers were built specifically for the MoD(PE) for use as test platforms on countless research programmes. Three Buccaneer S2Bs (XW986, XW987 and XW988) were completed in 1974, and were delivered directly to the RAE, XW986 and XW988 going to West Freugh, while XW987 was assigned to Farnborough. The former aircraft became semi-permanent residents at West Freugh, assigned to weapons development for a variety of aircraft types, including the Buccaneer itself. Eventually the aircraft were officially transferred to Farnborough, to join XW987, although they spent a great deal of time detached back to West Freugh, operating over the associated ranges in the Luce Bay area, or alternatively over the Larkhill ranges, while operating from Farnborough or

XW988 was one of a batch of three Buccaneer S2s manufactured for the Ministry of Defence Procurement Executive. The unusual colour scheme, comprising dark green, yellow and white patches, was designed to facilitate effective photographic calibration during flight trials programmes. After completing a total of 1,382 flying hours, the aircraft was sold to the Lincolnshire Military Collection.

XV344 joined the trials fleet at Holme-on-Spalding Moor after serving with the Fleet Air Arm. Its final days were served with the Ministry of Defence (Procurement Executive) at Farnborough, and in 1988 the aircraft began flight trials for the TIALD pod which is now coming into service with the RAF. During this period the aircraft was named Nightbird *and received suitable nose artwork. The aircraft was retired in 1994 and scrapped at Farnborough.*

Boscombe Down. One of the first tasks assigned to the aircraft was the testing of what was to become the JP.233 airfield denial pod for the RAF's Tornado force. A variety of munitions dispensers were test flown, and the anti-personnel and runway cratering munitions were also flown as part of the programme. The next main project was the Multi Function Bomb Fuse which was developed by Thorn EMI, who bought time on the aircraft to test their stores.

The Buccaneers were also used to fly 'proof drops' of weapons such as the BL.755 cluster bomb unit, normally flying a couple of drops each year to ensure that the systems still worked, and these were normally dropped on a soft target at West Freugh. XW987 was also fitted with a bomb door fuel tank to

enable the aircraft to operate as a re-fuelling tanker for MoD(PE) operations, whenever required. As RAE operations at Farnborough began to wind-down, the Buccaneers (like many other Farnborough aircraft) moved to Boscombe Down. These three purpose-built trials aircraft (as opposed to various other Buccaneers which were used at Boscombe Down) were completed to S2B standard although they had some unique features, as Squadron Leader D. Southwood recalls; "The back cockpit had been ripped out, and instead you had lots of switches to operate the various instrumentation systems and recorders associated with the test programmes. They also had additional pylons attached to the outer wings, and these were used to carry cameras which were mounted at different angles. They were traditional wet film cameras, running at 100 frames per second, and they would be used to film the separation of stores. They produced a bit of additional drag, maybe knocking-off five knots or so, but they didn't really affect anything. Because West Freugh's range was quite tight on safety, we had to have very precise release points, and for toss bombing we had a system whereby you pressed a trigger which started a timer going. This opened a 'gate' of one second, and the release pulse had to be within that gate, otherwise the store wouldn't be released. The release pulse was only generated at a given angle, so you had to pull six degrees per second to achieve it, so we had a pitch rate gauge in the cockpit too. It was real trick flying, and it was a big deal if you got all your bombs off in the timing gate. You pulled the trigger, pulled back on the control column, and you'd fly the pitch rate. If you got it precisely right, the release pulse was generated when the timing gate was open."

Squadron Leader Southwood continues; "For critical stores like the BL.755 we would fly down the range's attack track, and you had to fly precisely over a set of lights, and they would then trigger the release pulse. The drops at West Freugh were very carefully plotted to within a 20ft resolution, and there was quite a bit of professional pride involved in delivering the weapons accurately. It was a very gratifying job, not least because we got a chance to drop lots of bombs. On an operational Buccaneer squadron you would get maybe one high explosive thousand-pounder per year to drop, and maybe four inerts, whereas we would sometimes drop four bombs per sortie. You wouldn't always aim the bombs yourself, as many of the drops over Larkhill for example, were range-controlled releases. We operate a variety of fairly non-standard aircraft at

Boscombe Down, so the fact that the RAF had disposed of its Buccaneer fleet, didn't really influence our decision as to when our Buccaneers should be withdrawn. On the other hand, I think it fair to say that there was a gradual decline in the amount of work which required the Buccaneers and when we became an Agency, people started to rationalise expenditure, and the Buccaneers came under much more scrutiny. They started to become harder to justify, at least on paper, with the amount of flying they did. Even so, there was still work for them to do when they were withdrawn. They were very useful, especially because they had very long legs, and they could be flown at high speed. They handled in exactly the same way as standard RAF machines, as the camera pylons really didn't make any difference. The cameras didn't cover everything however. A fixed-lens camera could only illustrate maybe a tenth of a second at the moment of separation, after which the weapon would go out of the frame. We were sometimes more interested in the behaviour of the store for quite some time after separation, so we sometimes had another aircraft flying with us to fly camera chase. The Buccaneers themselves were also occasionally used as chase plane, because you could fly close formation at 550 knots on another aeroplane, whereas you certainly couldn't formate at that speed in a Hawk, and the rear cockpit in the Tornado has lots of equipment which makes it less than ideal for a camera chase. You could use the Jaguar T2, but it doesn't turn as well as the Buccaneer at high speed and you needed reheat to keep up the speed, which made position keeping very difficult. You also had stacks of gas to use in the Buccaneer, so it was a good aeroplane for that kind of work."

Unlike the RAF's (and FAA's) Buccaneers, the MoD(PE) Buccaneers rarely made public appearances, although

XW988 was flown by Squadron Leader Southwood, at the ETPS anniversary open day in 1988; "I actually planned to fly Phantom XT597 at the event, but the aircraft suffered a major engine surge during a practice rehearsal, and we could not get the engines changed in sufficient time. So the day before the event I did three practice displays in the Buccaneer, and as I'd been display flying the RAF's Buccaneer about four years previously, it was fairly easy to work out a decent display. But that was the only time that one of our Buccaneers was publicly displayed in the air." They did make a few static appearances however, at events such as the International Air Tattoo, where the bizarre colour scheme applied to all three machines created a great deal of interest. The result of a study at Southampton University, the Buccaneers were suitably painted to present the best colour and light contrast possible for camera tracking purposes, this being a striking dark green, black, white and yellow 'patchwork' over which serials and national insignia were added. XW987 was eventually repainted in the now-standard MoD(PE) 'Raspberry Ripple' colour scheme, although there is some doubt as to whether this was done by accident or design. Likewise, there is a persistent tale that the huge serial numbers applied across the bomb bay door were also placed there by accident, but there no longer appears to be any way of substantiating this tale. Certainly, the Buccaneer pilots didn't know anything about it, as Sqn Ldr Southwood comments; "When we went out to the aeroplane, the bomb door was nearly always open, but one day we looked at some air-to-air pictures of XW988, taken from West Freugh's Andover, and suddenly we saw the big serial number written right across the bomb bay, and

Making a rare public appearance for workers at Brough, XW988 spent her entire career with the MoD(PE), which is now the Defence Research Agency. The huge serial numbers applied to the bomb door (just visible) were reportedly painted by mistake after an MoD officer scribbled the serial across the drawing of the aircraft's proposed paint scheme. In reality, this is probably an 'urban myth', but whatever the true reason, the unusual serial application remained until the aircraft was retired.

April 1, 1976, and XX897 takes-off for the first time at Holme-on-Spalding Moor. Wearing an unusual pseudo-naval colour scheme, the aircraft was manufactured for the Royal Radar Establishment, and was operated from Pershore until the base closed, after which it was relocated to RAE Bedford. As part of the Tornado F2/3 radar trials programme, the aircraft was later fitted with a Tornado radar unit in an F2 nose cone. After being sold to a civilian buyer, it was registered as G-BUCC in anticipation of the aircraft's reappearance as a flying 'warbird'. Sadly, the Civil Aviation Authority have not seen fit to authorise civilian Buccaneer flying.

until then we'd had no idea that they were there! I remember thinking that it would be a dead give-away if we were ever cited in a low flying complaint. On the other hand, when we occasionally received such complaints, we'd ask what colour the Buccaneer was painted. When they replied that it was painted in standard RAF camouflage, we could claim complete innocence!"

The MoD's Buccaneer operations began to wind-down shortly after RAF operations ended. XW986 and XW987 were withdrawn in 1994, while XW988 continued flying from Boscombe Down until February 1995. All three were offered for sale, and while XW986 (now painted in 'Ripple' colours) was sold to Delta Engineering (who continue to maintain the aircraft in flyable condi-

tion), XW988 was sold to Mike Beachyhead in South Africa, where the aircraft (painted overall gloss black) is now part of his private collection of jet 'warbirds' used for airshow appearances, and for contracted work with the South African Air Force. XW987 was also sold to Mike Beachyhead, and after a long period of storage at Boscombe Down, the aircraft was ferried to RAF St Mawgan during March 1997. After being suitably prepared, XW987 then departed for South Africa, marked as ZU-BCR, on 1 April 1997. Of course, this relatively unpublicised take-off from St Mawgan was also the last time that a Buccaneer flew in British airspace, and as XW987 climbed away over the Atlantic, the Buccaneer's story was quietly and finally completed.

With just two Buccaneers remaining airworthy in the hands of a South African civilian, the Buccaneer's long and distinguished service career is over. Having enjoyed a successful but relatively uneventful career with the Navy (the service for which it was specifically designed), the Buccaneer realised its true potential with the Royal Air Force – the service that didn't want it. The Buccaneer proved itself to be an immensely strong, manoeuvrable and reliable aircraft which had a better low level speed, range and weapons-carrying ability than many other aircraft, including the F-111 (which the RAF had wanted) and the Tornado, which eventually replaced it in RAF service. The Buccaneer was still a potent warplane even at the time of its retirement, but the cost-effectiveness of assigning Tornados to the maritime strike role made the Buccaneer force an expense which could no longer be (or at least, didn't have to be) afforded. Blackburn's Roy Boot – a person who could rightly be afforded the title 'Mr Buccaneer' – sums up the aircraft; "For nearly 20 years from the time that I did the initial B.103 design in the Project Office, until I moved to Warton in 1978 with the last 12 years as Chief Designer, the Buccaneer formed a major part of my life. A Commanding Officer of a Buccaneer squadron in Germany said, 'So far as I can tell, everyone who has flown the Buccaneer has always ended up with a great love for the aircraft and it has its own personality which endears itself to everyone. It is well liked because of its inherent stability at low level where it was a sheer delight to fly. It earned and kept the respect of NATO allies, particularly on Flag exercises, where at 100 feet it scored over many other types.' That is exactly what we set out to achieve in the first instance, many years back, and these comments – coming from members of the service which for 14 years rejected the Buccaneer – give me particular pleasure."

Positively the last time a Buccaneer was seen in the air over the United Kingdom was when XW897 departed for South Africa from RAF St Mawgan on 1 April 1997 registered as ZU-BCR. Since repainted in an all-black colour scheme, the aircraft continues to fly under the ownership of Mike Beachyhead (Photo: Andrew March).

The Buccaneer S.Mk.2 described

General

The Buccaneer S. Mk 2A, 2B, 2C and 2D aircraft are low level, long range strike/attack/recce aircraft. The Mk 2A and 2B are RAF aircraft: the Mk 2C and 2D are RN aircraft and are equipped for carrier operation. The Mk 2A and 2C are pre–Mod 118 aircraft and the Mk 2B and 2D are post–Mod 1188 aircraft (Mod 1188 introduced provision for carriage of Martel missiles). The different marks of aircraft are mentioned here only when it is necessary to describe a difference between them. The aircraft are powered by two Rolls-Royce Spey Mk 101 axial flow bypass turbojet engines. Two crew members are carried, pilot and navigator, seated in tandem in a cabin which is pressurised for high altitude flight.

A capacious bay, located in the lower half of the centre fuselage, is enclosed by a large door upon which weapons and other stores are mounted. When Mod 1600 is embodied, this door can be replaced by a bomb door tank (Mod 5300) which carries fuel in addition to weapons and stores. The bomb door or bomb door tank rotates through 180 degrees to the open position, exposing the stores and thus providing a launching or dropping platform. Underwing stores can be carried on pylons fitted to both the inner and outer planes.

The mainplanes incorporate a power-operated, single-break folding mechanism between the inner and outer planes, the outer planes folding upwards and inwards over the centre fuselage. The fuselage nose cone is folded rearwards to reduce the length of the aircraft for stowage.

During manufacture the fuselage structure is built in the following three main sections:

a) The basic cabin structure consists of front and rear pressure bulkheads (spanned at the top by two longerons), vertical frames and longitudinal stringers. A sliding, one-piece canopy – which can be jettisoned in an emergency – surmounts the structure. Extending between the bulkheads is a pressure floor on which the crew members' ejection seats and equipment are installed. Below the floor is a housing for the nosewheel unit.

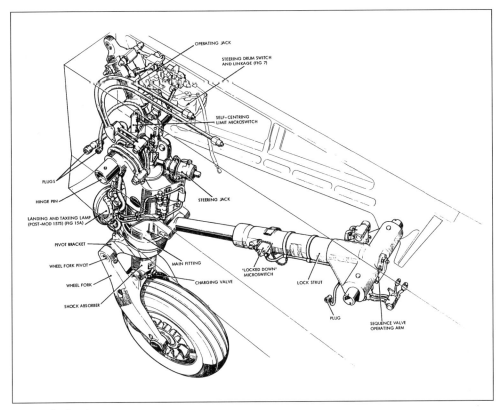

Nose wheel unit.

b) The centre fuselage, the main load-bearing structure, has three compartments arranged as follows:

1. An upper compartment, extending the length of the section, which is divided into eight integral fuel tanks.

2. Two lower compartments, the forward one of which is divided into two small equipment bays (housing hydraulic system components [front bay] and electrical equipment [aft bay]), and the large rear one forming the bomb bay.

c) At each extremity of the section is a bulkhead, between which are port and starboard longerons which run through the bomb and accessories bays. The fuel tank floor forms the roof for both lower bays; these compartments are separated by a substantial bulkhead. Reinforced frames are provided for the auxiliary, front and rear spar attachments.

A large bay in the rear fuselage accommodates radio and electrical equipment. Access is gained through a hatch positioned just forward of the housing for the arrester gear.

Each mainplane is a two-part assembly comprising inner and outer planes. The inner plane is attached to the centre fuselage section at three points – the auxiliary, front and rear spars. When assembled, the inner plane is classified as part of the centre fuselage and is not normally dismantled; small-span plain flaps are hinged to the trailing edge. The outer plane is of integral, stressed-skin construction, with an aileron, hinged to the trailing edge, extending the full span. The root ends of the outer plane spars are machined to form the hinge and latch fittings. Attachment fittings for wing pylons are provided on the inner and outer planes.

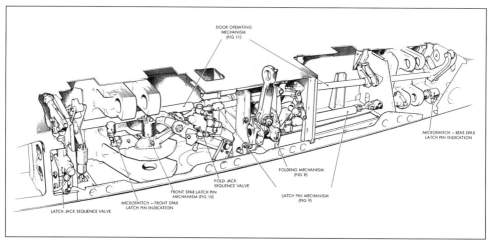

Wing fold mechanism diagram.

The tail unit comprises a large fin which is surmounted by an all-moving tailplane. A conventional rudder is hinged to the rear of the fin, while a trimming flap is hinged to the trailing edge of the tailplane. This flap is used in conjunction with an aileron droop mechanism and a blowing system for take-off and landing.

Tail unit structure.

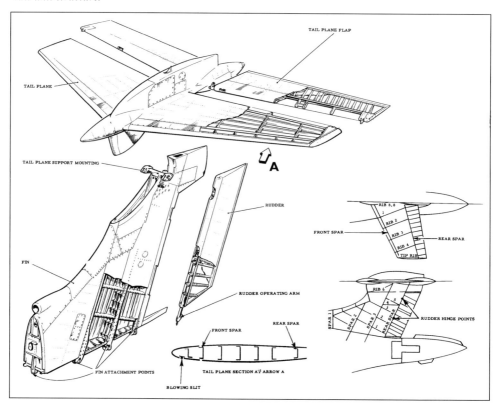

The landing gear is hydraulically-operated and comprises two main units which retract inwards, and a steerable nose-wheel unit which retracts rearwards. Hydraulically-operated disk brakes with anti-skid control, are fitted to the main wheels. A hydraulically-operated arrester hook and tail skid are fitted to all aircraft, and for carrier operation hold-back gear and two assisted take-off hooks are fitted to the fuselage of Mk 2C and 2D aircraft; all of these items are retractable when not in use.

The main flying control surfaces are controlled by an orthodox control column and rudder pedals, operation being effected by hydraulically-powered control units. Each power unit, one for each aileron, is fully duplicated by a tandem ram served by two independent hydraulic systems.

The wing flaps and airbrakes are also hydraulically-operated but are served by a different hydraulic system; provision is made for emergency operation.

Electrical actuators are connected to the three main control circuits to enable trimming to be effected. A single switch controls two electrical actuators which move the aileron droop mechanism and tailplane trimming flap, both surfaces functioning at a synchronised rate.

Hydraulically-operated feel units, controlled by pitot-static pressure, give simulated feel to the power-operated rudder and tailplane controls in relation to altitude and forward speed; this system is powered by the starboard flying controls hydraulic system.

The engines are installed one on each side of the fuselage centre section. The engine attachments comprise an inboard trunnion mounting on the engine horizontal centre line, a forward upper mounting which is attached to a cantilever beam extending from the bodyside, and a rear mounting linkage which is attached to a transverse beam in the upper nacelle structure.

Mounted on each engine are two accessories gearboxes, one driven from the engine low-pressure compressor shaft and the other driven from the engine

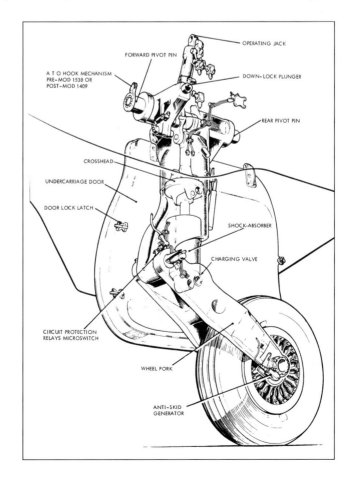

Main undercarriage unit.

Four 1,000lb HE bombs in the bomb bay.

high-pressure compressor shaft, and termed the left-hand and right-hand gearboxes, respectively. Included in the accessories driven by each engine right-hand gearbox is a constant-speed drive unit. These units in turn drive AC generators which provide the power for the aircraft electrical services.

Three tappings from the engine casing opposite the seventh stage of the HP compressor supply air pressure for the air bleed system. This system serves the blowing system, fuel system (for tank pressurisation, negative-g recuperators and fuel/no-air valves operation), windscreen rain clearance, hydraulic fluid reservoir pressurisation, constant speed drive unit (CSDU) oil tank pressurisation, CSDU oil ground cooling, engine bay cooling, radio bay air cooling and cabin air conditioning.

Subsidiary systems fed from the cabin air conditioning include windscreen demisting, windscreen washing, anti-g suits, accessories bay cooling, radome conditioning and pressurisation systems. A tapping from the top of the HP compressor supplies air for the engine anti-icing system.

Fuel is carried in eight integral tanks built into the upper compartment of the centre fuselage and coupled in pairs for supply purposes. Four of the tanks (master tanks) feed fuel direct to the engines, the other four serving as slave tanks to the master tanks. Fuel is transferred by air pressure from the slave tanks to replenish the master tanks as the fuel is consumed. The normal fuel capacity is increased when a bomb door tank (BDT) is installed. Fuel from this tank is transferred to the fuselage master tanks by electrically-driven pumps.

Overload tanks, comprising two jettisonable slipper tanks, one under each inner wing, and a bomb bay tank can be fitted. Fuel from these tanks is transferred by air pressure as fuel is used from the fuselage tanks.

A single pressure-refuelling coupling is provided for refuelling and defuelling on the ground. For air-to-air refuelling purposes, a refuel probe can be fitted to the nose of the aircraft.

From the tanks, fuel is supplied through hydraulically-driven flow proportioners, flowmeter transmitters and low-pressure cocks to the engines. An inter-tank transfer system and cross-feed system controlled by electrically-actuated cocks, together with pneumatically-operated negative-g recuperators, ensure that a fuel supply is always available, even when normal feed conditions cannot be maintained.

Four electrically-operated jettison valves allow fuel from all fuselage tanks to be discharged through a single outlet on the undersurfaces of the rear fuselage. Fuel in the overload tanks can be jettisoned through valve-operated outlets at the bottom rear of each tank. However, the jettison facility is removed from the bomb bay tank when it is fitted on a BDT and fuel from both tanks is jettisoned via the fuselage tanks jettison system.

To enable the aircraft to fulfil the role of an air-to-air refuelling tanker, a Mk 20E or C refuelling pod can be installed on a special pylon fitted to the starboard inner wing. When the aircraft is used as a tanker, fuel from the fuselage tanks can be transferred, through the pod, to the receiver aircraft. Fuel in the pod can also, if necessary, be transferred back into the fuselage tanks.

Power for the two flying controls hydraulic systems is supplied by two pumps, one on each engine right-hand gearbox. Each pump serves one half of each of the four powered control units so that, in the event of failure of either engine or pump, the flying controls remain operative.

Two more pumps, one on each right-hand gearbox, provide power for the general services hydraulic system. The general services include:

Landing gear
Nosewheel steering
Wheelbrakes
Wing flaps
Bomb door/BDT
Airbrakes
Wing-fold mechanism
Arrester hook
Tail skid
Fuel flow proportioners

This system can, under certain emergency conditions, supply hydraulic pressure to one of the two flying controls hydraulic systems.

A windscreen wiper, operated by an independent hydraulic system incorporating a pump driven by two electric motors, is also installed.

Two 30 kva, 200v, 400hz AC generators provide the primary source of electrical power. One air-cooled generator is driven by each engine through a CSDU. From the 200v AC supply, a 115v AC supply is

500lb HE bombs on tandem bomb racks. Designed for both FAA and RAF use, the racks were rarely used.

SAAF Buccaneer S.50 rocket pods.

obtained through a stepdown transformer, and a 28v DC supply obtained through two transformer rectifier units. A 24v lead-acid battery, located in the radio bay, is maintained fully charged off the main DC busbar. Should the generating system fail, the battery is automatically isolated from all but certain essential services.

Pitot and static pressures from the air-operated instruments are obtained from a pressure head on the leading edge of the port outer plane. The standby instruments and hydraulic feel systems are supplied with pitot pressure from a pressure head beneath the nose fuselage, true static being sensed by two static vents, one on each side of the folding nose.

The majority of the radio and electronic equipment is housed in the radio bay in the rear fuselage. Communication is by UHF and HF radio, the intercom system being incorporated in an associated centralised audio selector system.

A 36-rocket launching tube as used during the 1960s by FAA squadrons.

Gloworm rockets and two 1,000lb low drag HE bombs.

A podded, pressurised unit in the nose houses the scanner of a search radar installation, the nose cone being formed into a radome manufactured from resin-bonded glass cloth.

The integrated instruments, automatic pilot and electronic equipment combine with the radio and radar systems to form a control and navigational system and provide a weapon system for attack.

Type 6 MSB rocket-assisted ejection seats are fitted. A demand emergency oxygen set and a multi-service personal equipment connector, cater for the crew members services. Mod 1596 introduces a miniature detonating cord (MDC) system for the navigator and Mod 1480 introduces a similar system for the pilot. The systems operate independently of each other and are initiated when either firing handle on the respective ejection seat is pulled. Operation of an MDC system fractures the canopy transparency above the seat.

A 10-litre package unit, in the radio bay, contains liquid oxygen which is converted into gaseous oxygen for supply to the crew via Mk 17F or 17G regulators.

Fuel System

Eight integral fuel tanks extending the length of the centre fuselage, immediately above the bomb bay and accessories bay, supply fuel to the two engines. Post-Mod 1600 aircraft have provision for the installation of a bomb door tank. Fuel is transferred from this tank to the fuselage tanks by two electric pumps (normally only one is used). Overload tanks can be carried, these comprise two jettisonable slipper tanks to be installed under the inner wings and a tank to be mounted on the bomb door or bomb door tank The fuselage and overload tanks are pressurised by air from both engines. Two recuperators, one for each engine, ensure a supply of fuel to the engines under negative-g conditions for a limited time. Switches which close fuel/no-air valves in the master tanks can be used for fuel balancing. A switch controlling inter-tank transfer valves can be used to re-direct fuel flow as required. The supply to each engine can be interconnected by a cross-feed cock.

Air-to-air refuelling takes place through a probe fitted to the starboard

Flight refuelling 'buddy' pod and flash ejector pod.

side of the upper surface of the folding nose. The probe is connected to the forward end of the ground refuelling gallery. For operations not requiring air-to-air refuelling, the probe may be removed and the orifice blanked off. Flight refuelling is controlled by a 'Flight Refuel – On/Off' switch on the pilot's starboard console. Selecting this switch to 'On' isolates the overload tanks and bomb door tank (if fitted) fuel transfer circuits and connects the DC supplies required for operation of the refuel solenoids of all the refuel/defuel valves. The refuelling process is then automatically controlled by the tank high-level float switches. The overload tanks and BDT do not start to refuel until the fuselage tanks are full. The fuel-remaining indicator is reset by the fuel passing through the flow transmitter in the refuelling gallery. On completion of refuelling the 'Flight Refuel' switch must be selected to 'Off' or the transfer of fuel from all overload tanks and BDT will be prevented.

A streamlined pod, carried on a special pylon under the starboard inner wing is used to refuel other aircraft in flight. The pod receives its fuel from the aircraft fuel system and when not required for refuelling it acts as a normal wing tank. Operation of the flight refuelling pod is

Camera crate loaded into a Buccaneer S2 bomb bay.

automatic once certain settings and switch selections have been made. The pod has a self-contained hydraulic system for operating the hose drum and applying the brake, and a pneumatic system for emergency release of the emergency brake. A fuel pump is provided for pumping out the fuel and both it and the hydraulic pump are driven by a ram air turbine at the nose of the pod. The various electrical circuits are designed to make the refuelling operation as automatic as possible, except for trailing and winding-in the hose.

Engines

Two Spey Mk.101 engines are installed, one on each side of the fuselage at the inner wing root. The engine is a two-spool by-pass turbojet which has a four-stage low pressure (LP) compressor and a 12-stage high pressure (HP) compressor each driven by a two-stage turbine. The LP assembly is mechanically independent of the HP assembly, the LP shaft rotating inside the HP shaft. From the air inlet the air is drawn through the LP compressor; part of the air is then directed through the HP compressor and part through the by-pass duct. On leaving the HP compressor the air is directed through the combustion section which contains ten combustion liners and here the fuel is added. The mixture is ignited and the resulting gas is expanded through the turbines. From the turbines the gas passes to the exhaust mixer where it is mixed with the by-pass air flowing from the LP compressor. The total mass is expanded to atmosphere through the convergent propelling nozzle.

To maintain compressor stability in the lower speed range, variable incidence inlet guide vanes (IGV) and an HP compressor air bleed valve are fitted. When open, the valve permits air from a permanent bleed at the seventh stage to pass to the by-pass duct. The seventh stage bleed also provides air for the general services system and the blowing system for the boundary layer control. The pneumatically operated shut-off valves controlling the air supply to the mainplanes blowing system are supplied from the 12th stage; this stage also supplies air, on demand, for engine anti-icing purposes. An engine-driven HP pump supplies fuel to a fuel spray nozzle in each combustion liner. The pump is controlled by a single lever operating the HP cock and the throttle valve. Two gearboxes, one driven from the HP shaft and the other from the LP shaft, provide drives for accessories. The HP gearbox also receives the drive from an LP starter which, for starting purposes, is supplied with air from a Palouste starter, the latter being automatically controlled by the starting circuits. All the controls and indicators related to the engine systems are located in the pilot's cockpit.

Engine Air Bleed System
Both engines supply air through a common duct for mainplanes blowing. The following general services are supplied through another common duct:

Direct:
Tailplane blowing
Windscreen rain clearance
Radio bay hot air
Cabin air conditioning

Via a heat exchanger:
Fuel system
Main fuel tanks pressurisation
Fuel jettison system purging
Fuel/no-air valves operation
Wing tank pressurisation
Bomb bay tank pressurisation
Air-to-air refuelling pod pressurisation
Fuel recuperators operation
General services hydraulic system reservoir pressurisation
Radio bay air conditioning system

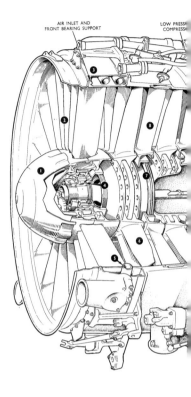

AIR INLET AND FRONT BEARING SUPPORT
1   Air inlet hub fairing
2   Inlet guide vanes
3   Anti-icing air manifold
4   Front bearing
5   Hot-air tube

LOW PRESSURE COMPRESSOR
6   Stage one rotor blades
7   Interstage air seal
8   Stage one stator vanes
9   LP compressor rotor drum
10 Oil feed tube
11 Oil return tube

COMPRESSOR INTERMEDIATE CASE
12 LP compressor rear bearing
13 Left-hand gearbox driving gear
14 Left-hand gearbox drive shaft
15 Right-hand gearbox driving gear
16 HP compressor front bearing
17 Internal gearbox
18 Outlet guide vanes
19 Variable inlet guide vanes

HIGH PRESSURE COMPRESSOR
20 Stage one rotor blades
21 Stage one stator vanes
22 Bleed valve
23 Air offtake bleed ports
24 HP compressor rotor shaft
25 Cooling air tube
26 LP compressor intermediate shaft.

DIFFUSER CASE
27 LP shaft thrust bearing
28 HP shaft thrust bearing
29 Liner airscoop
30 HP outlet guide vane
31 Hot-air manifold

COMBUSTION CASE
32 Fuel spray nozzle
33 Interconnector
34 Liner
35 Discharge nozzle

TURBINES
36 HP turbine bearing
37 HP turbine shaft
38 LP turbine shaft
39 LP cooling air manifold
40 HP1 nozzle guide vane
41 HP1 turbine blade
42 HP2 nozzle guide vane
43 HP2 turbine blade
44 LP1 nozzle guide vane
45 LP1 turbine blade
46 LP2 nozzle guide vane
47 LP2 turbine blade
48 LP turbine bearing

EXHAUST MIXER
49 LP turbine bearing housing spokes
50 Inner exhaust cone
51 Exhaust mixer annular nozzle

The Rolls-Royce Spey engine.

Each engine provides a direct supply for its own engine bay ventilation and constant speed drive unit oil cooling system.

Air is taken from each engine at three tappings off the HP compressor case opposite the seventh stage. The three bleeds merge within a common manifold beneath the rear of the engine, from which air is distributed through two large-bore ducts – one serving the mainplane blowing slits, and the other the general services system. All the controls and indicators related to the engine air bleed system are in the pilot's cockpit.

Flying controls

The flying controls are divided into main and auxiliary groups as follows:

Main control surfaces
(including trimmers)
1. Ailerons
2. Rudder
3. Tailplane

Auxiliary control
surfaces:
1. Mainplane flaps
2. Airbrakes
3. Tailplane flap

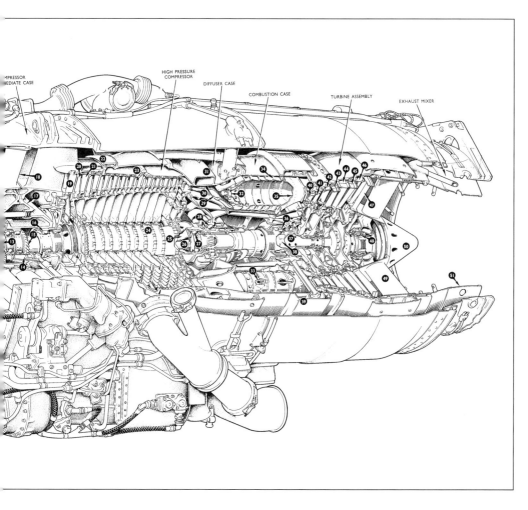

The main control surfaces are moved by powered control units (PCU) supplied from both flying controls hydraulic systems. The PCU are controlled by either manual demands by the pilot, via mechanical linkages, or an electrical input from the autopilot system. The autopilot system provides the following facilities:

1. Short period autostabilisation of the aircraft about the pitch, roll and yaw axes. This facility is normally in operation throughout the flight.

2. Automatic holding of the aircraft on any desired height, Mach number or heading. The heading lock facility is only available if the Mach lock or height lock mode is engaged. A standby yaw damper system is provided, but this is not used when the normal stabilisation yaw channel is engaged. A blowing system for boundary layer control is incorporated to give increased lift and control at low speed. Air from the engine air-bleed system is directed over the inner and outer mainplanes, mainplane flaps, ailerons and under the tailplane. To give feel to the controls, spring boxes are incorporated in the control linkages. Additional feel, relative to airspeed, is provided for the rudder and tailplane

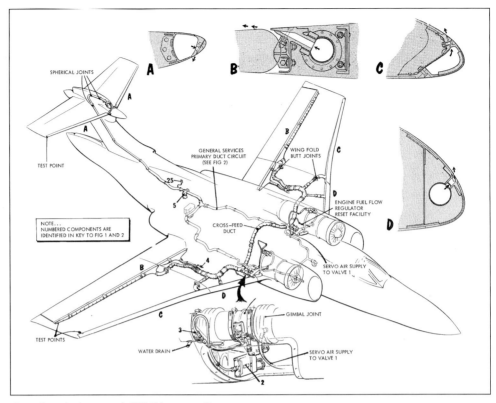

Boundary layer control (BLC) system diagram.

controls by hydraulic feel simulator units controlled by pitot pressure. Trimming is by electric actuators which act on the linkages between the controls (control column and rudder pedals) and the PCU. Both ailerons can be drooped, for use as additional flaps, while still maintaining normal differential control; the change in trim is approximately balanced by a tailplane flap which moves upwards. Aileron droop and tailplane flap are selected by the same lever switch. The control lever for the mainplane flaps is angled towards and has the same angular movement as the aileron droop lever, so that both levers can be used as one, when required. All the controls and indicators related to operation of the main control surfaces are in the pilot's cockpit. The airbrakes consist of two petals which are

hinged at their forward end and extend beyond the rear fuselage, forming a tail cone when closed. The airbrakes are hydraulically operated by power from the

The 1,000lb HE bomb twin carrier installation.

Tandem 1,000lb bomb pylon and Sidewinder missile installation (test flown in 1967 but not adopted by FAA).

normal side of the GS hydraulic system. Intermediate positions between 'in' and 'out' are obtained by releasing the operation switch which is spring loaded to the centre (off) position.

Undercarriage

The undercarriage comprises the port, starboard and nosewheel units, and the tailskid: all are operated by hydraulic power from the normal side of the GS hydraulic system. The undercarriage is controlled by three hydraulic selector valves, one for the leg jacks, one for the doors and up-locks, and one for the tail-skid jack. On Mk.2C and 2D aircraft, a deck take-off facility is provided to enable the pilot to select the undercarriage up immediately the aircraft is airborne and before the main oleo legs have fully extended. Nosewheel steering is available for 50 degrees to either side of the central trailing position. Steering is by a hydraulic jack powered by the normal side of the GS hydraulic system. The jack is controlled by an electrical drum switch which incorporates input and follow-up levers operated by the rudder controls

Rocket launcher for 36 x 2-inch projectiles.

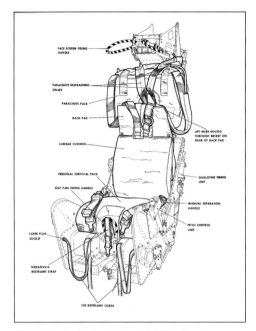
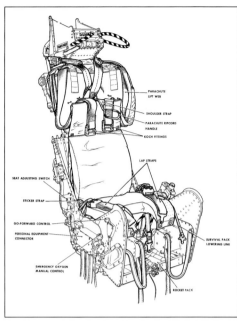

The Martin Baker Type 6 MSB ejection seat, port and starboard sides.

and nosewheel pivot bracket, respectively. The arresting hook is operated by power from the GS hydraulic system and is controlled by an up/down switch on the pilot's port control panel.

Ejection seats

An ejection seat Type 6 MSB1 Mk2 is provided for the pilot. A type 6 MSB2 ejection seat is provided for the navigator, the mark number depending upon the modification state as follows:

The Mk2 is the basic seat.

The Mk3 seat is identical to the Mk2 seat but with splayed thigh guards to provide greater knee clearance of the Martel TV display unit.

The Mk4 seat introduces an additional MDC breech unit fitted behind the seat to complement the navigator-initiated MDC system.

The Mk 5 seat is identical to the Mk4 seat, but with splayed thigh guards.

Attached to the underside of the seat pan is a multi-tubed rocket pack which sustains the thrust of the ejection gun giving a higher trajectory to enable ejection to be made from zero speed and zero height. The rocket tubes contain a solid propellant which is ignited by a firing body. A seat pan firing handle is fitted to the front of the seat as a primary or alternative method of initiating ejection. Leg restraint cords are provided to ensure that the seat occupant's legs are drawn back and held close to the seat pan during ejection. The miniature detonating cord (MDC) system enables the transparency above the navigator's station and pilot's station to be shattered before the seat passes through the canopy upon ejection. No separate controls are provided since the MDC is detonated by use of either the seat pan or face screen firing handle. A single sliding canopy, mounted on two jettison rails, encloses the tandem cockpits. The canopy is normally opened or closed by an electric actuator, controlled by a close/open level on the canopy control box on the pilot's cockpit starboard wall. The canopy can be jettisoned from three control positions, one above the pilot's instrument panel coaming, port side, one on the side of the navigator's port console and a third, external position on the port side of the front fuselage.

Aircraft limitations

The aircraft is cleared for operation in ambient temperatures not exceeding 40 degrees Celsius and is restricted to ground level ambient temperatures down to minus 10 degrees Celsius. Intentional spinning is prohibited. Intentional stalling is prohibited. Investigation of the 1g stall with the aircraft unblown in the 0-0-0 configuration is permitted but must not be continued beyond the ADD steady tone, the onset of buffet or engine banging, whichever occurs first. Investigation of the 1g stall in other configurations is prohibited. Inverted flight with negative-g is permitted for a period not exceeding 10 seconds. Deliberate sustained inverted flight is prohibited. Looping manoeuvres in the vertical plane are restricted to a half loop with a roll off the top. The limitations for this manoeuvre include a maximum AUW of 51,000lb, a maximum entry altitude of 7,000 feet, and a minimum entry speed of 530 knots with full power on entry.

Rolling with no external stores, the rudder autostabiliser or standby yaw damper and aileron autostabiliser must be engaged at all times. Use of rudder in rolling manoeuvres must be kept to a minimum. The application of further forward or back stick from the initial condition during rolling manoeuvres is prohibited.

Single engined flying may be carried out unblown throughout the full aircraft envelope, and blown up to 7,000 feet. In symmetric or rolling flight the angle of attack is not normally to be increased above that corresponding to buffet onset, ADD steady tone, engine disturbance or normal acceleration limits. However, on entry to toss manoeuvres penetration beyond buffet onset is permitted as necessary to follow the strike sight display, and in this case, audio onset or 16 units ADD is not to be exceeded at speeds greater than 0.75M.

Napalm tanks (flown during carriage trials but not officially part of FAA or RAF weapons fit for the Buccaneer).

XK527 carrying four Martel anti-radar missiles during trials from Holme-on-Spalding Moor in 1981.

Maximum speed limitations
Clean aircraft – 580 kt
Aircraft with pylons without stores, or with practice bomb carriers without stores – 580kt
With pylons and bare tandem beams – 560kt
Arresting hook lowering – 400kt
With aileron gearing set for low speed – 300kt
Undercarriage down – 225kt
Airbrakes – no restriction

Maximum AUW at take-off with blow on is 59,000lb, Normal landing AUW for a two-engined landing with blow off is 39,000lb.

Dimensions
Wing span – 44ft 0in
Area – 514.7 sq ft
Fuselage length – 63ft 5in
Height – 16ft 3in
Tailplane span – 14ft 3in

Landing gear
Wheelbase – 20ft 8in
Wheel track – 11ft 10.5in

Weights
Empty – 29,980lb
Maximum external load – 16,000lb
Internal fuel load – 12,480lb

Engines
Two Rolls-Royce Spey RB.168-1A Mk.101 non-afterburning turbofans
Thrust rating, each – 11,100lb

Performance
Maximum speed at sea level – 691 mph
Maximum strike range with external fuel and normal weapons load – 2,300 miles
Combat radius with full weapons load (hi-lo-lo-hi) – 600 miles
Take-off distance at maximum AUW – 3,400 ft
Landing distance – 3,150 ft

APPENDIX II

Buccaneer production

A Paveway laser-guided bomb and designator pod being test flown on XK527 at Holme-on-Spalding Moor.

XK486 (NA.39)
First flew 30/04/58 RAE Bedford. Trials aircraft. To Holme-on-Spalding Moor (HOSM) 09/04/58. Crashed on test flight due to engine failure 05/10/60 at Little Weighton, crew ejected.

XK487 (NA.39)
First flew 12/09/58 (HOSM). Trials aircraft. Transferred to Ferranti 1960 for radar development associated with Buccaneer and TSR.2. Fitted with TSR.2 radome. Withdrawn 1967, burnt at Farnborough on dump 07/68.

XK488 (NA.39)
First flew 13/11/58. Trials aircraft. Engine trials with Bristols at Filton and de Havilland at Hatfield. Retired to Fleet Air Arm Museum; on display at Yeovilton 1998.

XK489 (NA.39)
First flew 28/01/59. Trials aircraft. HOSM and A&AEE Boscombe Down. Canopy off tests and flight trials. Withdrawn and scrapped HOSM 1964.

XK490 (NA.39)
First Flew 23/03/59. Trials aircraft. Hot weather trials Malta 1959. Crashed Lyndhurst 12/10/59 after pilot lost control. Crew killed.

XK491 (NA.39)
First flew 29/05/59. Trials aircraft. Fitted with retractable refuelling probe. First spin tests. Ejection system trials. Withdrawn and scrapped HOSM 1966.

XK523 (NA.39)
First flew 29/07/59. Trials aircraft. Bomb release

24-tube rocket projectile pods.

trials 1960-61. Deck landing trials HMS *Victorious* 1960. A&AEE 02/63. Withdrawn and scrapped HOSM 1966.

XK524 (NA.39)
First flew 04/04/60. Trials aircraft. Handling research. Performed 8.9g pull 27/06/61. Extended chord ailerons. Crashed HOSM 13/05/65 due to tailplane stall. Crew ejected (first to eject using canopy miniature detonating chord system).

XK525 (NA.39)
First flew 15/07/65. Trials aircraft HOSM. PEE Foulness. RAE West Freugh. Withdrawn and burnt West Freugh dump 1992.

XK526 (NA.39)
First flew 29/08/60. Trials aircraft HOSM. First to S1 standard. Converted to S2 standard, first flight in this configuration 18/04/63. A&AEE 7/67. Withdrawn 1982, allocated 8684M. RAF Honington gate 1987.

XK527 (NA.39)
First flew 12/10/60. Trials aircraft HOSM. Converted to S2 standard. Hawker Siddeley and BAe trials aircraft. S2D modifications 29/10/66. Withdrawn 1991, allocated 8818M, battle damage repair airframe, RAF Lossiemouth. Scrapped Lossiemouth 1993, nose section preserved New Milton.

XK528 (NA.39)
First flew 21/11/60. Trials aircraft HOSM.

A&AEE 7/62. Crashed during weapons trails flight, Luce Bay 30/06/66.

XK529 (NA.39)
First flew 02/01/61. Trials aircraft HOSM. Crashed during catapult launch, HMS *Hermes* deck trials 31/08/61. Crew killed.

XK530 (NA.39)
First flew 15/02/61. Trials aircraft HOSM. RAE trials Farnborough, ground instructional airframe 1971. To RAE Bedford by road 16/04/73. Scrapped Bedford 03/90.

XK531 (NA.39).
First flew 18/05/61. Trials aircraft HOSM. To Royal Navy 700Z Flight Lossiemouth ('LM/680'). 809 NAS ('LM/227'). NASU 03/10/67, withdrawn Lossiemouth, allocated 8403M. To Winterbourne Gunner by road, NBC compound. Scrapped 1992.

XK532 (NA.39)
First flew 31/05/61). Trials aircraft HOSM. To Royal Navy 700Z ('LM/681'). 809 NAS ('LM/228'). 736 NAS ('LM/632'). RNEC Manandon 10/05/67, allocated 886M. Preserved Inverness.

XK533 (NA.39)
First flew 16/06/61. Trials aircraft HOSM and A&AEE. To Royal Navy 700Z Flight ('LM/682'). 809 NAS ('LM/229'). Crashed during single engine approach, Moray Firth 21/10/63. Cockpit with East Fortune Museum of Flight.

Camera crate (foreground) and flash crate (rear) in a Buccaneer bomb bay. The camera crate was used by the FAA and occasionally by the RAF. The flash crate was never used operationally.

XK534 (NA.39)
First flew 19/08/61. Trials aircraft HOSM. To Royal Navy 700Z ('LM/683'). 809 NAS ('LM/233'). 736 NAS ('LM/633'). To AES Arbroath 22/09/66. Withdrawn Arbroath 11/03/69.

XK535 (NA.39)
First flew 29/11/61. Trials aircraft HOSM. To Royal Navy 700Z ('LM/685'). Final development batch aircraft. 736 NAS ('LM/637'). Crashed on approach to Lossiemouth 18/08/62 ('LM/684'). A&AEE, PEE Shoeburyness 22/10/85. Pendine range 07/91. Scrapped 1992.

XN922 (S1)
First flew 23/01/61. First production standard aircraft. Delivered 19/02/62 A&AEE. Hot weather trials, Libya. Crashed Boscombe Down 05/07/62. To AIU Lee on Solent 21/02/63. Scrapped at Lee on Solent.

XN923 (S1)
Delivered 30/03/62. RAE trials West Freugh. 700Z 07/05/62. AHU Lossiemouth 03/07/62. A&AEE 05/08/63. Hawker Siddeley Brough 12/06/67. Boscombe Down. Withdrawn and transported to Vallance Collection, Charlwood, current 1997.

XN924 (S1)
DD 19/04/62. Royal Navy 736 NAS ('LM/220').

801 NAS ('R/115'). 809 NAS ('LM/220'). AES Arbroath 13/03/67. Scrapped at Arbroath.

XN925 (S1)
DD 29/05/62. Royal Navy. 801 NAS ('R/116'). 809 NAS ('LM/221'). 736 NAS ('LM/640'). Instructional airframe at Lossiemouth 03/09/69. To Catterick, crash & rescue training. Destroyed 1988.

XN926 (S1)
DD 19/06/62. Royal Navy. 801 NAS ('R/117'). 809 NAS. 736 NAS. RNAY Sydenham 17/07/66. 736 NAS. NASU Lossiemouth 16/05/68. To Pendine ranges, scrapped 1992.

XN927 (S1)
DD 13/07/62. Royal Navy 801 NAS ('R/118'). 809 NAS ('LM/223'). AHU Lossiemouth 18/02/64. Crashed near Elgin 25/03/64.

XN928 (S1)
DD 16/07/62. Royal Navy 801 NAS ('R/119'). 809 NAS ('LM/224'), 736 NAS ('LM/641' and 'LM/631'). St Athan instructional airframe 31/03/70, allocated 8179M. To Wales Air Museum, Rhoose. Scrapped 1996. Nose to Phoenix Aviation, Bruntingthorpe.

XN929 (S1)
DD 04/10/62. Royal Navy 801 NAS ('R/120'). AHU Tengah 28/11/63. RNAY Belfast 07/10/64. 736 NAS 02/12/66. 800 NAS ('E/108'). Withdrawn Lossiemouth, allocated 8051M. Scrapped 1991, Elgin. Nose to RAF Cranwell.

XN930 (S1)
DD 07/02/63. Royal Navy 801 NAS ('R/121'). 800 NAS ('E/106') 28/02/66. 736 NAS

A WE177 bomb on the port station in a Buccaneer S2 bomb bay.

A WE177 on the Buccaneer S2's port station. Note bomb bay fairing designed for the WE177.

('LM/632') 13/02/69. NASU Lossiemouth 18/01/71, allocated 8180M. To Honington Battle Damage Repair Flight. Scrapped Hanningfield Metals 1991.

XN931 (S1)
DD 21/12/62. Royal Navy 801 NAS ('V/122'). Crashed Singapore 15/11/64.

XN932 (S1)
DD 08/01/63. Royal Navy 801 NAS ('R/115'). 800 NAS ('E/109') 06/04/65. Withdrawn 23/03/67 to Lee on Solent.

XN933 (S1)
DD 24/01/63. Royal Navy 801 NAS ('V/116'). 736 NAS 23/09/66. NASU Lossiemouth 26/09/68. To PEE Pendine. Destroyed 1992.

XN934 (S1)
DD 04/02/63. Royal Navy 736 NAS ('LM/633'). 801 NAS ('V/117'). 736 NAS ('LM/631') 08/10/65. To Lee on Solent 15/05/68. To Predannack fire dump 10/92, destroyed 1993.

XN935 (S1)
DD 16/02/63. Royal Navy 801 NAS ('V/118'). AHU Tengah 03/01/64. 801 NAS ('V/124') 09/07/64. Crashed Singapore 19/08/64.

XN942 (S1)
DD 11/03/64. Royal Navy 801 NAS.

XN945 (S1)
DD 28/07/64. Royal Navy 801 NAS. 736 NAS 30/05/67.

XN948 (S1)
DD 01/03/63. Royal Navy ('V/119'). Aircraft

ditched near HMS *Victorious* off Changi, Singapore, 26/11/64.

XN949 (S1)
DD 15/01/63. Royal Navy 736 NAS ('LM/641'). 809 NAS 21/01/63. RNAHU Tengah 10/10/63. 801 NAS ('V/120') 07/12/63. 736 NAS ('LM/641') 08/10/65. Crashed Moray Firth 08/08/65.

XN950 (S1)
DD 31/01/63. Royal Navy 809 NAS 05/09/63. 736 NAS ('LM/635') 27/03/65. Crashed on overshoot from Lossiemouth, Sweet Hillock Farm 28/03/66.

XN951 (S1)
DD 02/03/63. Royal Navy 809 NAS. 800 NAS ('E/101') 27/04/64. 736 NAS 16/11/70. Crashed on overshoot at Lossiemouth 01/12/70.

XN952 (S1)
DD 19/02/63. Crashed HOSM 19/02/63.

XN953 (S1)
DD 22/03/63. Royal Navy 800 NAS ('E/107'). 801 NAS ('V/115') 02/04/65. 736 NAS 22/07/65. NASU Changi 07/01/66. 800 NAS 26/05/66. 736 NAS ('LM/637') 09/01/70. NASU Lossiemouth 22/01/70. To St Athan, allocated 8182M. To SAH Culdrose A2655 ('SAH-23'). To fire dump Predannack, destroyed 1992.

XN954 (S1)
DD 01/04/63. Royal Navy 801 NAS ('V/123'). AHU Tengah 26/11/63. 736 NAS ('LM/631') 14/03/69. NASU Lossiemouth 21/01/71. SAH Culdrose 30/07/71. Dumped off HMS *Ark Royal* for RN safety film 14/04/74.

XN955 (S1)
DD 28/03/63. Royal Navy 801 NAS ('V/124').
AHU Tengah 22/06/64. A&AEE C Squadron
14/07/67. NASU Lossiemouth 15/02/68. SOC
25/02/69. To PEE Foulness, destroyed 1992.

XN956 (S1)
DD 22/04/63. Royal Navy 801 NAS. 800 NAS
('E/100') 17/03/64. 801 NAS 21/04/65. 736
NAS 21/04/66. To Laarbruch for Battle Damage
Repair Flight, allocated 8059M 06/90 (marked as
15 Sqn 'K'). Scrapped 1992.

XN957 (S1)
DD 24/04/63. Royal Navy 801 NAS. 809 NAS
28/01/65. 736 NAS ('LM/640') 27/03/65.
NASU Lossiemouth 26/02/71. To FAA Museum,
Yeovilton 01/90 ('LM/630').

XN958 (S1)
DD 03/05/63. Royal Navy 801 NAS. 800 NAS
('E/111') 09/08/65. Crashed off Singapore
20/11/65.

XN959 (S1)
DD 10/06/63. Royal Navy, to A&AEE. 800 NAS
('E/103') 13/03/64. 736 NAS 02/06/67. 803
NAS ('LM/610'). NASU Lossiemouth
23/01/68. To PEE Foulness. Destroyed 1992.

XN960 (S1)
DD 04/07/63. Royal Navy 809 NAS ('LM/225').
800 NAS ('E/100') 14/07 65. 801 NAS ('V/121')
22/11/68. NASU Lossiemouth 22/04/68. To
RAE Farnborough. PEE Foulness, destroyed 1992.

XN961 (S1)
DD 28/06/63. Royal Navy 809 NAS. 800 NAS

('E/108') 15/10/64. 736 NAS ('LM/634')
08/04/65. Crashed Helmsdale 25/06/65. Crew
killed.

XN962 (S1)
DD 09/07/63. Royal Navy 809 NAS ('LM/235').
800 NAS ('E/110') 25/09/64. 736 NAS
('LM/635') 26/05/69. NASU Lossiemouth
20/01/71. Scrapped 1972, nose to RAF
Exhibition Flight.

XN963 (S1)
DD 29/07/63. Royal Navy 800 NAS ('E/104').
803 NAS ('LM/612') 16/10/67. NASU
Lossiemouth 29/02/68. To PEE Foulness,
scrapped 1992.

XN964 (S1)
DD 27/08/63. Royal Navy 801 NAS ('V/118').
800 NAS 16/07/65. 736 NAS 06/12/65. 803
NAS ('LM/613') 31/01/68. NASU Lossiemouth
1971. To Newark Air Museum.

XN965 (S1)
DD 04/09/63. Royal Navy 809 NAS ('LM/225').
800 NAS 11/08/64. 736 NAS ('LM/636')
10/01/66. AHU Lossiemouth 29/06/66. 736
NAS 27/10/70. To PEE Pendine range.
Destroyed 1992.

XN966 (S1)
DD 25/09/63. Royal Navy 809 NAS ('LM/226').
809 NAS 08/11/63. Crashed on runway,
Lossiemouth 24/01/64.

XN967 (S1)
DD 02/10/63. Royal Navy 809 NAS. 736 NAS
27/03/65. NASU Lossiemouth 26/01/70. To

The Rolls-Royce Spey engine installation during construction at Brough.

XK527 carrying four Martel anti-radar missiles during trials from Holme-on-Spalding Moor in 1981. The HOSM title was applied in Day-Glo orange.

Above: *XK527 carrying a pair of 17BC dispenser pods during flight trials in 1978.*

Another picture of XK527 with two SG357 munitions dispenser pods pictured during flight trials from Holme-on-Spalding Moor in 1979.

The HB876 munitions dispenser pod fitted in the Buccaneer's bomb bay, 1979.

A close-up view of the twin HB876 dispenser during trials on XW988 in 1980.

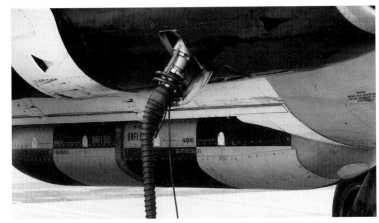

A close-up view of the 17BC munitions pod during trials at Holme-on-Spalding Moor. This pod was not adopted for RAF use.

Flambards Theme Park, Helston ('E/103'). Dismantled 1995, nose section to private collection, Mucklebridge, 1996.

XN968 (S1)
DD 16/01/63. Royal Navy. To A&AEE 23/01/64. 800 NAS ('E/105') 12/03/64. 736 NAS 03/03/69. Crashed into forest near Lossiemouth 08/12/71.

XN969 (S1)
DD 13/11/63. Royal Navy 800 NAS ('E/106'). AHU Lossiemouth 21/06/65. Crashed south of Khormaksar 09/10/65.

XN970 (S1)
DD 03/12/63. Royal Navy 800 NAS ('E/107'). 800 NAS 25/06/65. Crashed Beira, Mozambique (operating from HMS *Eagle*) 25/03/66.

XN971 (S1)
DD 13/12/63. 800 NAS ('E/102'). 736 NAS 02/06/67. 803 NAS 03/07/67. NASU Lossiemouth 09/09/68. NASU Sydenham 1970. RAE West Freugh 17/09/70 as spares source. Scrapped 1972.

XN972 (S1)
DD 15/01/64. Royal Navy. 809 NAS. 800 NAS ('E/108') 15/09/64. 801 NAS ('R/122') 05/04/65. 736 NAS ('LM/642') 22/07/65. SOC 21/09/71. To PEE Foulness, destroyed 1992, nose section to RAF Exhibition Flight.

XN973 (S1)
DD 02/12/63. Royal Navy. To A&AEE. AHU Tengah 02/12/64. 800 NAS ('E/108'). 801 NAS ('R/119') 03/02/65. 736 NAS ('LM/643') 27/06/66. NASU Lossiemouth 06/10/70. To BAe Warton 1988 ('LM/633'). Destroyed 1994.

XN974 (S2A)
DD 18/06/64. MoD. To A&AEE. HOSM trials aircraft. To BAe Warton. Yorkshire Air Museum.

XN975 (S1)
DD 13/07/64. MoD(PE) trials, weapons evaluation. RAE West Freugh. RRE Pershore. RAE Bedford 11/05/77. RAE Farnborough 10/73. Crashed 14/06/78 following near miss with a German civilian helicopter, near Bruggen.

XN976 (S2B)
DD 31/08/64. First service aircraft for Royal Navy. A&AEE 05/09/65. HMS *Hermes* 15/03/67. To RAF 09/71. 237 OCU. Modified to S2B standard. 12 Sqn 01/75 ('NF'). BAe 02/87.

12 Sqn. Crashed 09/07/92 following PFCU failure, 50 miles east of RAF Leuchars.

XN977 (S2B)
DD 27/10/64. 700B Flight ('230/LM'). 801 NAS ('230/H'). To RAF 02/75. 12 Sqn. 237 OCU (04/76). Converted to S2B standard. 15 Sqn ('G') 14/11/80. Heavy landing 08/03/82, placed in long term storage. Scrapped at Shawbury 10/91.

XN978 (S2B)
DD 04/11/64. 700B Flight ('726/LM'). 801 NAS ('231/LM') 26/10/67. 800 NAS ('114/E') 25/11/68. To RAF 03/71. 12 Sqn. Crashed near Creil, France, 05/06/71.

XN979 (S1)
DD 20/11/64. 700B Flight ('727/LM'). 801 NAS ('232/V'). Crashed off Lizard Point, 09/06/66. Cockpit section with 2157 Sqn (Mitcham) ATC.

XN980 (S2)
DD 17/01/65. 736 NAS ('652/LM'). 801 NAS ('233/V'). 800 NAS 31/08/67. 736 NAS. Crashed 03/03/69 following collision with XV159, 10 miles south of Wick.

XN981 (S2B)
DD 04/02/65. 801 NAS ('234/V'). 809 NAS ('026/R'). 800 NAS ('115/E'). To RAF 06/71. 237 OCU. 12 Sqn. Returned to RN 809 NAS ('026/R'). To S2B standard. Returned to RAF. 208 Sqn 04/79. 12 Sqn. Scrapped Lossiemouth 03/94.

XN982 (S2A)
DD 03/03/65. 809 NAS ('024/R'). Damaged at Cecil Field, USA. 19 MU 07/78. Placed in storage at Farnborough. To Brough by road 06/82. Fatigue test specimen. Scrapped at Brough 07/92.

XN983 (S2B)
DD 29/03/65. RNAY Sydenham. 12 Sqn 29/08/72. 237 OCU 01/73. 12 Sqn 01/78. 15 Sqn 02/79. 208 Sqn 03/84. 12 Sqn 05/84. Stored Shawbury, scrapped 02/94.

XT269 (S2).
DD 26/04/65. 700B Flight ('236/LM'). 809 NAS ('031/R'). Rolled off deck of HMS *Ark Royal* 15/02/72. Not recovered.

XT270 (S2B)
DD 04/05/65. 700B Flight ('237/LM'). 801 NAS ('237/H'). 800 NAS ('107/E'). Transferred to RAF 22/12/70. 12 Sqn 02/71. 237 OCU 05/73.

Converted to S2B standard. 237 OCU 06/76. 208 Sqn 10/76. St Athan store 08/81. Stored Shawbury 02/06/83. Scrapped 10/91.

XT271 (S2A)
DD 11/05/65. 700B Flight ('240/LM'). 800 NAS ('105/E'). To RAF. 12 Sqn 07/73. 237 OCU 12/73. 208 Sqn 02/75. 15 Sqn 02/78. 16 Sqn 05/78. 237 OCU 06/79. Stored St Athan 01/84. 237 OCU 13/05/87. 12 Sqn 28/03/88. Scrapped Elgin 04/93.

XT272 (S2A)
DD 05/07/65. 801 NAS ('241/H'). 736 NAS. 800 NAS. To MoD(PE) 08/71. Marshalls Cambridge 1973. Tornado nose modification. To BAe Warton and RAE Farnborough. Withdrawn and stored at Bedford. Scrapped at Farnborough 10/92.

XT273 (S2A)
DD 14/07/65. 801 NAS ('242/V'). 800 NAS ('113/E'). 809 NAS ('025/R') 22/05/70. To RAF. 237 OCU 06/75. 208 Sqn 09/75. 237 OCU 17/08/77. St Athan 21/11/79. 12 Sqn 16/05/88. 208 Sqn 29/06/88. 12 Sqn 06/07/88. Scrapped Elgin 10/92.

XT274 (S2A)
DD 16/07/65. 800 NAS ('103/E'). 736 NAS. 809 NAS. To RAF. 12 Sqn. 03/04/74. 237 OCU 08/12/75. St Athan 22/06/77. 208 Sqn 31/08/77. 237 OCU 04/03/83. To Abingdon BDRF 21/05/85 (8856M). Pendine Range 12/89. Destroyed Pendine 06/95.

XT275 (S2B)
DD 29/07/65. 801 NAS ('235/H'). 736 NAS. 801 NAS. 809 NAS 28/01/73. To RAF. 208 Sqn 06/09/74. Bitteswell 05/11/76. To S2B standard 22/09/78. 15 Sqn ('A') 15/11/78. St Athan store 15/08/80. To storage at Shawbury 15/06/83. Scrapped 10/93.

XT276 (S2B)
DD 24/09/65. 801 NAS ('242/H'). 800 NAS 06/05/70. To RAF. 12 Sqn 25/04/72. 237 OCU 01/05/73. To S2B standard 31/10/75. 12 Sqn 05/11/75. 15 Sqn 19/08/80. 16 Sqn ('S') 26/08/80. Cat.3 accident at Laarbruch 01/01/82. St Athan storage 30/06/82. Shawbury storage 08/06/83. Catterick fire section 08/06/86. Destroyed 01/87.

XT277 (S2B)
DD 25/08/65. 801 NAS ('243/H'). 809 NAS ('320/H') 22/01/66. 800 NAS ('101/E'). To RAF. 12 Sqn 19/04/73. To S2B standard 19/02/75. 237

OCU 29/03/76. To Shawbury store 10/08/83 (8853M). To 2SoTT Cosford 23/10/85. Scrapped at Cosford. Nose to Bruntingthorpe.

XT278 (S2A)
DD 04/10/65. 809 NAS ('321/H'). 800 NAS ('104/E'). To RAF. 208 Sqn 11/09/74. 12 Sqn 06/01/77. 15 Sqn 04/03/77. 208 Sqn 05/05/77. 237 OCU 15/02/78. Grounded due to fatigue. To St Athan 23/07/80. To Catterick 31/03/83. Scrapped at Catterick 03/84.

XT279 (S2B)
DD 26/10/65. 809 NAS ('322/H'). A&AEE 08/06/66. 809 NAAS 09/05/68. 800 NAS ('102/E') 27/07/70. To RAF. 12 Sqn 42/11/72. 237 OCU 16/08/74. To S2B standard. 15 Sqn ('C') 17/11/80. 16 Sqn (gloss black colour scheme). To St Athan storage 12/03/84. 208 Sqn 07/10/86. Scrapped at Lossiemouth 12/05/92.

XT280 (S2A)
DD 02/11/65. 809 NAS ('323/H'). 736 NAS 05/12/71. To RAF. 16 Sqn 03/08/81. 12 Sqn 06/03/84. 208 Sqn 03/07/84. 12 Sqn 09/12/86. 208 Sqn. Scrapped at Lossiemouth 03/94.

XT281 (S2B)
DD 11/11/65. 809 NAS ('324/H'). 736 NAS 13/09/66. 801 NAS ('237/E'). To RAF. 237 OCU 27/09/71. To S2B standard 20/11/72. 12 Sqn 11/04/73. Grounded at Cold Lake. Shipped to Lossiemouth 17/10/80 (8705M) ('ET') weapons loading trainer. Scrapped at Elgin 10/92.

XT282 (S2)
DD 23/11/65. 809 NAS ('325/H'). 800 NAS ('102/E'). Crashed 31/08/70 following hydraulic failure over Moray Firth.

XT283 (S2A)
DD 07/12/65. 809 NAS. 800 NAS ('111/E') 09/01/67. 809 NAS 30/01/70. To RAF. 208 Sqn 17/12/75. 237 OCU ('G') 24/01/77. To Lossiemouth, 237 OCU ('GC'). A&AEE 24/09/87.

XT284 (S2A)
DD 13/12/65. 736 NAS. 809 NAS 21/03/66. 736 NAS 06/03/69. 809 NAS 17/04/72. To RAF. 208 Sqn 10/01/75. 15 Sqn 20/12/76. 237 OCU ('H') 25/11/77. St Athan storage 21/12/83. Transferred to Abingdon BDRF 21/05/85 (8855M). Destroyed Abingdon.

XT285 (S2A)
DD 20/12/65. 736 NAS. 809 NAS 30/08/66. 736 NAS 25/07/68. To Marshalls Cambridge

('Tornado nose refit). MoD(PE) Warton 72. Crashed 05/07/78 near West Freugh.

XT286 (S2A)
DD 06/01/66. 800 NAS ('112/E'). 809 NAS ('022/R'). To RAF. 12 Sqn 10/03/74. 237 OCU. 16 Sqn 03/01/80. St Athan storage 28/09/83. 208 Sqn 31/10/86. Station Flight Lossiemouth 02/11/87. 208 Sqn 16/11/87. To Abingdon. By road to Shawbury, scrapped 08/93.

XT287 (S2B)
DD 02/02/66. 801 NAS ('230/H'). 809 NAS ('033/R'). To RAF. 237 OCU 15/03/71. To S2B standard 08/08/73. Transferred to Navy 809 NAS 09/08/73. Transferred to RAF, 15 Sqn ('F – *McRoberts Reply*') 05/08/80. 16 Sqn, St Athan storage 13/03/84. 12 Sqn 30/01/85. 208 Sqn ('ES') 22/03/85. 237 OCU ('G') 21/03/88. 12 Sqn 17/10/88. Scrapped at Lossiemouth 12/05/92.

XT288 (S2B)
DD 18/02/66. 800 NAS ('102/E'). To RAF. 12 Sqn 12/04/72. 237 OCU 22/01/73. To S2B standard. 12 Sqn 01/10/75. 208 Sqn 05/01/79. BAe Holme-on-Spalding Moor 01/08/80. 12 Sqn 20/08/87. A&AEE. To Lossiemouth (9134M). Withdrawn 03/94. To East Fortune museum.

XV152 (S2A)
DD 27/04/66. 809 NAS ('024/R'). 736 NAS. 803 NAS 30/07/68. To RAF. 208 Sqn 30/12/74. 237 OCU 23/09/77. St Athan storage 04/02/81. Transported to Swanton Morley (8776M) 31/03/88.

XV153 (S2)
DD 29/04/66. 801 NAS ('232/V'). Crashed in Subic Bay 06/10/66 during evaluation flight from HMS *Victorious*.

XV154 (S2A)
DD 19/05/66. 800 NAS ('106/E'). 809 NAS ('021/R'). To RAF. 237 OCU 07/03/75. St Athan store 12/06/84. To Lossiemouth (8854M) BDRF. Scrapped 09/92.

XV155 (S2B)
DD 26/06/66. 801 NAS ('233/H'). To RAF 02/10/69. 12 Sqn. 237 OCU 09/01/73. To S2B standard 01/08/75. 12 Sqn 11/05/76. A&AEE 29/03/79. St Athan storage 12/09/80. To Brough 01/10/81 (8716M). Fuselage used for tests, transferred to MoD(PE) 06/01/84. Scrapped Macclesfield.

XV156 (S2A)
DD 16/06/66. 800 NAS ('100/E'). 809 NAS 16/09/69. To RAF. 208 Sqn 15/10/74. 237 OCU 20/09/77. St Athan store 21/01/81. Withdrawn St Athan (8773M), Battle Damage Flight. Destroyed at St Athan 07/91.

XV157 (S2B)
DD 28/06/66. 800 NAS ('107/E'). To RAF. 12 Sqn 16/06/70. Transferred to RN 736 NAS 11/01/71. Modified to S2B standard 19/07/72. To RAF. 12 Sqn 19/07/72. 237 OCU 30/04/73. 208 Sqn 13/09/76. 12 Sqn 28/11/79. St Athan store 14/10/80. Transferred to Shawbury 11/05/83. Scrapped 10/91.

XV158 (S2)
DD 22/07/66. 736 NAS ('655/LM'). Ditched 20/05/68, Moray Firth, following hydraulic failure.

XV159 (S2)
DD 29/07/66. 800 NAS ('101/E'). 736 NAS ('641/LM'). Crashed 03/03/69 in North Sea, 10 miles east of Wick, following collision with XN980.

XV160 (S2B)
DD 17/08/66. 800 NAS ('104/E'). 803 NAS ('610/LM'). To RAF. 237 OCU 12/03/73. To S2B standard 11/05/76. 208 Sqn 11/02/76. 12 Sqn 21/11/79. To St Athan store 10/12/80. 16 Sqn ('X') 12/08/81. Crashed 20/09/82 off Sardinia after stalling during an attack manoeuvre.

XV161 (S2B)
DD 01/09/66. 800 NAS ('105/E'). 809 NAS 17/04/70. To RAF. 208 Sqn 02/10/74. To S2B standard 11/02/77. 208 Sqn 09/01/79. St Athan store 12/09/80. 208 Sqn 02/12/80. 12 Sqn ('AF') 08/07/83. Allocated 9117M, scrapped Lossiemouth 03/94.

XV162 (S2B)
DD 21/09/66. 801 NAS ('232/H') ('240/H'). To RAF. 12 Sqn 11/05/72. Crashed in North Sea near Bridlington 13/06/72.

XV163 (S2A)
DD 30/09/66. 800 NAS ('110/E'). 809 NAS 30/01/70. To RAF. 237 OCU 08/05/75. 208 Sqn 01/09/75. St Athan store 07/03/84. 237 OCU 17/06/88. Shawbury store 02/94. Scrapped 03/92. Nose section preserved at Bruntingthorpe.

XV164 (S2)
DD 01/11/66. 801 NAS ('235/H'). Crashed 16/09/69 at Beinn Ruadh, south of Strathy Point.

XV165 (S2B)
DD 27/10/66. 803 NAS ('610/LM'). 800 NAS 29/10/68. 809 NAS 07/03/69. 801 NAS 28/04/69. To RAF. 12 Sqn 09/07/70. To S2B standard 23/05/73. 12 Sqn ('BF') 11/10/85. 237 OCU 21/03/88. Stored Shawbury, scrapped 02/94. Cockpit section sold.

XV166 (S2B)
DD 25/11/66. 736 NAS. To RAF. 237 OCU 04/06/71. To S2B standard 16/01/73. 16 Sqn 14/06/73. 15 Sqn ('FF') 17/10/75. Crashed on approach to Honington 04/03/76.

XV167 (S2A)
DD 06/12/66. 801 NAS ('236/H'). Crashed on launch from HMS *Hermes* 29/01/70.

XV168 (S2B)
DD 13/12/66. 801 NAS ('231/H'). To RAF. 12 Sqn 28/10/71. To S2B standard 07/07/72. 12 Sqn 15/12/72. 12 Sqn ('CF') 10/06/85. 208 Sqn ('VS') 11/06/85. 237 OCU 13/10/86. 208 Sqn 03/92. To Brough 15/10/93. On display.

XV332 (S2B)
DD 16/01/67. 801 NAS ('233/H'). 809 NAS ('026/R'). To RAF. 12 Sqn 04/02/72. 237 OCU 04/10/72. 15 Sqn 08/11/73. To RN 809 NAS 02/04/74. To RAF, modified to S2B standard. 216 Sqn 22/10/79. 12 Sqn 01/08/80. 208 Sqn ('RS') 02/09/83. 237 OCU 10/06/86. Reserve Op. Granby aircraft (*Dirty Harriet*). To Cottesmore 03/94. To Marham 05/04/94, last RAF Buccaneer flight.

XV333 (S2B)
DD 27/01/67. 809 NAS ('030/R'). 801 NAS ('234/H'). To RAF. 12 Sqn 13/12/71. 237 OCU 14/11/72. 16 Sqn 14/08/73. To RN 02/04/74. To S2B standard, 15 Sqn 27/11/78. 16 Sqn 16/08/79. St Athan store 16/09/80. 12 Sqn 15/10/81. 208 Sqn 19/05/86. To Yeovilton for display 23/03/94.

XV334 (S2B)
DD 06/02/67. 801 NAS ('234/H'). 736 NAS 20/08/68. To RAF. 12 Sqn 08/12/72. To S2B standard 05/11/75. 237 OCU 28/06/76. 12 Sqn 01/06/78. 15 Sqn ('D') 01/06/78. St Athan store 13/02/81. To Shawbury store 05/05/83. Scrapped 10/91.

XV335 (S2A)
DD 14/02/67. 736 NAS ('656/LM'). Crashed North Minch 01/07/68.

XV336 (S2A)
DD 28/02/67. 800 NAS ('115/E'). 801 NAS

('238/LM'). To RAF. 12 Sqn 08/11/72. 237 OCU 15/01/73. MoD(PE) 14/03/78. 208 Sqn 04/04/78. St Athan store 24/09/80. To Shawbury store 13/04/83. 12 Sqn 02/89. To Shawbury store, scrapped 10/91

XV337 (S2C)
DD 10/03/67. 800 NAS ('101/E'). 809 NAS 24/07/72. To MoD(PE) 10/73. Weapons trials A&AEE. Withdrawn 06/84. BDRF Abingdon ('8852M'). To St Athan, scrapped 08/92.

XV338 (S2A)
DD 29/03/67. 736 NAS. 801 NAS ('236/H'). To RAF. 12 Sqn 27/12/72. 237 OCU 02/10/74. To St Athan store 29/01/81. Broken up 14/01/83. Cockpit to Honington ('8774M'). To Pendine Range 07/91.

XV339 (S2A)
DD 07/04/67. 736 NAS ('643/LM'). 809 NAS 29/04/68. To RNAY Sydenham 24/05/71. Crashed 06/10/72 during test flight.

XV340 (S2B)
DD 26/04/67. 809 NAS. 736 NAS 30/09/69. 801 NAS ('235/H'). To RAF. 16 Sqn 04/06/73. 12 Sqn 13/03/75. 208 Sqn 23/06/77. 15 Sqn 19/01/79. To Brough for fatigue tests ('8659M') 31/03/80. To Abingdon 22/08/80. To Honington BDRF 17/09/80. To Farnborough 06/07/83. To Pendine Range 07/91.

XV341 (S2B)
DD 01/05/67. 800 NAS ('113/E'). To RAF. 12 Sqn 06/07/73. 237 OCU 09/09/74. To S2B standard 06/12/76. 208 Sqn 03/08/78. 15 Sqn 02/10/81. 16 Sqn 07/83. MoD(PE) Holme-on-Spalding Moor 14/11/83. 12 Sqn ('RF') 02/04/85. Crashed on landing at Lossiemouth 14/06/85. Remains to Brough 03/02/86.

XV342 (S2B)
DD 16/05/67. 803 NAS. 736 NAS 23/05/68. 800 NAS 29/04/70. To RAF. 12 Sqn 24/01/73. 16 Sqn 11/09/80. 237 OCU 26/01/81. 16 Sqn 08/04/81. St Athan store 13/03/84. 208 Sqn 09/10/88. Scrapped Lossiemouth 04/93.

XV343 (S2A)
DD 16/05/67. 800 NAS ('111/E'). 809 NAS ('033/R'). Crashed near Honington 12/04/73.

XV344 (S2)
DD 09/06/67. 800 NAS ('105/E'). 809 NAS. To MoD(PE) trials, Holme-on-Spalding Moor. Cranfield 09/80. To Kemble for respray. RAE

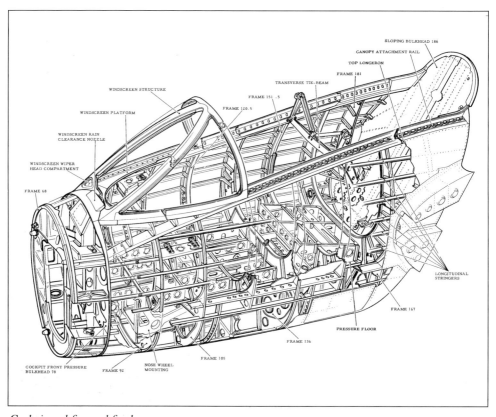

Cockpit and forward fuselage structure.

Farnborough trials then Boscombe Down. To DERA Farnborough 1/98 for display.

XV345 (S2B)
DD 03/07/67. 800 NAS ('103/E'). To RAF. 12 Sqn 14/05/73. 237 OCU 24/08/73. To S2B standard 13/09/76. 208 Sqn 07/08/78. 16 Sqn 30/03/79. 15 Sqn 31/07/79. Crashed near Nellis AFB 07/02/80 following fatigue failure.

XV346 (S2)
DD 18/07/67. 801 NAS ('233/H'). 736 NAS ('656/LM'). Ditched near Tarbat Ness, 13/02/69.

XV347 (S2)
DD 15/08/67. Initially to RN, transferred to RAF 12 Sqn 02/10/69. Destroyed following engine fire during taxying, Lossiemouth 09/12/71.

XV348 (S2B)
DD 06/09/67. To RN, transferred to RAF. 12 Sqn 02/10/69. 15 Sqn 04/07/73. 16 Sqn 10/07/73. 12 Sqn 19/08/75. 237 OCU 22/08/75. Crashed after striking power cables, Glomfjord, Norway 31/10/77.

XV349 (S2B)
DD 07/09/67. 736 NAS. To RAF. 12 Sqn 02/10/69. To S2B standard 06/07/72. 15 Sqn 12/06/73. 12 Sqn 08/12/75. 237 OCU 17/05/76. 12 Sqn 08/08/79. To St Athan store 04/08/80. To Shawbury store 20/04/83. Scrapped 10/91.

XV350 (S2A)
DD 19/09/67. To RN, transferred to RAF 01/01/69. Trials aircraft Holme-on-Spalding Moor. A&AEE 12/81. BAe Scampton 11/88. Withdrawn 1993, to East Midlands Aero Park, Castle Donington.

XV351 (S2D)
DD 03/10/67. 809 NAS ('030/R'). Crashed over Wash 11/11/74.

XV352 (S2B)
DD 30/04/68. To MoD(PE) 01/07/72. 208 Sqn 18/10/76. Cat 3 accident 14/02/84. 208 Sqn ('TS') 11/10/85. 237 OCU 13/05/86. 208 Sqn 30/03/88. 237 OCU ('FC') 02/89. Op. Granby ('Tamdhu') 10 mission symbols ('U'). St Athan

07/04/94. Scrapped, nose section privately owned.

XV353 (S2B)
DD 24/10/67. 800 NAS ('112/F'). 809 NAS ('031/R'). To RAF. 12 Sqn 21/01/71. To S2B standard 28/05/73. To RN 809 NAS. To RAF 27/11/78 12 Sqn. 208 Sqn 01/07/83. Station Flight Lossiemouth 11/09/87. 208 Sqn 07/10/87. Scrapped Lossiemouth 02/94.

XV354 (S2A)
DD 08/11/67. 803 NAS ('614/LM'). 809 NAS 22/05/70. To RAF. 208 Sqn 22/05/75. 237 OCU 06/03/78. To St Athan store 14/01/81. To Manston 31/03/83.

XV355 (S2A)
DD 29/11/67. 803 NAS. 800 NAS ('112/E'). 801 NAS ('112/H') 21/06/69. 800 NAS ('115/E') 28/07/69. To RAF. 12 Sqn 26/10/72. 237 OCU 02/10/73. 208 Sqn 07/11/75. 237 OCU 09/11/84. 12 Sqn 01/11/87. 208 Sqn 06/01/88. Scrapped Lossiemouth 12/05/92.

XV356 (S2B)
DD 13/12/67. 800 NAS ('114/E'). To RAF. 12 Sqn 08/12/72. To S2B standard. 237 OCU 14/01/75. 208 Sqn 11/01/78. 15 Sqn ('B') 31/01/79. St Athan store 15/08/80. To Shawbury store 22/06/83. Scrapped 10/91.

XV357 (S2A)
DD 05/01/68. 803 NAS ('612/LM'). 809 NAS ('034/R') 19/05/70. To RAF. 208 Sqn 22/04/75. 237 OCU 20/07/77. St Athan store 08/06/80. To Farnborough 28/02/84. PEE Foulness 04/91. Nose to RAF Exhibition Flight.

XV358 (S2D)
DD 14/02/68. 800 NAS ('101/E'). 736 NAS 26/01/72. 809 NAS ('035/R') 31/01/73. RN. Det. Honington 03/05/77. To RAF ('8658M') 18/11/78. RAF Bruggen BDRF 12/09/80.

XV359 (S2B)
DD 28/02/68. 800 NAS ('100/E'). 809 NS ('035/R'). To RAF 15/12/78. To S2B standard 15/03/82. 12 Sqn ('EF') 03/84. 208 Sqn ('VS')

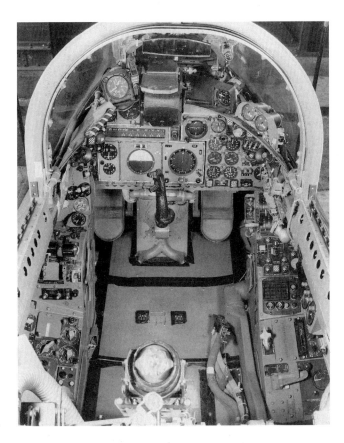

The Buccaneer S2 front cockpit.

02/87. ASF Lossiemouth. To RNAS Predannack
31/03/94.

XV360 (S2A)
DD 10/04/68. 803 NAS ('613/LM'). 800 NAS
('105/E'). To RAF. 12 Sqn 14/08/72. 237 OCU
15/10/73. Crashed into sea near Covehithe,
29/07/75.

XV361 (S2B)
DD 02/05/68. 800 NAS ('114/E'). 809 NAS
('021/R'). To RAF 18/11/78. To S2B standard
28/11/78. 15 Sqn 06/01/82. 12 Sqn 04/07/83.
A&AEE 28/09/83. 12 Sqn 30/09/83. 208 Sqn
08/09/86. To Aldergrove 18/04/94. To Ulster
Aviation Society, Langford Lodge.

XV863 (S2B)
DD 25/07/68. 809 NAS ('036/R'). MoD(PE)
Holme-on-Spalding Moor 10/06/73. To RAF. 16
Sqn 17/01/80. 237 OCU ('CC') 07/11/84. 208
Sqn 05/11/85. 237 OCU 29/10/87. Op. Granby
(*Sea Witch Debbie*) 6 mission symbols ('S').
Gate guard Lossiemouth ('9115M').

XV864 (S2B)
DD 05/09/68. 809 NAS. 736 NS 11/05/70. 809
NAS 23/11/73. To RAF. 16 Sqn 11/05/79.
Grounded at Nellis, shipped to UK 24/03/80. St
Athan store 02/09/80. 16 Sqn 22/07/82. 237
OCU 02/11/83. 12 Sqn ('KF') 01/03/84. To
Manston 05/04/94.

XV865 (S2B)
DD 01/10/68. 736 NAS ('652/LM'). 809 NAS
('022/R'). To RAF 27/11/78. 216 Sqn 28/01/80.
208 Sqn 01/08/80. St Athan 08/03/85. 208 Sqn
('BS') 17/07/85. 12 Sqn 28/05/86. 237 OCU
03/06/86. 208 Sqn 10/89. Withdrawn at
Lossiemouth ('9226M'), scrapped.

XV866 (S2B)
DD 11/11/68. 809 NAS ('024/R'). 736 NAS
('653/LM'). A&AEE 26/03/74. To RAF. 16 Sqn
('Y') 27/09/79. To St Athan store 12/08/80.
Shawbury store 25/05/83. Scrapped 10/91.

XV867 (S2B)
DD 06/12/68. 803 NAS ('611/LM'). 736 NAS

The Buccaneer S2 rear cockpit.

*The Buccaneer S2
front port console.*

18/12/69. 809 NAS 26/10/73. To RAF. 16 Sqn 11/12/79. To S2B standard. 237 OCU 27/10/81. 208 Sqn 04/11/83. 12 Sqn 16/04/84. 237 OCU 15/04/86. 12 Sqn 08/05/86. Station Flight Lossiemouth 03/09/87. 208 Sqn 07/10/87. Undercarriage collapse on landing at Leeming 10/09/93. Scrapped on site.

XV868 (S2B)
DD 14/01/69. 809 NAS ('025/R'). 803 NAS ('610/LM'). To RAF. 12 Sqn 24/05/79. Cat 3 accident 26/08/81. 12 Sqn ('EF') 11/08/82. 208 Sqn 23/10/85. 12 Sqn 08/08/88. Scrapped Elgin 12/05/92.

XV869 (S2B)
DD 06/03/69. 809 NAS ('020/R'). Holme-on-Spalding Moor, A&AEE 04/03/74. To RAF 27/11/78. 208 Sqn 06/09/79. 12 Sqn ('MF') 13/03/85. 237 OCU 11/11/88. 12 Sqn 02/89. To Shawbury store 01/03/90. Scrapped 02/94.

XW525 (S2B)
DD 20/01/70 to RAF. Retained by Hawker Siddeley. 12 Sqn 02/12/74. 237 OCU 06/08/75. 208 Sqn 06/08/76. Crashed Claerwen Reservoir after losing tail section, following near miss 27/04/77.

XW526 (S2B)
DD 30/04/70. On loan to Ministry of Technology 30/04/70. 12 Sqn 08/07/70. 15 Sqn 19/11/70. 237 OCU 12/01/76. 16 Sqn ('Y') 18/05/76.

Crashed at Osnabruck 12/07/79 following fatigue failure.

XW527 (S2B)
DD 30/06/70. 12 Sqn 06/07/70. 15 Sqn 11/12/70. 16 Sqn 14/03/73. 12 Sqn 23/05/77. Retained by 12 Sqn. To St Athan 07/04/94. Scrapped, nose section privately owned.

XW528 (S2B)
DD 31/07/70. 12 Sqn 05/08/70. 15 Sqn 19/11/70. Collision with XW536 over North Sea 16/06/75. Grounded 02/80. To St Athan by road 20/08/80. To Coningsby BDRF 21/05/85 ('8861M').

XW529 (S2B)
DD 30/09/70. MoD(PE) 05/07/84. A&AEE weapons trials. To Lossiemouth. Scrapped Elgin 10/92.

XW530 (S2B)
DD 31/10/70. 15 Sqn 12/01/71. 16 Sqn 19/02/73. 208 Sqn 05/11/79. 12 Sqn ('HF') 01/11/84. Op. Granby (*Glenmorangie*) 12 mission markings. Withdrawn 02/94. To Buccaneer Service Station, Elgin, on display.

XW531 (S2B)
DD 30/11/70. 15 Sqn 04/12/70. 12 Sqn 11/01/71. 237 OCU 01/04/71. 15 Sqn 15/04/71. 12 Sqn 26/11/74. Crashed off Norwegian coast 29/10/76.

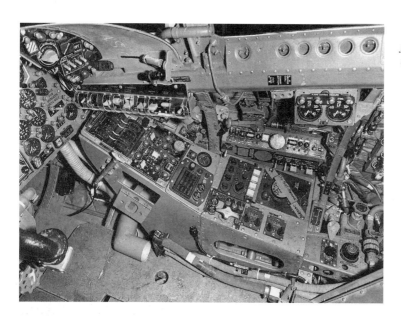

The Buccaneer S2 front starboard console.

XW532 (S2B)
DD 31/12/70. 15 Sqn 08/01/71. Crashed 25/03/71 Venlo, Netherlands.

XW533 (S2B)
DD 26/02/71. 15 Sqn 10/03/71. 16 Sqn 05/03/73. 216 Sqn 11/05/79. 12 Sqn 01/08/80. 15 Sqn 26/04/83. 237 OCU 03/11/83. 208 Sqn 08/04/88. 237 OCU 02/89. Op. Granby (*Fiona – Miss Jolly Roger*) 11 mission symbols ('A'). Scrapped Elgin 09/92.

XW534 (S2B)
DD 31/03/71. 237 OCU 06/04/71. 15 Sqn 06/10/72. 16 Sqn 27/07/78. 15 Sqn 21/08/78. 16 Sqn ('Z') 18/03/81. To St Athan store 28/09/83. To MoD(PE). 12 Sqn 10/89. To Shawbury store, scrapped 10/92.

XW535 (S2B)
DD 07/05/71. 237 OCU. 15 Sqn 06/10/72. 16 Sqn 08/01/73. Crashed near Gutersloh, Germany 24/11/73, following near miss.

XW536 (S2B)
DD 11/06/71. 237 OCU. 15 Sqn 30/11/72. 16 Sqn 08/01/73. 15 Sqn ('E') 24/04/75. Crashed in North Sea 16/06/75 following collision with XW528.

XW537 (S2B)
DD 23/07/71. 237 OCU. 15 Sqn 03/01/71. 16 Sqn 24/05/77. 237 OCU 12/03/81. Crashed on approach to RAF Wattisham 04/03/82.

XW538 (S2B)
DD 28/08/71. 237 OCU. 16 Sqn 02/05/73. Grounded at Nellis, shipped to Brough 04/80. To Abingdon 22/08/80. BDRF Lossiemouth ('8660M'). Scrapped 12/85.

XW539 (S2B)
DD 19/10/71. 12 Sqn. Crashed in Irish Sea off Isle of Man 04/01/72.

XW540 (S2B)
DD 08/12/71. To MoD(PE) 21/12/71. 15 Sqn 01/05/72. 208 Sqn 01/02/79. 216 Sqn 26/03/79. 12 Sqn 01/08/80. 208 Sqn 01/07/83. 12 Sqn 22/08/83. 237 OCU 28/05/86. 12 Sqn 04/11/86. Crashed 17 miles off Duncansby Head 22/04/87.

XW541 (S2B)
DD 07/12/71. 15 Sqn. 16 Sqn 15/11/72. 15 Sqn 11/04/74. St Athan store 13/10/80. To Honington store 27/11/84. Weapons trainer Honington ('8858M'). To PEE Foulness 02/91.

XW542 (S2B)
DD 24/12/71. 15 Sqn. 16 Sqn 14/02/73. 216 Sqn 26/03/79. St Athan wing transplant 12/09/80. 12 Sqn 01/05/81. 208 Sqn 01/07/83. MoD(PE) 31/08/84. 12 Sqn 14/05/86. 237 OCU 27/10/86. 237 OCU 11/88. 208 Sqn 10/89. Scrapped Lossiemouth 02/94.

XW543 (S2B)
DD 19/05/72. 15 Sqn. 16 Sqn 10/05/73. St Athan wing transplant 17/09/80. 16 Sqn

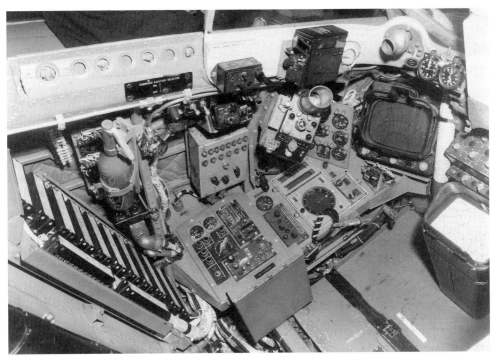

The Buccaneer S2 rear port console.

The Buccaneer S2 rear starboard console.

25/01/82. 237 OCU ('E') 04/11/83. To St Athan store. 12 Sqn 02/89. Hydraulic failure at St Mawgan 14/05/92. Scrapped on site.

XW544 (S2B)
DD 23/06/72. 15 Sqn. 16 Sqn 12/10/79. To Shawbury store. To 2SoTT Cosford ('8857M') 23/10/83. Withdrawn 21/05/85. Privately owned.

XW545 (S2B)
DD 14/08/72. 15 Sqn ('L'). 16 Sqn 28/11/73. Holme-on-Spalding Moor 18/01/80. To St Athan store 27/11/81. To Lossiemouth BDRF ('8859M'). To Pendine Range 03/90.

XW546 (S2B)
DD 30/09/72. MoD(PE). 15 Sqn 10/10/72. Wing transplant Bitteswell 14/11/80. 16 Sqn ('L') 05/08/83. 237 OCU 02/12/83. ASF Lossiemouth ('E'). Scrapped Elgin 04/93.

XW547 (S2B)
DD 31/10/72. 15 Sqn. 12 Sqn 09/12/74. 237 OCU 29/09/76. 12 Sqn 01/06/78. 216 Sqn 27/06/79. Wing transplant Bitteswell 23/10/80. 12 Sqn 28/04/81. St Athan 20/04/82. 208 Sqn ('JS') 01/07/83. 12 Sqn 20/04/88. Op. Granby (*Pauline – Guinness Girl/The Macallan*). 11 mission symbols ('R'). To Cosford 20/01/93, on display ('9169M').

XW548 (S2B)
DD 01/01/73. 15 Sqn. 16 Sqn 11/01/74. 208 Sqn 25/10/76. 16 Sqn 12/10/76. Crashed near Volkel, Netherlands, following in-flight fire 03/02/77.

XW549 (S2B)
DD 14/02/73. 15 Sqn. 16 Sqn 23/02/73. 12 Sqn 05/12/79. St Athan store 30/07/80. To Kinloss BDRF ('8860M'). Stored Kinloss.

XW550 (S2B)
DD 30/03/73. 15 Sqn. 16 Sqn 12/11/76. 15 Sqn 31/08/78. 16 Sqn ('X') 08/09/70. To St Athan store 15/08/80. Scrapped, nose section privately owned.

XW986 (S2B)
DD 25/01/74. MoD(PE). To West Freugh. Weapons trials. To Farnborough 03/75. To Boscombe Down. Withdrawn 09/94. Sold to Delta Engineering. Stored, Kemble.

XW987 (S2B)
DD 15/03/74. MoD(PE). Weapons trials. West Freugh. To Farnborough. To Boscombe Down.

Withdrawn 02/95. To Mike Beachyhead, South Africa. Active.

XW988 (S2B)
DD 16/05/74. MoD(PE) West Freugh. Weapons trials. To Farnborough. To Boscombe Down 01/04/83. Withdrawn 08/94. To Mike Beachyhead, South Africa. Active.

XX885 (S2B)
DD 30/04/74. 16 Sqn. 15 Sqn 27/07/77. 12 Sqn 09/02/79. 216 Sqn 27/03/79. St Athan wing transplant 17/12/80. 208 Sqn 06/08/81. 12 Sqn 04/05/84. 208 Sqn 29/06/88/ Withdrawn ('9225M'). Op. Granby (*Famous Grouse – Hello Sailor*) 7 mission symbols. To Enstone, Oxfordshire.

XX886 (S2B)
DD 14/06/74. 16 Sqn. 216 Sqn 30/05/79. To Honington, weapons trainer. Scrapped Honington.

XX887 (S2B)
DD 29/08/74. 15 Sqn. Withdrawn 02/80. Weapons trainer Laarbruch. To St Athan store. Shawbury store 19/02/83. Scrapped 10/91.

XX888 (S2B)
DD 21/11/74. 15 Sqn. 16 Sqn ('Z') 15/03/79. St Athan store 11/09/80. To Shawbury store. Scrapped, nose section to Dundonald.

XX889 (S2B)
DD 31/12/74. MoD(PE). 16 Sqn 13/02/75. 15 Sqn 20/06/77. 12 Sqn 09/03/82. 208 Sqn ('WS') 31/10/83. 237 OCU 01/12/86. 237 OCU 24/10/88. 12 Sqn 01/11/88. Op. Granby (*Longmom*) 14 mission symbols ('T'). To Lossiemouth.

XX890 (S2B)
DD 07/04/75. 15 Sqn ('K'). Crashed at Laarbruch 18/08/77.

XX891 (S2B)
DD 17/07/75. 16 Sqn 03/08/83. Crashed 2 miles from Laarbruch 11/08/83.

XX892 (S2B)
DD 14/08/75. 16 Sqn. 237 OCU ('F') 15/03/84. 237 OCU ('FC') 03/12/84. 208 Sqn 04/08/86. 12 Sqn 07/10/87. 208 Sqn 10/89. Op. Granby (*Glenlossi*) 8 mission symbols ('I'). Scrapped Lossiemouth 03/94.

XX893 (S2B)
DD 21/10/75. 16 Sqn. 15 Sqn ('H') 13/06/77. 16

Sqn 17/08/77. 237 OCU 19/10/84. Op. Granby reserve. Scrapped Lossiemouth 03/94.

XX894 (S2B)
DD 05/12/75. 15 Sqn. 16 Sqn 30/10/78. 15 Sqn ('M') 03/80. 12 Sqn 02/09/81. 208 Sqn ('HS') 13/12/85. 237 OCU 09/08/88. Op. Granby (*Aberlour*) 7 mission symbols ('O'). 809 NAS markings ('020/R'). To St Athan 07/04/94. To Bruntingthorpe.

XX895 (S2B)
DD 05/12/75. 12 Sqn. 208 Sqn 28/11/79. 15 Sqn 05/09/80. 237 OCU ('B') 17/01/84. St Athan 15/10/84. 237 OCU ('BC'). 12 Sqn 15/04/86. 237 OCU 06/05/86. 12 Sqn 09/05/88. 208 Sqn 15/07/88. Op. Granby (*Glenfiddich – Lynn/Jaws*) 5 mission symbols ('G'). Withdrawn Lossiemouth. On display, Woking.

XX896 (S2B)
DD 21/01/76. 12 Sqn. St Athan store 17/12/79. To Shawbury store 06/07/83. Scrapped 09/91.

XX897 (S2)
DD 22/04/76. MoD(PE). To Marshalls Cambridge, Tornado F2 nose fit. RRE Pershore. RAE Bedford. Withdrawn 06/95. To civilian owner, Bournemouth.

XX898 (S2B)
DD 17/06/76. 12 Sqn. 208 Sqn 20/02/80. 12 Sqn 01/08/80. Crashed on approach to RAF Lossiemouth 17/06/82.

XX899 (S2B)
DD 29/09/76. 208 Sqn. 15 Sqn 01/09/80. 237 OCU ('JC') 03/10/84. Op. Granby (*Laura Laser Lips/Linkwood*) – ('P'). Scrapped Lossiemouth 10/93. Nose section privately owned.

XX900 (S2B)
DD 24/11/76. 208 Sqn. 216 Sqn 09/04/79. 12 Sqn 12/03/82. 208 Sqn 25/02/86. To St Athan store. To Bruntingthorpe 10/94.

XX901 (S2B)
DD04/01/77. 208 Sqn. To Lossiemouth 208 Sqn ('GS') 01/07/83. 12 Sqn 21/01/87. 237 OCU 15/05/87. 208 Sqn 24/02/88. Op. Granby (*Kathryn the Flying Mermaid/Glen Elgin*) 9 mission symbols ('N'). To Elvington via Kemble.

XZ430 (S2B)
DD 05/05/77. 208 Sqn. 237 OCU 12/02/81. 208 Sqn 24/03/81. St Athan 16/12/81. 208 Sqn ('DS') 18/07/83. Crashed 20 miles east of Fraserburgh 20/05/84.

XZ431 (S2B)
DD 23/07/77. 208 Sqn. 12 Sqn 01/08/80. A&AEE 10/05/83. 208 Sqn ('PS') 09/08/83. Station Flight Lossiemouth 06/08/87. 208 Sqn 28/09/87. 237 OCU 21/12/88. 208 Sqn 02/89.

XZ432 (S2B)
DD 06/10/77. 15 Sqn. 216 Sqn 26/03/79. 208 Sqn 01/08/80. MoD(PE) 05/12/83. 208 Sqn ('CS') 09/12/83. 237 OCU 10/06/85. 12 Sqn 22/05/86. 237 OCU 15/09/88. Scrapped Elgin 10/92.

SAAF S.Mk.50

411
DD 01/12/65 24 Sqn. Crashed 04/01/73, stalled during flight refuelling.

412
DD 01/12/65 24 Sqn. To gate guard, Waterkloof.

413
DD 01/12/65 24 Sqn. Hydraulic failure, crashed into impalas on landing 30/08/83.

414
DD 01/12/65 24 Sqn. To SAAF Museum, Swartkop 04/04/91.

415
DD 01/12/65 24 Sqn. Crashed during night exercise over sea 16/10/69.

416
DD 01/12/65 24 Sqn. To SAAF Museum, Ysterplatt.

417
DD – Crashed during delivery flight over sea, following stall 03/11/65.

418
DD 01/12/65 24 Sqn. Crashed 14/10/70 after being damaged by 400kg para-bomb during drop trials.

419
DD 01/12/65 24 Sqn. Crashed near Danger Point following collision 24/11/72.

420
DD 01/12/65 24 Sqn. Crashed near Danger Point following collision 24/11/72.

421
DD 03/10/66 24 Sqn. To SAAF Museum, Swartkop 04/04/91.

422
DD 01/12/66 24 Sqn. To National Museum of Military History, Johannesburg (by road) 10/03/92.

423
DD 03/10/66 24 Sqn. Crashed off Scottburgh 03/08/78 following double flame-out during night exercise.

424
DD 03/10/66 24 Sqn. Crashed Roedton during night exercise 07/05/79.

425
DD 01/12/66 24 Sqn. Crashed near Lyndenburg 18/07/78 following stall.

426
DD 03/10/66 24 Sqn. Crashed Grootfontein 29/12/75 following collision.

A tantalising glimpse of what could have been; a Blackburn general arrangement drawing of the P.150, an advanced development of the Buccaneer with engine reheat, a thin wing and an updated navigation/attack system – the ultimate Buccaneer.

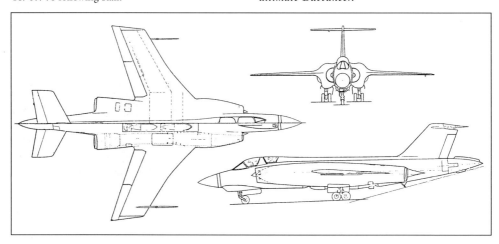

Index

188, Bristol 13
510, Supermarine 17
A-3 Skywarrior, Douglas 62
A-4 Skyhawk, Douglas 11, 12
A-6 Intruder, Grumman 84
Abingdon BDRF, RAF 187, 189
Admiralty 9, 11, 26, 80
Airbrake petals 26, 34, 35
Akrotiri, RAF 114, 128
Aldergrove 15, 192
Alford, W. H. (Bill) 36
Alpha bombs 91
Angola 88, 92, 94
Anson, Lt-Cdr E. R. 51
Area rule, 26
Ark Royal, HMS 63, 67, 68, 81, 82, 126, 182, 186
Arms embargo 87, 106
Armstrong Siddeley 20
Armstrong Whitworth 11, 12, 21, 22
Arrester gear 32, 37, 44, 74, 86
AS.30 missile, Nord 84, 90, 91, 93, 95, 96
AW.52, Armstrong Whitworth 21
AW.166, Armstrong Whitworth 13, 21
AW. 168, Armstrong Whitworth 12, 13

B.103, Blackburn 17, 19, 22
B.136, Blackburn 85
BE33, Bristol 20
Beachyhead, Mike 160, 161, 196
Bedford, RAE (Thurleigh) 29, 31, 32, 35, 37, 44, 160, 179, 180, 187, 197
Beirut 114, 128, 130
Beverley, Blackburn 22
BL.755 cluster bomb 157, 158
Blackburn 11, 17, 22, 47, 55, 84, 87, 112
Blue Parrot radar, Ferranti 24, 27, 56, 68, 112, 154
Bolt, Adm. A. S. 10
Boot, Roy 17, 18, 23, 35, 44, 47, 54, 60, 78, 86, 107, 118, 161
Boscombe Down, A&AEE 23, 29, 32, 36, 38, 42, 48, 70, 109, 122, 157, 160, 179, 190, 196
Boulton-Paul 117
Boundary layer control (BLC) 20, 46, 52, 55, 140, 174
Brawdy, RNAS 65
British Aerospace 109, 122, 125, 126, 154
British European Airways (BEA) 55
Brooke-Smith, Tom 15
Brough factory 17, 25, 27, 28, 30, 46, 48, 50, 64, 97, 102, 117, 125, 126, 154, 156, 159, 189
Brown, Lt-Cdr 'Ossie' 46
Bruntingthorpe 181, 187, 197
BS55, Bristol Siddeley 55
BS605, Bristol Siddeley 86
Buccaneer 2* 77, 78
Buccaneer Mk.3 76

Buccaneer S.Mk.50 85, 197
Buccaneer Service Station 193
Bullpup missile 67, 68, 82

Camera crate 56, 113, 170, 181
Camm, Sir Sydney 11, 44
Canberra, English Electric 88, 91, 93, 107
Carrier operations 16, 67
Catapult launching 18, 37, 44, 46, 68, 72, 81
Catterick, RAF 77, 181, 187
Civil Aviation Authority (CAA) 135, 160
Cockpit 105, 106, 190-195
Cold War 9, 44
College of Aeronautics, Cranfield 15
Comet, de Havilland 116
Cosford, RAF Aerospace Museum 126
Cottesmore, RAF 129, 156
Crashes 37, 45, 46, 63, 78, 80, 86, 106, 121, 122, 124, 127, 153, 179-198
Cross, Lt K. B. 63
Cutlass, Chance-Vought 16, 17

Davies, Wg Cdr G. 109
de Havilland 12, 20, 34, 46, 55, 179
Deck trials 36, 38, 39, 40, 44, 46, 63
Defence Research Agency (DRA) 103, 156, 159
Delta Engineering 160, 196
Desert Storm 126, 131
Dunn, Trevor 46

Eagle, HMS 60, 62, 63, 67, 73, 76, 79, 186
East Midlands Aero Park 97, 109, 191
East Fortune Museum of Flight 180, 188
Egypt 119
Ejection seats 48, 77, 169, 176
Elvington, RAF 36, 48, 92
Enterprise, USS 62
ETPS 159
Exercise Shopwindow 52

F-104G Starfighter, Lockheed 84
F-111K, General Dynamics 7, 81, 107, 110, 111, 113, 115, 161
Fairey 11, 13, 14, 22
Fairey Delta 2 13, 21
Falkland Islands 101
Farnborough, RAE 20, 156, 157, 179, 180, 183-186, 189, 190, 192, 196
Field, Stan 54
Fleet Air Arm 7, 15, 51, 59, 64, 75, 82, 86, 98, 111, 116, 134, 135, 153
Fleet Air Arm Museum 99, 179, 183, 189
Fletcher, Air Vice Marshal Peter 111
Flight simulator 136
Flutter testing 32
Fly-by-wire 35
Flying controls 172
Foulness, PEE 183, 186, 192, 194

Fozard, John 12
Fuel tanks 44, 45, 63, 112, 113, 119, 166, 169
Fuel system 40, 48, 169

Gannet, Fairey 21, 73
German Navy 84
Germany, RAF 8, 119, 127, 149, 161
Gibraltar 62, 63, 140
Glen Fruin 50
Gloster 18
Gloworm rockets 169
Gnat, Folland 49
Goose Bay 63, 119
Green Cheese 10, 16, 24, 43
Grounding 121, 122, 124, 125, 127
Gulf War 98, 102, 125, 126, 129, 149
Gyron, de Havilland 20
Gyron Junior, de Havilland 12, 13, 20, 25, 47, 51, 54, 55, 69, 74

Hardened aircraft shelter (HAS) 98, 101, 128, 136, 139
Harrier, BAe 51
Harvey, Capt. Ernie 88, 90
Hatfield 34, 179
Hawk, BAe 51, 137, 158
Hawker 11, 21, 22
Hawker Siddeley Aviation 44, 84, 107, 112, 119, 180, 193
Healey, Denis 75, 107
Helston Aero Park (Flambards) 54, 186
Hermes, HMS 44, 46, 49, 62, 67, 78, 180, 186, 189
Higgs, Cdr G. 63
Hill, Prof. Geoffrey 15
Holme-on-Spalding Moor 28, 32, 41, 42, 46, 53, 58, 68, 91, 110, 154, 157, 160, 178, 179, 184, 187, 189, 193
Honington, RAF 109, 113, 115, 116, 119, 127, 128, 153, 180, 192, 194
Hot weather trials 63
Howard, Lt-Cdr David 64
HP.88, Handley Page 17, 22
Hunter, Hawker 23, 32, 44, 65, 66, 114, 116, 124, 127

In-flight refuelling 47, 62, 65, 66, 82, 85, 104-106, 141, 149, 167, 169
International Air Tattoo 159
Iraq 131
Isoclinic wing 15

Jaguar, SEPECAT 131, 133, 135, 154, 158
Javelin, Gloster 18, 32
Johannesburg, National Museum 198
Johnson, Rear Adm. J. 96
Joyce, John 37
JP.233 pod 131, 157

Keith-Lucas, David 14
Kirov class cruiser 151, 152

Laarbruch, RAF 8, 111, 116, 124, 127, 131, 183, 187, 196
Lancaster, Avro 7
Langebaan, AFB 105
Langkloof 86
Langley, Virginia 32
Larkhill range 156, 158
Laser designators 132
Leeming, RAF 82, 193
Lexington, USS 63, 72
Lightning, English Electric/BAC 120, 147
Lincolnshire Military Collection 156
Lossiemouth, RNAS/RAF 47, 52, 53, 59, 61, 63, 72, 86, 97, 98, 101, 115, 116, 127-129, 132, 134, 137, 140, 151, 153, 155, 180, 187, 190-194, 197

Marham, RAF 129, 155, 156, 189
Marias, Capt. Dries 88, 90
Marshalls of Cambridge 187, 197
Martel missile, Matra 77, 108-112, 115, 125, 145, 150, 153, 154, 162, 178, 184
Martin Baker 48, 176
Mears, Lt-Cdr David 64
Merlin, Rolls-Royce 15
Meteor, Gloster 13, 18, 21, 22, 31, 33
Middleton, Lt-Cdr L. 62
Millet, Paul 63
Miniature detonating cord (MDC) 50, 169, 176
Ministry of Aviation 55, 84
Ministry of Defence (Procurement Executive) 80, 124, 155, 157, 159
Ministry of Supply 15, 18, 21, 22, 24, 47
Mirage F1, Dassault 88, 91, 92, 94

N114T, Blackburn 17
NA.39, Blackburn 17, 19, 23, 107
NACA 18, 36
Napalm tanks 65, 177
National Physical Laboratory, 18
NATO 9, 135, 137
Naval Staff Requirement NA.39 10
Nellis AFB 119, 122, 124, 127, 190, 192, 194
Newark Air Museum 183
Night attacks 71, 91
Nightingale, Dave 45
Norway 137
Nose art 125, 126, 129

Operation Granby 126, 131, 189, 191-194, 196, 197
Operation Northern Wedding 114
Operation Pulsator 114, 128, 131
Operation Reindeer 88
Orpheus, Bristol Siddeley 55
Oxley, Lt-Cdr G. 63

P.145, Blackburn 109, 112, 118
P.149, Blackburn 117
P.150, Blackburn 107, 198
P.151, Armstrong Siddeley 20
P.1108, Hawker 11, 12
P.D.1, Shorts 15
P.D.13, Shorts 14, 16, 21
Panther, Grumman 18

Parker, G. R. I. (Sailor) 35, 45
Patuxent River, NAS 71
Paveway system 117, 118, 125, 126, 128, 131, 132, 150, 153, 179
Pearson, Jack 59
Pendine, PEE 181-183, 187, 189, 196
Pensacola, NAS 44, 63
Percival 11
Pershore, RRE 160, 186, 197
Phantom, McDonnell 28, 35, 68, 81, 107, 113, 120, 130, 147, 159
Pitchfork Flt Lt /Wg Cdr G. 65, 113, 115, 120, 127
Predannack, RNAS 182, 192

RA.19, Rolls-Royce 16
Radloff, Maj. Joham 88
RAF Exhibition Flight 183, 186
Ray, Wg Cdr Dave 125
RB.115, Rolls-Royce 12, 22
RB.162 lift engine, Rolls-Royce 117
RB.163 Spey, Rolls-Royce 55, 57, 58, 64, 70, 107, 111, 152, 162, 171-173, 178, 183
Reconaissance missions 93, 94
Red Angel 11
Red Beard (see Target Marker Bomb)
Red Flag Exercises 119, 120, 122-124, 126, 127, 138, 154, 161
Rice, Lt Bill 53
Roberts, Lt-Col David 131
Rocket assisted take-off 85, 92, 106
Rolls-Royce 12, 25, 55-58, 60
Rotodyne, Fairey 21
Rowe, N. E. 18
Royal Air Force (RAF) 7, 11, 65, 82, 87, 103, 107, 111, 113, 120, 131, 153
Royal Naval Test Unit 46
Royal Navy (RN) 7, 44, 55, 59, 71, 72, 75, 84, 95, 134,

SAAF Museums 106, 197, 198
S.B.1, Shorts 15, 21
S.B.4 Sherpa, Shorts 15, 16, 21
S.C.1, Shorts 21
Sapphire, Armstrong Siddeley 17, 18, 20
SBAC Display, Farnborough 2, 15, 33, 52, 62
Scampton, RAF/BAe 97, 191
Scimitar, Supermarine 12, 18, 33, 44, 51, 71
Sea Eagle missile 108, 151-155
Sea Hawk, Armstrong Whitworth 13, 21, 84
Sea King, Westland 135
Sea Vixen, de Havilland 33, 51, 65, 66, 73
Seamew, Shorts 21
Shackleton, Avro 90, 96, 105, 136
Shawbury, RAF 100, 104, 127, 154, 187, 188, 189, 191, 193
Shoeburyness, PEE 181
Shorts 11, 14, 21, 22
Sidewinder missile 118, 121, 130-132, 134, 150, 175
Silver Castle 105
Simonstown 83, 85
SNEB rocket pod 72, 112
South African Air Force (SAAF) 83, 85, 113, 160
South African Navy 87
Southwood, Sq Ldr D. 157-159

Specification B.35/46 14
Specification ER.134T 13, 21
Specification M.148T 10, 12, 14, 16, 21, 22
St Athan, RAF 82, 155, 186-192, 196, 197
St Mawgan, RAF 100, 102, 115, 160, 161, 196
Stamper, John 47
Sturgeon, Shorts 15
Sverdlov class cruisers 9, 10
Swift, Supermarine 23
Sydenham, RNAY 15, 181, 186, 189

Tain weapon range 80
Target Marker Bomb (TMB) 10, 24, 25, 36, 40, 42-44, 63, 73, 82, 112, 150
Taylor, LT-Cdr A. 63
Todd, Lt J. 65
Tornado, Panavia 51, 80, 128, 131, 135, 139, 145, 151, 153, 155, 158, 160, 161
Torrey Canyon, VLCC 64, 65, 95, 96
Toss bombing 42, 44, 62, 63, 73, 91, 115, 150, 158
Trident, de Havilland 55
TSR.2, BAC 7, 10, 77, 83, 107, 110, 111, 179

Ulster Aviation Society 192
Ultra-Light, Fairey 21
Undercarriage 53, 112, 163, 165, 175
US Air Force 24, 107, 119
US Mutual Weapons Development Prog. 32, 84
US Navy 18, 62, 71, 84, 107

Valiant, Vickers 11, 47
Vallance Collection 181
Van der Stel 86
VC10, Vickers 102, 139, 141, 149
Vernon, HMS 50
Victor, Handley Page 11, 14, 44
Victorious, HMS 36, 38, 39, 62, 63, 67, 112, 180, 182, 188
Voodoo, McDonnell 26
Vulcan, Avro 7, 11, 14, 117

Wafra 90, 95, 105
Wales Air Museum 181
Warton, BAe/MoD(PE) 155, 161, 186, 188
Wasp, Westland 83, 85
Waterkloof, AFB 86, 90, 95, 105, 199
Watson, Bernard 31
WE177 42, 82, 111, 112, 116, 150, 181, 182
Wessex, Westland 79
West Freugh, RAE 44, 80, 156, 157, 159, 180, 186, 188, 196
West Raynham, RAF 65
Westland 11, 16, 22
Whitby class frigates 85
Whitehead, Derek 30, 31, 38, 39, 59
Wilson, Harold 87, 96, 110
Winton, Lt-Cdr J. de 61
Woodford factory 154
Wyvern, Westland 16, 22

Yeovilton, RNAS 44
Yorkshire Air Museum 72, 186

Zambia 91, 92

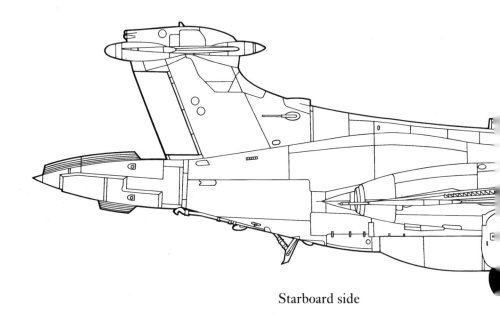

Starboard side

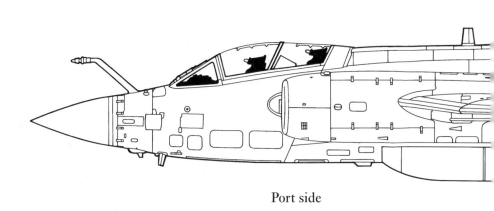

Port side

Drawn by Terence Wong-Gane